Partial Visions

Richard M. Merelman

Partial Visions

Culture and Politics in Britain, Canada, and the United States

The University of Wisconsin Press

The University of Wisconsin Press
114 North Murray Street
Madison, Wisconsin 53715

3 Henrietta Street
London WC2E 8LU, England

Library of Congress Cataloging-in-Publication Data
Merelman, Richard M., 1938–
    Partial visions: culture and politics in Britain, Canada, and the
United States / Richard M. Merelman.
    300 pp.   cm.
    Includes bibliographical references and index.
    ISBN 0-299-12990-X   ISBN 0-299-12994-2 (pbk.)
    1. Politics and culture – United States. 2. Politics and
culture – Canada.
    3. Politics and culture – Great Britain. 4. United States –
Politics and government.
    5. Canada – Politics and government.
    6. Great Britain – Politics and government.
    7 United States – Popular culture.
    8. Canada – Popular culture.
    9. Great Britain – Popular culture. I. Title.
E183.M47   1991
306.2 – dc20   91-9089
                        CIP

For Sally Hutchison

Contents

Preface

The question of culture's role in politics arose as early as Plato's decision to expel poets from his Republic. But, despite Plato, today's poets — the wordsmiths and image makers of popular culture — occupy positions of great power in democratic societies. I argue in this book that Britain, Canada, and the United States have spawned cultural visions which tend to frustrate the realization of democracy. I therefore call these visions *partial*. These partial visions are contained in forms of popular culture: television situation comedies, magazine advertisements, social studies texts, and corporate publications. As an ensemble, popular culture constitutes collective representations of two basic relations in liberal democratic discourse: the relations of public to private and of the collectivity to the individual. These partial visions are paradoxes: indispensable, yet incomplete; revelatory, yet distorted; idealized, yet inequitable. Ultimately, however, these visions hinder public opinion and political debate from accomplishing the democratic project.

Chapter 1 of this study describes how political institutions and histories in Britain, Canada, and the United States provide distinctive matrices for cultural development, and how these matrices shape "conflictive democratic participation," an indispensable feature of modern democracy. Chapter 2 utilizes symbolic anthropology to conceptualize forms of popular culture as narratives of liberal democracy. Chapters 3 through 5 describe the partial visions of liberal democracy in American, Canadian, and British popular culture. Chapter 6 describes the way public opinion and political debate in Britain, Canada, and the United States reflect and project these partial visions. Chapter 7 discusses the implications of this study for issues of change, meaning, and power in liberal democracies.

The narratives of popular culture frame politics in liberal democracies, just as surely as the Catholic mass frames the Church spiritual and temporal, or ritualized cargo systems frame life among the Zinacantan Indians of Mexico (Kertzer 1988: 57). The reader should therefore be under no illusions: because they are *partial*, the cultural visions of liberal democratic politics in Britain, Canada, and the United States ultimately must alter if democracy is fully to flower.

Acknowledgments

Aspects of this project have been supported by the University of Wisconsin–Madison Graduate School and by a Hawkins Professorship in the Department of Political Science. I am grateful both to the Graduate School and to my colleagues in Political Science for their encouragement and assistance.

Magda Ghanima, then of the University of Maryland, helped me as a research assistant to get the project up and running. Finessa Ferrell-Smith served as my project assistant in Madison and ably laid the foundation for chapter 6. Merely listening to her Oklahoma twang pitting itself over the phone against the BBC English of secretaries in London was worth the price of admission. Melanie Grant in London taped many of the British television programs I rely upon; Glen Luff of the Canadian Broadcasting Corporation, Toronto, and Fred Headon of the Canadian Association for the Social Studies helped me secure Canadian materials. Phyllis Miller deserves a special place in heaven for deciphering my mysterious hieroglyphic amalgam of typed manuscript and handwritten revisions, entering this script on the appropriate floppy discs, and giving me back beautiful copy. All this she did quickly, with good humor, and much patience for the vagaries of quixotic scholarship.

Judith Tuttle of the University of Wisconsin–Madison Memorial Library benignly evaded the call of duty in permitting me flexibility in the use of library materials. I have vexed Judy for years, and I hope I don't get her into trouble by thanking her publicly.

Many students, friends, and colleagues risked their health by reading an earlier, quite heavy, version of the manuscript. They provided me the ideal body of feedback, unsparing, yet kindly. These unindicted co-conspirators are: Peter Eisinger, Murray Edelman, Gina Sapiro, Paula Mohan, Fred Greenstein, Bill Gormley, Eric Gorham, Leon Epstein, and Dan Levin. They are, of course, absolved from what follows.

I want particularly to express my gratitude to Crawford Young, not only for his exemplary reading, but also for his unflappable optimism about this project. I only hope Crawford's optimism wasn't founded on the fact that I had written the thing, and not he. Barbara Hanrahan, of the University of Wisconsin Press, was similarly a bulwark during a long period of review.

Part of chapter 3 appeared as "Sitcoms and Citicorp: On the Cultural Construction of American Liberalism," *Journal of American Culture* (Spring, 1987): 41–56; much of chapter 2 and a small bit of chapter 7 appeared as "On Culture and Politics in the United States: A Perspective from Structural Anthropology," *British Journal of Political Science* (October, 1989): 465–93. Both pieces have been somewhat rewritten for this study.

Mere words cannot do justice to the feelings which only she to whom this book is lovingly dedicated elicits.

Partial Visions

CHAPTER ONE

Three Liberal Democratic Cultures

Introduction: Democratic Possibilities and Group Conflict

However else one may characterize it, democracy surely implies some form of popular rule. And popular rule requires widespread popular participation in politics (Pennock and Chapman 1975). Whether through direct action or through a process of representation, a public must help determine its political fate if that public is to enjoy democratic empowerment. Partly because the root meaning of *democracy* is "popular rule," as democracy has spread, its promises of popular rule have embraced ever-larger categories of persons. For example, in the United States the concept of democracy originally meant the dangerous rule of an untutored, unpropertied — and possibly unstable — majority over a "respectable," propertied, reliable minority. However, as the idea of democracy became popular in the United States, and as enfranchisement and citizenship rights gradually encompassed formerly disenfranchised groups, the concept of democracy shrugged off its lower-class, disreputable, majoritarian associations and transformed itself into a process whereby majority and minority somehow combined forces to rule through representative mechanisms (Pennock 1979). A vision of consensual democracy thus replaced a democracy of group conflict (see Sartori 1987: 88–89).

But this transformation of the democratic concept from conflict to consensus has not proven to be an unambiguously happy development. The difficulty is this: in its earlier incarnation, as the power of the poor majority over the rich minority, democracy promised (or threatened) greater equality between social classes (Hanson 1985). Equality promotes political participation, for where equality reigns, no segment of the population is systematically disadvantaged in the pursuit of political power. So by motivating people to act politically, equality promotes democracy. But modern democratic states have appropriated the rhetoric of democratic empowerment without delivering on the promise of equality. Indeed, not only do many remain disadvantaged, but the goal of equality itself has also faded. Therefore, the participation necessary to democratic empowerment lags.

In addition, "Modern states . . . however seriously they may take

3

social or economic equality . . . are precluded by their very structure from giving more than token recognition to the ideal of political equality. Modern state structures concentrate power to a degree which no ancient state could have begun to emulate . . . " (Dunn 1979: 12–13). In short, even when states *do* strive for social equality, they must monopolize power so as to limit political democracy. We face a paradox: without social equality, there is incomplete political democracy; but to achieve social equality, a state structure must be so entrenched and powerful that no popular force can control it. Therefore, the political participation necessary to realize democracy dwindles either because of the power of want (the absence of social equality) or because of the want of power (the absence of political equality). And, to repeat, without sustained political participation, democracy as popular rule fails (Dahl 1985).

Of course, political participation has virtues other than popular rule. These include, *inter alia*, self-development (Nagel 1987: 11–12); the reforging of institutional power (MacPherson 1973: chap. 6); the psychological well-being conveyed by effective democratic action; and increased satisfaction with governmental performance (Pennock 1979: 465). Yet these benefits are secondary because they depend upon widespread political participation in the promotion of popular rule. Unless political participation actually increases popular rule, it will be revealed as a sham, and its secondary benefits will quickly vanish. For this reason, I intend to concentrate upon political participation as an aid to popular governance.

To be sure, political participation is not the sole defining quality of a democracy. Choice, majority rule, and minority rights are also required (Sartori 1987: 24–25). Yet political participation is necessary, if not sufficient, to popular rule. A major task for democratic theory, then, is to discover those conditions which promote political participation and which, therefore, favor democracy (for an attempt, see Held 1987).

Concerning political participation as a goal, Jane Mansbridge argues that an approach such as the one I have taken threatens to become "adversarial." Adversarial theories presuppose that pervasive group conflict will promote political participation. Mansbridge disagrees. Adversarial democracy is anticommunitarian; it subjects the will of one group in a society to the will of another, and therefore always disappoints losers (Sandel 1984; Mansbridge 1980). Losers therefore often leave the struggle.

Moreover, adversarial democracy sometimes allows a majority to deprive a minority of its legitimate rights, including the coveted right to participate. Adversarial democracy thus reduces the actual number of persons enjoying self-governance over time through a combined process of exclusion and recurrent defeat. Also, by accepting group conflicts as a given, adversarial democracy prevents a shared public interest from emerging. Ultimately, by institutionalizing and legitimating conflicting group interests, adversarial democracy destroys the fellow-feeling which generates political participation (for a critique, see Kelso 1978: chap. 8; Hart 1978).

Mansbridge argues that democratic participation need not be adversarial. Instead, she claims that high levels of political participation may emerge without group conflict. If citizens are connected to each other socially and share common goals, they will spontaneously celebrate and protect these goals through democratic action. Thus, group conflict will fade, and democratic participation will grow.

I disagree with this assessment. Mansbridge confuses cause and effect; her communal democracy is the *consequence* of prior agreement, not its creator. She demonstrates only that where there are no adversaries, adversarial democracy need not exist. Not only is this proposition true by definition, but the circumstances themselves are also rare, and can be found only in small communities (Dahl and Tufte 1973). Once communities enlarge, divisions of substantive interest always create opposing political forces, and political participation can no longer reflect an unadulterated public interest.

It follows, therefore, that in industrial democracies increased political participation requires conflicting group interests. But are the two phenomena linked causally? Does the perception of group conflict stimulate political participation? Although empirical evidence on this point is divided, most studies support the position that group conflict stimulates political participation (Jackman 1987: 405–24). Certainly the logic of the argument is straightforward: the power of each individual person is less in large than in small regimes; moreover, the individual's sense of spontaneously sharing interests with all his fellow citizens decreases as the size of the polity increases. Given these twin phenomena, it follows that (all other things being equal) people will participate less in large polities than in small. What then does motivate participation in large polities? A logical answer is membership in a group smaller than the polity as a whole, one in which the individual perceives a vital interest against nonmembers. In large polities more people participate in order to protect themselves or to impose their will on adversaries in conflict than to share in a national consensus. Ultimately, therefore, it is group contest and struggle which stimulate political participation in

6   Three Liberal Democratic Cultures

modern democracies (See also Dahl 1986: 244–245; Connolly 1987: 8; Barber 1984: 25).

My own position may be simply put. I define democracy as a system of rule in which there is widespread political participation among citizens; majority preferences rule in decision-making; governments implement policies favored by a majority; and citizens enjoy "moral equality" (Nagel 1988: 76), which protects the right of minorities to participate in politics. I argue that group conflict promotes these four components of the democratic project. I call the optimal form of group conflict *conflictive democratic participation*.

It is often pointed out that not all group conflict promotes democracy. I agree. The examples of countries such as Sri Lanka, India, and Israel, among other prominent cases, provide ample testimony to the many destructive forms group conflict can take in societies which aspire to democracy. There *is* some optimal form of group conflict that promotes democracy (Hart 1978). But I argue only that group conflict is *necessary* to democracy, not that it is *sufficient*. I discuss the form of group conflict I consider most helpful in a later section (p. 15).

Skeptics about the value of group conflict also point out that nonconflictive politics may not be the most important reason for widespread political apathy. As Mancur Olson and Anthony Downs have demonstrated, considerations other than the structure of group conflict often influence a "rational judgment" in favor of nonparticipation (Olson 1965; Downs 1957). These factors, too, must be addressed if increased democratic participation is to become a reality.

But these critics often overlook the fact that group conflict apparently helps to overcome rational nonparticipation (Miller et al. 1981: 203–13). Of course, the relationship is complex because, in already divided societies, political participation no doubt encourages people to perceive the group conflict that already exists and to develop in turn an ideology of conflict which stimulates further participation, and so on. Yet self-government through democratic processes is limited as much by the widespread absence of articulate ideological frameworks as by rational nonparticipation. More to the point, ideologies which encourage political participation are themselves "rational" reactions to the structure of group conflict.

It is also true that appropriate political institutions must focus group conflict in order for political participation to increase. People must not only perceive group conflict, but must also articulate such conflict through interest groups, mass movements, and especially political parties. Where party competition and party organization deteriorate, participation in politics languishes, a central insight supported empirically by numerous writers, most notably V. O. Key and Walter Dean Burnham (Key 1956; Epstein 1986: 255–56).

These, however, are secondary considerations to the many writers who argue the primary point that "too much" or "the wrong sorts of" conflict ultimately pose a danger to democratic regimes. Much recent democratic theory claims that vigorous group conflict often destroys a necessary consensus on the individual and group rights which are indispensable in a democracy. So there is a dilemma: unless group conflict exists, there will be too little participation to support self-government; but "too vigorous conflict" will tempt some groups to repress others, thereby reducing participation and destroying democracy (Huntington 1968).

But I feel these arguments demonstrate only that political participation, like other components of democratic regimes, is complex. However, no one disputes the fact that every account of democracy accepts widespread public participation. Because political participation is fragile and even volatile, democracies are fragile and occasionally volatile; but fragility and volatility in no way detract from the importance of political participation in helping to enhance democracy. After all, one must risk being burned in order to build a warming fire.

Moreover, arguments against "too much" participation are in an important sense simply beside the point. Once a regime proclaims itself democratic, it invites evaluations by reference to the amount and quality of political participation it achieves. The legitimacy of democracies suffers when citizens regularly eschew opportunities for political participation. When only a bare majority of eligible citizens in the United States vote in the most important of American elections — that for President; when only minorities vote in off-year elections (as in 1982, when 33.7 percent of the electorate voted); when barely 10 percent of the public take part in political organizations between elections; when the social group most advantaged by the equally distributed franchise (the working class) still votes 30 percent less frequently than the middle class (Cohen and Rogers 1983: 33); then the boasts of democratic regimes must fall on deaf ears. Nonparticipation in politics creates a no-man's land of disputed and uncertain legitimacy within which democratic regimes are vulnerable to internal and external opposition. If bitter group conflicts among a highly mobilized population threaten democratic institutions, so also does widespread apathy, which mocks protestations of true democracy.

To summarize, democracy requires widespread participation in governance. In large polities, such participation usually requires the perception and articulation of group conflict. Therefore, democracies have an interest in group conflict and in protecting and encouraging institutions which mobilize this conflict. To the degree that democratic regimes succeed in this endeavor, they move towards fuller realization of their democratic possibilities; to the degree that they do not, they blight the promise of democracy.

Democratic Limitations and Group Conflict: Four Perspectives

If it is a truism that democratic regimes have not fulfilled their aspirations toward political participation, nowhere is this proposition more dramatically or paradoxically illustrated than in the United States, where despite the diffusion of higher education to increasing numbers of people, the elimination of legal barriers to political participation, and the spread of affluence, political participation—for example, in the form of interest groups—remains pressure from a tiny minority of unrepresentative, wealthy people (Schlozman 1984: 1006–32). Thus, not only is political participation limited, but it is also dominated by a most unrepresentative few persons (but see Berry 1989: chap. 2).

Contemporary scholars have pursued the problem of limited and skewed political participation through institutional, economic, social-psychological, and cultural approaches. Of these four, it is the last two with which this study deals. I argue in this study that certain qualities of a society's popular culture subtly prepare people either to seek out political participation and welcome group conflict or to resist political participation and to reject group conflict. Often, the latter occurs, to the detriment of political participation. I do not argue that *only* culture and social psychology explain political participation. Each approach to political participation has some validity, though each is limited both empirically and logically. I do contend, however, that the most popular approaches—institutional, politico-economic, and social-psychological— depend upon cultural support. For this reason, cultural factors are integral to all forms and motives of political participation. Let me explain.

The institutional approach claims that appropriate political mechanisms are required to increase both the range and amount of political participation. For example, Wolfinger and Rosenstone (1980) argue that easier registration arrangements would substantially increase voting in America. Many years ago, Key (1956) argued that party primaries factionalize and personalize politics, reduce citizen attention to issues, and eventually reduce voter turnout. Burnham (1970) argues that introduction of the Australian ballot weakened the capacity of American parties to mobilize voters. Powell (1986: 17–43) argues that single-party, winner-take-all voting districts limit voting participation. Advocates of proportional representation argue that legislative representation of minority-party candidates encourages voter participation, since fewer people have to choose between wasting a vote and voting for a candidate who is the least unpalatable alternative (for a review, see Jackman 1987: 405–24).

Yet the effects of these institutional features on voting are uncertain. No single set of political institutions has been shown to promote such participation uniformly. Instead, particular institutional factors are more or less powerful in different settings. For example, party primaries in the city of New York affect voter participation quite differently from party primaries in Mississippi. Under conditions of severe group conflict, proportional representation may actually serve as a conciliating force by representing the small number of moderate citizens. By contrast, under the same conditions, single-member districts may promote antagonism by forcing members of the principal conflict groups "to stay with their own" (Dahl 1966: chaps. 11–12). Thus, group antagonism — and therefore political participation — responds differently to identical institutional mechanisms. Moreover, institutions affect mainly voting. When one considers the volume or quality of political debate, for example, institutions retreat to a subsidiary position.

Not surprisingly, therefore, in the last thirty years, students of political participation have turned for help to social psychology. Social-psychological explanations focus on the attitudes and beliefs of individual persons rather than on the features of political institutions (see Abramson 1983). Yet the attitudinal approach has also proven limited. Problems of measurement have shown themselves stubbornly daunting. Moreover, the number of promising participation-related attitudes seems infinite. And even where there exists a reliable relationship between an attitude and an act of political participation, causality is by no means clear (Barry 1970). Finally, even deeply held attitudes usually explain only some forms of political participation, or the same form under some conditions but not under others, or some levels of participatory intensity better than others (see, for example, Hochschild 1984).

More reductionist in their treatment of political participation are theories of rational choice. Two such theories have led the way: that of Anthony Downs and that of Mancur Olson. Downs applies his arguments mainly to elections. He states that "skilled politicians whose main goal is to win will take similar stands on issues about which a majority might become passionate . . . and converge toward the median on any position that is a dominant concern to most voters" (Nagel 1987: 113). Voters at the extreme will either settle for the mainstream candidate nearest to (though still far from) their own position, or else abstain entirely. Many will abstain, as will many moderates who are indifferent between two candidates very like each other (but see Crewe and Searing 1988: 361–85).

Olson's theory extends to all forms of political participation, not just voting. Olson (1965) argues that in organizations that pursue collective benefits (i.e., benefits which all members can share equally, regardless of individual contribution), political participation is inherently limited. Under these conditions, the "natural" human desire to get something for nothing predisposes each person to abstain from participating while profiting from the efforts of others, who presumably *do* participate. Also, because people calculate that the value of their personal contribution to attaining a successful collective outcome is meager, they may rationally abstain from acting. In sum, regardless of attitudinal preferences or institutional form, large conflict groups pursuing collective goals will have difficulty motivating their supporters to participate.

But, despite his efforts to do so, Olson does not help us understand instances of high participation in the pursuit of collective goals. Nor does he explain values such as altruism that have been shown experimentally to compensate for the antiparticipatory factors he describes (Douglas 1986; Marwell and Ames 1979: 1335–60; 1980: 926–37). Olson also ignores the fact that in some cultures, nonparticipation is almost shameful. And where there is significant group conflict over goals, individuals may feel a strong sense of solidarity with those who share their views — so much so, in fact, that they may participate regularly despite the limitations of their individual contributions (for example, Fantasia 1988).

Finally, neither Downs nor Olson explains how people decide what actually *constitutes* a "contribution," or what an "acceptable" calculus of costs and benefits is, or whether it is right to profit from the efforts of others. *Contribution, cost-benefit calculi,* and *morality* are all matters of cultural variation. In some cultures the acceptable ratio of personal reward to collective effort may be low; in others it may be high. To a Protestant, giving a gift to a friend may be a selfless act; to a Buddhist, the same gift may establish an enduring relationship of reciprocity and patronage (for a range of views, see Bailey 1971). Without considering culture, rational-choice explanations of participation lose much of their power, as do institutional and social-psychological explanations (see also Scitovsky 1976).

So we arrive at cultural explanations, that is, explanations involving subjective phenomena, such as political values, which characterize whole societies as well as specific individuals. In the next chapter I provide an elaborate treatment of the culture concept, but for now I wish to explore one promising cultural explanation, involving the idea of liberalism. I will argue that a heritage of liberalism has combined with unique historical circumstances to produce in Canada, Britain, and the United States quite distinct cultures of political participation. Each of these cultures is a combination of three orientations towards politics: (1) an orientation towards the group or the individual as the central *unit* of culture and politics; (2) a *temporal* orientation in the form of static or dynamic relations between cultural units; and (3) a *spatial* orientation towards either the vertical or the horizontal, or, in political terms, toward the hierarchical or the egalitarian (Laponce 1981; for comparison, D'Andrade 1984: 88–123).

I will argue that in Canada the culture of political participation is dominantly group-oriented, somewhat dynamic, and divided between a hierarchical model of Parliamentary politics and an egalitarian model of dualism involving British and French cultural groups. In Britain the culture of political participation is a generally static, hierarchical model of group solidarity, revolving around social class. In the United States the culture of political participation is fluid, egalitarian, and individualistic. Of the three cultures, the United States produces the least amount of what I call conflictive democratic participation, Canada a modicum of such participation, and Britain the most.

Liberal Democracy and Conflictive Democratic Participation: An American Perspective

In the United States, liberalism—with its emphasis on individualism, market preference, and the dispersion of governmental power—powerfully undercut both feudal/reactionary and socialist challenges (Hartz 1955; Lipset 1963, 1989). The absence of a feudal past prevented the upper class, which might have challenged liberalism either on self-interest or on moral grounds, from ever standing a chance. Disappointed defenders of the British Crown fled to Canada. Later, romantic aristocrats in the South fell to Northern force of arms. Hence, a reactionary, antiliberal alternative never developed in the United States.

Nor did a serious, working-class, socialist challenge to liberalism develop, for a triumphant liberal bourgeoisie was secure enough from feudal reaction to open political and social opportunities to workers. Selective mobility, an expanding land frontier, and political enfranchisement eroded working-class hostility to liberal politics (Lipset 1963). Ethnic rivalries and occasional repressive measures further weakened the socialist movement. Thus, because it avoided challenges on left and right, the liberal majority was able to lapse into a prolonged participatory languor; rarely challenged, its participatory ardor cooled steadily from the late nineteenth century onward. Encased within the liberal consensus, American politics became a struggle between Tweedledum and Tweedledee; as a result, the realization of democratic possibilities through group conflict gradually diminished.

Of course, American liberalism did not envision — nor did it create — a conflict-free political universe. But the central political conflict that liberalism presented was that of vulnerable individuals resisting tyrannical, repressive governments. As Graeme Duncan (1978: 59–75) and Benjamin Barber (1984) have argued, liberalism places center stage the attempts of individuals to protect their rights against government invasion. What have been the consequences of this individualistic emphasis so far as political participation is concerned?

As Duncan argues, individuals who feel little kinship with each other often feel helpless and apathetic in the face of government power (1978: 59–75). Alone and isolated, individuals are too weak to protect their rights; as a result, political participation suffers. The main alternative to this scenario — one eagerly embraced by liberal democrats in the United States — is a politics of interest groups and voluntary associations. As Schattschneider (1960) has pointed out, however, this system is defensive, costly, and inegalitarian. Pluralism virtually assures that it will be mainly people with money and leisure who sustain political participation over time. Ultimately, therefore, pluralism consists primarily of defensive actions undertaken intermittently by a minority of comparatively comfortable citizens, rather than assertive actions undertaken regularly by large representative majorities.

Moreover, the individualism promoted by American liberalism eventually took the form of Social Darwinism (Lukes 1973: chap. 4), which protected the economic inequalities that are inevitable under corporate capitalism. But, as we have seen, prolonged inequality discourages political participation, especially among the disadvantaged. In the United States, individualism became the right to stand or fall in competition with others, and this definition, by protecting inequality, did not foster political participation (Lukes 1973: part 1).

There is also the participatory effect of liberal economics to be considered. Liberalism promotes economic well-being through the medium of the market and through the use of private property. These twin emphases assume that people—primarily males until the mid-nineteenth century—gain their primary satisfactions as owners of private property or as private consumers. Therefore, liberalism encourages political avoidance unless or until the political realm interferes with the private sphere. By privatizing social life, liberalism helps to create citizens who are efficient producers and self-indulgent consumers, but not public-spirited citizens devoted to political participation

Although there is much in these condemnations of liberalism's effect on political participation, liberalism's critics may have exaggerated their arguments. The problem is that critics ignore cleavages within the liberal tradition which might promote democratic participation. Surely there is tension between Locke's property-protecting liberalism of possessive individualism and Mill's liberalism of self-development (MacPherson 1973: essay 1). After all, the accumulation of property in a few hands impedes self-development for all, since property provides necessary security for the self to develop freely. Therefore, even in thoroughly liberal regimes, such as that of the United States, the protection of private property could conceivably become an issue capable of stimulating significant political participation.

Or consider the utilitarian/individualistic calculus in liberalism. Contrary to liberalism's critics, this calculus contains a rationale for recurrent conflict between rich and poor. The poor gain more utility from each unit of consumption than do the rich, for by definition the poor consume fewer units to begin with (Page 1983). Therefore, the poor have a strong interest in the egalitarian redistribution of goods. Meanwhile, the rich—though perhaps less motivated to protect their goods than the poor are to confiscate them—enjoy advantages which reduce the political costs they must pay in order to defend themselves against encroachments by the poor. The result of this logic should lead us to expect continual struggle between rich and poor.

Finally, liberalism does not sanction the *unlimited* expansion of individual rights within an inviolable private sphere. Even in the United States, liberals admit that public needs sometimes take precedence over private preferences (for example, Okun 1975). For this reason, groups wishing to expand the area of privacy for themselves—homosexuals or

Christian Scientists, for example—often confront public restrictions. Other groups wishing to expand public control over private beliefs—supporters of prayer in the public schools, for example—also push their case (for a review of the problem in education, see Gutmann 1987). In sum, disagreements about the public/private divide could stimulate democratic participation in all liberal systems, including the United States.

Finally, the American liberal tradition never eliminated all group antagonisms that stimulate political conflict. From the Revolution to the Civil War, North and South represented clearly articulated, opposed cultural visions (Norton 1986; Kelley 1979). The North visualized a future of industrial growth, commercial expansion, and urban prosperity; the South visualized a future of agrarianism, commercial restriction, and racial stratification. Culturally, the South represented a feminine image of organic evolution; the North represented a masculine image of mechanical, contrived, forced development (Norton 1986). Around this cultural cleavage, political participation flourished but could not resolve the struggle. Following the Civil War, racial and ethnic antagonisms continued to characterize American life. In our time, such antagonisms may actually have multiplied. Traditional racial conflict still erupts in the United States, and new forms of ethnic discrimination have entered American life (Kinder 1986: 151–71). Today Hispanics and Asians import their own particular grievances into American politics; as a result, an issue such as bilingual education can quickly engage Americans (Stein 1986). Finally, issues related to gender, such as the right to an abortion, also galvanize political participation. Thus, it is now possible to create political participation around wholly new issues.

Despite these arguments, liberalism does usually restrict political participation, not just in the United States, but elsewhere. Liberalism generally favors the individual against the group; yet strong groups promote participation. Liberalism generally favors minority rights against majority rule and the lone person against the united community; but participation is greater (by definition) when majorities act than when minorities act, and participation is also greater within a united community than among a set of isolated individuals. Liberalism supports the market; yet the market, by creating inequality, reduces political participation. On balance, therefore, liberalism usually deters fully developed, democratic participation. Only on the comparatively infrequent occasions when group antagonisms overcome these tendencies, as in the immigration- and religion-driven conflicts of the nineteenth-century United States, is this logic reversed.

Yet liberalism need not necessarily have these effects. Liberalism contains two theoretical dichotomies around which group conflict sometimes revolves: the public/private dichotomy and the individual/collectivity dichotomy. Liberal regimes promote struggle over whether public or private entities should make decisions and allocate resources. Liberal regimes also promote struggle over the rights of the individual versus the individual's responsibility to a collectivity.

What I call *conflictive democratic participation* often revolves around these two axes. Because these axes are fundamental to liberal theory, debate about them tends to galvanize group-based political participation. However, such participation, though quite intense, will usually promote democracy, for both axes legitimize the individual — either as a *private* person or as an individual possessing rights against a collectivity. Thus, liberalism protects moral equality, which is the fourth component of my definition of democracy (see page 6). In practice, therefore, when conflictive democratic participation embodies the very essence of liberalism, it can also motivate the group-based political participation that is necessary to democracy.

By debating issues and mobilizing citizens, mass movements and interest groups — which abound in the United States — advance conflictive democratic participation. Yet over the long term, strong political parties promote most conflictive democratic participation. Parties forge the particularistic concerns of mass movements and interest groups into general programs which often take a position on public/private and individual/collectivity questions. Moreover, parties produce governing majorities of politicians; mass movements and interest groups cannot. Finally, parties can use elections and candidates to mobilize more citizens than can mass movements or interest groups. Therefore, on balance, conflictive democratic participation ultimately depends more on political parties than on mass movements or interest groups.

The cultural forces which might promote conflictive democratic participation presuppose the communication of a particular subjective consciousness among democratic citizens. In the United States, for example, potentially powerful divisions (e.g., race or class divisions) can only stimulate participation if citizens comprehend and respond to pertinent stimuli. Citizens must perceive conflicts between private and public demands; or respond differentially to arguments for and against the redistribution of economic power; or recognize a conflict between individual rights and collective responsibilities; or identify personally with the many regional, ethnic, and racial subcultures which could trigger conflictive democratic participation. In short, a cultural theory of conflictive democratic participation attempts to identify a citizenry seized by appropriate attitudes and immersed in subjective cultures which transmit such attitudes.

Unfortunately, we know little about how cultural forces influence conflictive democratic participation in the United States. For example, in most empirical studies, the strongest single determinant of political participation turns out to be social class (Natchez 1985: 134; Wright 1976). Psychological phenomena function in the studies mainly as conduits of *structural* inequalities; they play only a minor independent, formative role themselves. And higher-order *cultural* factors never appear at all (Verba, Nie, and Kim 1978).

By omitting culture, the contemporary portrait of participation implicitly rejects certain classic historical treatments, such as that of Tocqueville, who attributed the widespread political participation he observed in America to certain "habits of the heart"— a complicated cultural mix of trust, community-mindedness, conventionality, and mutual suspicion (see also Bellah et al. 1985). In Tocqueville's account American culture was the arch which held together social classes, political institutions, and political participation. Our task is to recover and reexamine the cultural influences Tocqueville first identified.

Liberal Democracy and Conflictive Democratic Participation in Great Britain

The effect of liberal culture on conflictive democratic participation hinges in large part upon the particular categorical distinctions liberal culture establishes between social groups. The clearer such categories are, the easier it is for people to believe that their own personal fates are bound up with the group struggle, and the more likely people are to enter the fray.

In the United States, liberalism often masks group divisions. For example, Republicans promote private property for corporations, but they promote public control over the private lives of certain groups, such as homosexuals and single mothers on welfare. Meanwhile, Democrats promote government regulation of corporations, but they argue for a sharp distinction between the family and the polity. Thus, American liberalism is a weak categorizer (for a quite different perspective, see Durkheim and Mauss 1963).

But liberalism assumes different shapes in different national settings. In particular, internal lines of conflict differ from one liberal society to another. What lines of cleavage appear salient in the British version of liberalism?

As compared to liberal democracy in the United States, certain aspects of British liberal democracy contain an "elitist" quality. By elitism, I refer to the attitudes of entrenched social groups which have historically and customarily exerted political domination. Indeed, elitism predated and to some degree fostered both liberalism and capitalism in Britain. As Colin Leys explains it, "in Britain many features of the pre-capitalist state were carried over into the nineteenth century and beyond. The common element . . . was the 'representative patrician' nature of the state apparatus" (Leys 1983: 44). In Britain, as opposed to the United States, the emergence of liberalism did not require an entirely new institutional structure. After all, British liberalism did not have to overturn an imperial elite, as was true in the United States. Therefore, the cleavage between a traditionally powerful elite and a less powerful citizenry remains more salient in British politics than in American politics (Beer 1969).

Lest we conclude that today elitism has been confined to the right wing of British politics, consider Labour party politics. As Beer points out, until 1982, "under the traditional [Labour] structure, a person wishing to be nominated could have asked party members . . . to elect his supporters to the ward committees, which in turn would have chosen the members of the management committee vested with the power of nomination. That is how it had been done before the days of the direct primary in the United States" (Beer 1982: 167). By comparison, in the United States, party primaries began to dissolve residual elite power as early as the Progressive period.

Another difference between the British and American versions of liberal democracy revolves around the power of centralized government. In the United States, hostility to centralized political power remains strong (Lipset and Schneider 1987: 17); the American liberal tradition emphasizes federalism, which fragments political power in order to keep the individual secure. By contrast, centralized power enjoys considerable strength in Britain; Britian is a unitary, not a federal system. Moreover, by fusing executive and legislature, the doctrine of parliamentary sovereignty guarantees coherent Cabinet government, as opposed to the fragmentation of authority which the balance-of-powers doctrine creates in the United States. In Britain, Cabinet decisions enjoy virtually automatic support by a working party majority in Parliament. As Richard Rose puts it, "Armed with the authority of the Cabinet and support from the majority party in the House of Commons, the Prime Minister can be certain that nearly all legislation introduced during the year will be enacted into law" (1985: 93). Therefore, Cabinet, Prime Minister, and majority party together form a unified center of power in Britain; no comparably powerful force exists in American politics.

Nor need Parliament compete with the judiciary. Because there is no written constitution in Britain, justices cannot brandish a written document against the decrees of Parliament. By contrast, America's written Constitution makes the decisions of other political institutions essentially provisional, open to judicial review. The result of judicial intervention in the United States, of course, is a less centralized, less predictable central government.

Further political fragmentation in the United States results from the different voting districts and staggered elections of senators and representatives, as well as from the adoption of direct elections to the Senate after 1912. Significantly, in the same era when the American Senate established itself as a powerful electoral competitor to the House, competition between legislative institutions declined in Britain. During the nineteenth century, the House of Lords often thwarted the legislative will of the House of Commons, but the Parliament Act of 1911 abolished the right of the House of Lords to veto legislation from the Commons. Further centralization of power naturally resulted. Today, calls for the elimination of the House of Lords are common in British politics; one could hardly imagine a similar call for abolishing the U.S. Senate.

A related element of centralization in Britain involves the administration of public policy. Administrative departments in Britain are better insulated from citizen pressure than are their counterparts in the United States (for a journalistic study, see Bruce-Gardyne 1986). In part, this phenomenon reflects the fact that a strong British state developed prior to the administration of modern welfare programs. For example, local governments in Britain have played little role in determining welfare benefit levels. Therefore, Whitehall ministries have great power in welfare administration, as compared with the American practice of allocating some welfare administrative responsibility to state and local governments. Administrative centralization may also be traced to mechanisms of elite recruitment, which traditionally direct many graduates of prestigious universities (chiefly Oxford and Cambridge) into the higher reaches of the civil service. The result is a merger of social elitism with centralized power.

These forces of centralized recruitment have been complemented by other civil service powers. For example, in Britain, powerful civil service undersecretaries enjoy permanent appointment. Most win not only the trust but also the dependence of their ministers, who, because they move frequently among Cabinet and sub-Cabinet positions, must rely on the longer experience of their undersecretaries. By contrast, department deputy- and undersecretaries in the United States are political appointees with little independent influence. Therefore, they can neither enhance the power of centralized government nor insulate themselves from electoral pressures. Moreover, the absence of an American-style Open Files Law and the pro-concealment pressures of the Official Secrets Act permit English ministers to control the flow of information to Parliament and to the British public (Christolph 1984). Its control of information further allows the civil service to support centralized power.

In sum, British liberal democracy is a more sharply demarcated model of hierarchical authority than is American liberal democracy. The British version of liberal democracy encourages citizens to allocate distinctly different roles to themselves and their leaders, and to see politics primarily in terms of discrete structures (e.g., Parliament, civil service) and formal position (Beer 1969). By contrast, in the United States a hierarchy of legitimate authority has never fully emerged to provide as clearly demarcated a model of politics. Instead, from the Jacksonian period onward, decentralization, fragmented institutions, and occasional populist movements have brought citizens and institutions together in fluid and unstable forms. In the United States, because there were fewer clear, categorical differences between citizens and their leaders, political participation spilled across institutional boundaries. But in Britain, Parliamentary sovereignty and centralized authority prevented participation from blurring the dichotomies between leaders and led, or from transgressing institutional perimeters.

American political participation has been shaped not only by the fluidity of political institutions, but also by the fact that political action does not expose people to fundamental reprisals. The Bill of Rights intervened between the citizen and politics, so that political participation rarely jeopardized citizenship. As a result, at least one clear categorical distinction did develop in American politics: the distinction between individual rights and government power.

By contrast, as Rose points out, the British tradition includes no equivalent to the American notion of individual rights (1985: 138). Neither a written constitution, nor court decisions, nor Parliamentary enactments have produced a clear conception that an individual possesses by right a sphere of inviolate freedom. True, custom and tradition have enshrined in Britain many of the same rights Americans legally enjoy—rights to free speech, for example, or to *habeas corpus*. But the individual as a formal possessor of unalienable rights is less central to British culture than to American culture.

For this reason, when the British choose to participate politically, they may well seek out an established group of like-minded people, rather than strike out as independent political entrepreneurs. Lacking a legal *imprimatur*, the English participant may feel more personally vulnerable than the American. Thus, the institutional hierarchies of the British political model may be reproduced within a sharply demarcated group model of political participation, and the fragmented individualism of the American political model—particularly the absence of strong, autonomous government institutions—may be reproduced in fluid, poorly demarcated forms of political participation.

The differential legitimacy of hierarchy in the two societies also affects political recruitment. For example, American politicians have traditionally attempted to portray themselves as "of the people," not members of any clearly defined social class. Consider Robert Dole's reference to his humble origins as he contested the wealthy George Bush. Dole's attack forced Bush to argue that he too had worked to make his future. As Bush's response suggests, a "social cachet" may sometimes be the political kiss of death in the United States. Indeed, not even liberal Democrats from working-class backgrounds are allowed to justify their politics as a form of class solidarity. They favor the working *man*, not the working *class*.

By contrast, British politicians often profit from proudly avowing their class origins. The reverence which working-class Labour supporters directed toward Ernest Bevin derived in part from his steadfast loyalty to and frequently enunciated pride in his class of origin (see, in particular, Bullock 1960). Similarly, Tory leaders such as Winston Churchill, Harold Macmillan, Anthony Eden, and Alec Douglas-Home epitomized both in policy and in self-presentation the aristocracy which spawned them. Unlike George Bush, they felt no need to give up their accents in order to succeed politically.

Given Britain's less egalitarian character, it should not be surprising that liberalism has encountered more of a challenge in that country than in the United States. British liberalism's strongest competitor, of course, has been socialism as represented by the Labour party. But liberal individualism has also faced considerable opposition from Conservative collectivism and paternalism (Krieger 1986: chap. 3). Meanwhile, in the United States, not only has socialism never become the ideology of a main political party, but there has also never been a struggle between mercantile and landed interests for control of the Republican party. Instead, mercantile wealth dominated the purchase of land, and quickly turned most agriculture into an extension of a capitalistic economy. Those farmers left out of politics were not the "gentry," but the beleagured small holders whose attempt to gain power as a distinct class failed in 1896. In the United States, therefore, land could not function as a symbol of family tradition or as a repository of pre-industrial social relations (for an exception, see Gaventa 1980). Today the real estate development, the shopping mall, and the corporate farm symbolize the fate of agriculture in the Republican party. By contrast, in Britain, the country house, the manor, and the village green, until the rise of Mrs. Thatcher, symbolized agriculture in the Conservative party.

Partly for this reason, liberal democracy took on more collectivist forms in Britain than in the United States. As early as the time of John Stuart Mill, British liberalism had already reached beyond individual competition in search of a larger social vision. In the late nineteenth century (a time when individualistic competition, Social Darwinism, and Progressivist technocracy thoroughly triumphed in the United States), British liberalism turned to Idealist philosophers, such as T. H. Green, who attempted to move liberalism away from pure individualism (Vincent and Plant 1984; Freeden 1986). Consider a representative liberal thinker of the time, Hobson, "who . . . recognized that each individual in feeling and in action . . . is both an individual and a member of social groups. The science of economics should, therefore, consider all members of society and all facets of their existence, for the individual and collective development of all members of society was the goal of an ideal economic system" (Weiler 1982: 171–72). Thus, by the early twentieth century, British liberals had concluded that liberalism must adapt itself to the British culture of clear classification, hierarchy, and group struggle.

By contrast, Progressivism was the closest American equivalent to this late-nineteenth-century British liberal critique. Like New Liberalism in Britain, American Progressivism recognized the dangers of unbridled competition and uncontrolled markets. But American Progressivism relied upon science and moral exhortation to end monopolies and political corruption. In so doing, it destroyed Populism's ambiguous group challenge to economic power, "neutralized" the conflict between workers and capitalists, sanitized the political parties, and stirred immigrants into the American melting pot. Progressivism attempted to homogenize American life rather than accept class division as a starting point for conflictive democratic participation (for example, De Brizzi 1983).

The Progressive movement exemplifies a characteristic American method for generating collective action, namely, altruistic motivation — described as early as in Tocqueville. This view refuses to accept group conflict as potentially positive; however, though productive of volunteerism, it cannot sustain political participation as effectively as does ideologically or theoretically based group conflict.

The key question is whether the British model of bounded hierarchy generates a cultural predisposition toward conflictive democratic participation. I shall argue that the British model does in fact generate such a predisposition.

Consider first the nexus between class and politics. To speak of British politics as more class-based than American politics is a cliché, perhaps even a misleading cliché during an era of party "dealignment" (Sarlvik and Crewe 1983). Nevertheless, the cliché retains considerable truth. Compare, for example, the strength of labor unions in Britain and the United States. In 1978, 55 percent of all British employees were members of unions, as compared to only 22 percent in the United States (Leys 1983: 115). Unions traditionally transmit images of class to workers; the weakness of the American union movement is perhaps the most important indication of how American liberal individualism influences contemporary American politics. Meanwhile, union power, though waning, continues to inscribe group hierarchy on contemporary British politics.

In addition, a strong regional component now abets British class politics. Until recently, British politics was more nationally homogeneous than American politics. Aided by a national press emanating from London, by an economy with few distinctive regional components, and by weak local governments, British politics has traditionally been freer of geographical variations than American politics. Today, however, a longstanding North-South cultural cleavage has expanded in Britain (Butler and Kavanaugh 1988: 284).

This regional shift has intensified British class/party differences. The North has become much poorer than the South, a fact which stimulates Labour success in the North. This region/class overlap contrasts sharply with the cross-cutting effects of regionalism in the United States. For example, the wealthy white Southern presence long kept conservatism alive in a "naturally" progressive Democratic party. Similarly, Republican sentiments among lower-middle-class rural and small-town North-erners confined Democratic support mainly to large cities (for a general treatment, see Lunch 1987). Today, while regional factors increase class/party cleavages in Britain, regionalism disrupts class/party cleav-ages in the United States, as the Sun Belt phenomenon suggests.

When we turn from class and region directly to parties, the distinc-tions between the American and British versions of liberal democracy again emerge sharply. For example, the concept of a political "indepen-dent" makes little sense to the British voter; indeed, investigators of vot-ing in Britain do not even bother to employ the concept (see, for ex-ample, Franklin 1985). In Britain, the operative model of politics assumes that party stability and party membership are the norm; therefore, "in-dependence" disturbs the model's categorical system. By contrast, in the United States the label *independent* is almost as meaningful as that of *Republican* or *Democrat*. All party-relevant labels in the United States refer to *psychological* identifications, which can be as easily al-tered as they were forged in the first place. The difference between the two party systems is captured by the fact that one pays dues and carries the membership card of a political party in Britain. By contrast, one "contributes money" in America. In Britain, at least in their organiza-tional guises, the parties resemble permanent institutions rather than voluntary, fluid organizations, as in the United States.

Indeed, in Britain even the concept of *government* is identified with the concept of party. "When a national survey asks people to say what first comes to mind when the word government is mentioned, three-fifths reply in terms of representative institutions, namely Parliament and parties" (Rose 1985: 72). The public's association of government with a ruling Parliamentary party virtually assures the party system a central place in British politics. This conception is quite different from that in the United States, where "government" tries to stand "above" party conflict. Thus, in summary, class polarization, party strength, and regionalism galvanize and reinforce the hierarchical cultural model of British liberal democracy.

Finally, let us consider the question of ideology. It is well known that most people in advanced industrial societies do not organize their politi-cal ideas along a single left-right dimension of ideology (for example, see Sniderman and Tetlock 1986a: 62–97). But there remains a mean-ingful difference between the British electorate, which still confronts a major party pledged to socialism, and the American electorate, whose "left" party avoids socialism like the plague. Surely there must be some ideologically significant difference between the British public, 39 percent of which responds favorably to the symbol of socialism (Rose 1985: 152), and the American public, whose most leftward-leaning elites fall ideologically to the *right* of Swedish industrialists (Verba and Orren 1985: 256)! In Britain debate about capitalism and socialism continues to generate participation in politics; in the United States, where no such debate exists, conflictive democratic participation suffers.

A useful test of my argument to this point involves racial politics. In the late 1940s, significant numbers of West Indians began to enter Britain, where, as citizens of the Commonwealth, they enjoyed a right of domicile. They were followed in the 1960s by many Pakistanis and Indians, and in the early 1970s by Ugandan Asians. A polarized racial politics in Britain soon developed, culminating in the formation of an anti-immigrant, pro-repatriation political party—the National Front—and in an inflammatory speech by a Conservative government minister, Enoch Powell, who prophesied "rivers of blood" in British streets if unrestricted immigration continued. Several Acts of Parliament both preceded and followed Powell's speech. These Acts, in effect, deprived most Commonwealth citizens of an assured right to settle in Britain. Eventually, the stream of New Commonwealth immigration to the British population slowed and stabilized (for a brief overview, see McLean 1982: 35–36).

In percentage terms, black immigrants to Britain do not approach the population of American blacks, much less that of recent Asian and Hispanic immigrants (legal and illegal) in the United States. Still, their numbers were sufficient to create racially polarized British politics. As Krieger observes, "Blacks may be British citizens, but the whites won't let them be part of the English nation" (1986: 103).

My intention is not to debate comparative degrees of racism in Britain and the United States. Certainly there is more than enough racial hatred to go around in both countries. Rather, my point is that blacks entered a British society characterized by a hierarchical, group-based cultural model of politics. Therefore, it is no surprise that, though small in numbers, blacks encountered strong resistance. By contrast, in the United States during these same years, racial polarization has ebbed and flowed. In the 1950s and early 1960s, the civil rights movement integrated public schools and reduced racial discrimination in hiring, in occupational recruitment, in public facilities, and in voting (for a history, see Williams 1987). But this period of integration (i.e., category breakdown) ended in riots and despair in the later 1960s. The 1970s saw modest renewals of joint black and white efforts towards desegregation, in the form of affirmative action programs, scattered-site housing, and the slow growth of a sizable black middle class. But then repolarization occurred around the "benign neglect" policies of the Reagan administration. Most recently, of course, the first black presidential contender, Jesse Jackson, mounted an impressive national campaign which attracted many white voters.

Thus, in the United States, a large racial minority has struggled to define itself as a unified group within a culture where group boundaries are often not clear, group appeals not entirely legitimate, and hierarchical models of politics unpopular. Of course, race remains the most stubbornly fixed group element in American politics. Even so, fluidity, instability, and uneven racial progress are natural consequences of the American cultural model (for relevant attitudinal data and theory, see Schuman, Steeh, and Bobo 1985), just as the virtual political exclusion of black immigrants is a natural consequence of Britain's hierarchical, group-based model.

Some observers now suggest that Britain has entered a period of populism, and has become more like the United States. Alleged symptoms of this shift are the revolt against party elites in both major parties, the emergence of the Social Democrats, the student revolts of the 1960s, the growth of racial disorder, widespread disenchantment with the current party system, and resurgent nationalism in Scotland and Wales (see Studlar and Waltman 1984). How closely these developments resemble American-style populism is uncertain. Certainly there are today more opportunities for grass-roots participation in British politics than ever before, including public inquiries, novel experiments with economic democracy (for a relevant study, see Ursell 1983: 327–53), and candidate reselection in the Labour party. Yet the basic cultural template of British politics — a hierarchical, group-based model of politics — constricts and shapes such efforts, just as historically it tempered the individualizing effects of British liberalism. Thus, British politics continues to expect groups as such to mount more conflictive democratic participation than is characteristic in the United States.

Liberal Democracy and Conflictive Democratic Participation in Canada

It is tempting to describe Canadian liberal democracy as an uneasy synthesis of American individualistic fluidity and British group hierarchy. But such a characterization gives us little analytic purchase, for it leaves unanswered the question of whether there is a distinctly "Canadian" quality to this synthesis. This analytic problem is compounded by the fact that the Canadian political system is in great flux, more so than that of the United States or Great Britain. Constitutional conferences of great significance are at this writing very much on the Canadian political agenda. Even "Canadian identity" itself is still a matter of heated debate (for an excellent study, see Verney 1986). Thus, contrasts between Canada and its British and American cousins defy any simple, "composite" characterization.

Our task is further confounded by the complex history of liberalism in Canada. Before the American Revolution, "the scanty English-speaking population of Canada-to-be . . . was fundamentally American in outlook" (McRae 1964: 234). But the American Revolution brought to Canada a British Loyalist resistance to American-style liberalism (Horowitz 1966: 143–71; Conway 1988: 381–96). Yet, unlike the British Conservatives whose political views they shared, these new Canadians found themselves living "in the atmosphere of the frontier" (McRae 1964: 236). No wonder Canadian liberal democracy did not copy British or American models; instead, the antirevolutionary circumstances of its history created a distinctly Canadian culture of liberal democracy, one with a strong admixture of Burkean conservatism (see Lipset 1989: chap. 1).

Of course, the chief reason Canadian liberal democracy is not a simple composite of British and American models is that it confronts a sizable, historically prior, regionally entrenched French minority that still shares only partially in the liberal model. Not only did French settlements in Quebec, New Brunswick, and Western Canada attempt to evade British control, but they also rejected the French Revolution. French Canada was essentially pre-Revolutionary in tradition (Pelletier 1988: 265–83), bound to a repudiated French monarchy and to a vanished French empire. French Canada was not the France of *liberté, égalité, fraternité*, the France created by the Revolution of 1789. Instead, it was the France of the *ancien régime*.

The unique character of Canadian liberal democracy thus inheres in the effort to adjust British and American concepts to the French-Canadian challenge. Douglas Verney (1986) identifies the most difficult problem in this respect when he asks if liberalism's characteristic individualism, political equality, and national sovereignty can be achieved when a substantial body of citizens prefers religious corporatism, minority rule in certain places (i.e., Quebec), and attenuated national sovereignty.

Some writers (e.g., Presthus, Kornberg) have characterized Canadian politics as "consociational" (Presthus 1973). But consociationalism provides more genuine group power sharing on national issues than is characteristic of Canada. Consociationalism appears to develop more in small countries (Belgium, Holland, Lebanon) than in countries as large as Canada. Our primary concern therefore is first to sketch the major classificatory qualities of Canadian liberal democracy, and only thereafter to apply appropriate terminology to the Canadian model.

Three components of the British model play an important role in Canada: Parliamentarianism, elitism, and deference. Both at the national and the provincial levels, Canada is a Parliamentary system complete with Cabinet government. Indeed, the Canadian imposition of Parliamentarianism in Quebec—where a different model predated the British amalgamation of Upper and Lower Canada in 1840—testifies to the centrality of the Westminster model to an understanding of Canadian liberal democracy.

Yet there are also deviations from the majoritarianism and party government of the Westminster model. For example, under the terms of the British North America Act of 1867, the Parliament at Ottawa lacked full sovereignty, since Canada legally remained subject to the power of the British Governor-General. Indeed, Canada remained officially a British colony until 1948: only in the 1980s did a Canadian Constitution supersede the British North America Act. In a sense, therefore, Canada remained a colony into our own time.

In addition, as a "co-equal," though numerically smaller, "founding people," the French in Canada enjoy a position which conflicts with the majoritarianism of the Parliamentary model. As Verney points out, customs mandating French representation in Cabinet (especially in Liberal party cabinets) early on modified the Parliamentary model, for in strictly majoritarian terms French interests would not necessarily have been represented. In addition, the British North America Act of 1867 assured the English-speaking minority in Quebec its own schools; elsewhere, to assure that English-speaking rights not be withdrawn in Quebec, French minorities in several provinces received similar, though often unimplemented, assurances from Anglophone majorities (Verney 1986: 269–71). Obviously special protection for the rights of identifiable minorities does not accord with the majoritarianism of the British model.

Understandably, given these unique conditions, the Canadian political system has never achieved the ideological and partisan clarity of its British forebear. Instead, Liberals and Progressive Conservatives—the two dominant parties—resemble each other more closely than do British Conservatives and Labour. Though supporting policies of social welfare and reform, the Liberals have, unlike British Labour, resisted socialism, and have quite loose ties to labor unions (Horowitz 1966:

143–71). Moreover, historically, Liberals have reserved a special place in the party for French Canadians both within and outside Quebec; in short, Liberals have never become predominantly a class-based party. Finally, the Canadian tradition of provincial autonomy and the sheer size of Canada have militated against the clear national party distinctions characteristic of Britain.

Yet socialism—though less important than in Britain—is still a major force in Canada, as it is not in the United States. The development of agrarian radicalism in Western Canada, especially in Alberta and British Columbia, spawned the Cooperative Commonwealth Federation and its successor, the New Democratic Party (NDP). Both parties have long held minority blocks of seats in Parliament and enjoyed majority power in some prairie provinces. Recently the NDP enjoyed an upsurge in popularity (see "Testing Time for the NDP," *Maclean's*, 15 August 1988: 12). Moreover, the Parti Quebecois also incorporates some explicitly socialist elements in its platform. While neither party is wholly socialist, each endorses some socialist policies, including selective nationalization of industry. But, as contrasted to Britain, these parties remain institutionalized minorities which contest the two dominant parties. Still, in sharp contrast to the United States, they have secured a firm legislative position.

The second British component of Canadian politics is elitism. As early as the 1800s "Family Compacts" of linked mercantile aristocracies enjoyed considerable power in British Canada. According to McRae (1964), there was a "substantial similarity between the Family Compacts and the American colonial oligarchies before the Revolution" (see also Lower 1958: 140). But in Canada there was no revolution against colonial rule, as in the United States; therefore, no popular force challenged the Family Compacts. As a result, it proved easy for Parliamentary authority in Canada to forge an early and uncontested alliance with traditional mercantile elites. Other factors also contributed to this elitest development; as Hockin puts it, "an authoritarian tradition in Quebec, the lack of a revolutionary history, the use of the Royal Canadian Mounted Police to police the opening of Canada's west (in vivid contrast to the American 'wild west'), and much of Canada's constitutional, economic and political thought, also show a blend of conservatism and faith in the state" (1975: 14).

Thus, while Americans adopted fluid forms of voluntary participation and a weak state, Canadians reacted to insecurity (such as the frontier experience) by erecting a strong state and informal social discipline. Meanwhile, in Quebec, a preliberal clerical tradition kept power out of the hands of the "habitant." Finally, within British Canada, a strong commercial elite, with close ties to the British Crown, successfully resisted American "plans" for the incorporation of Canada into an expanding American empire. This success reinforced elite power and further restricted mass participation. As recently as 1973, Presthus could still characterize Canadian politics as nonparticipatory, because of the control French and British elites enjoyed in accommodation with each other (1973: 8).

Two important aspects of the Canadian liberal democratic model were the strong state tradition and the comparative absence of constitutionally stated, judicially protected individual rights. The strong state tradition orginated in a British-style civil service shielded from popular political pressures. As Hockin explains, the British practice of appointing Canadian civil servants directly from London has never entirely disappeared (though Ottawa is now the source); additionally, American-style suspicion of bureaucrats as a class never fully took hold (Hockin 1975: 162; see also Flaherty 1988: 99–129). A strong, secure bureaucracy allowed the Canadian state to undertake initiatives of the sort Americans have resisted, such as the formation of a Canadian Broadcasting Corporation charged specifically with promoting national unity (Dick 1983: 129), and the nationalization of Canadian airlines. The Canadian civil service could also promote welfare-state reforms successfully while simultaneously entering into full partnership with Canadian industry; by contrast, in the United States both developments occurred in an almost *sub rosa* fashion.

The British model also retarded the development of legally protected, constitutionally explicit individual rights. As Verney puts it, "the notion of parliamentary (or legislative) supremacy meant that the courts were never to pass judgment on the validity of parliamentary statutes as being repugnant to the common law" (1986: 132–33). In the twentieth century, Canadian courts have been reluctant to rule on the constitutionality of important government acts; for example, during the Manitoba school crisis, local judicial authorities first attempted to avoid a decision on the constitutional merits of the case, next reluctantly opposed the Manitoba legislature, and then ultimately lost ignominiously (Verney 1986: 275). Even "the Federal Court Act of 1970 . . . did not on the whole improve the citizen's recourse against Federal administrative agencies. The Act does not require boards, beyond the rules of natural justice, to conduct hearings according to any minimum standards of procedure or to what an American might call 'due process'" (Hockin 1975: 143). Though in 1982 Canada adopted a Bill of

Rights similar in some respects to that of the United States, the historical point remains that the individual/state cleavage—a principal divide in American politics—appears less salient in Canada.

In other respects, such as decentralization and institutional fluidity, the Canadian liberal democratic model resembles the American model. As a political entity, Canada gradually added provinces on terms which very much resemble the early, strong American versions of "states' rights." In Canada, as in the United States, education remains a provincial rather than a federal responsibility—so much so that, until recently, provincial politics hindered a national bicultural solution to French/English friction. While some provinces (e.g., Ontario) generally complied with the Royal Commission on Biculturalism and Bilingualism's (1969) recommendations for the protection of linguistic minorities, others (e.g., British Columbia) proved quite resistant (Soucie 1987). Federal government pressure has yet to overcome all these provincial barriers.

The most dramatic manifestation of provincial power in Canada is the pattern of periodic consultations between the Prime Minister and provincial authorities over the terms of confederation. Such forums are unimaginable even in the United States; certainly they provide ample opportunity for individual provinces and whole regions (especially the West) to promote their own interests within the unsettled confederational arrangement (Axworthy 1988: 129–55). As a result, Canadian regionalism flourishes—wholly apart from the French/English conflict.

Provincial power creates provincial party systems with quite different priorities from the national party system. In national politics the Liberals have usually supported a pan-Canadian republic within which French and English Canadians would subordinate themselves to a stable Canadian national identity. But in Quebec the Liberal party attempted to insulate the "habitant" from the high tides of English nationalism. Outside Quebec, Liberalism was expansionist and individualistic; within Quebec, it was restrictive and corporatist. The situation resembles that of southern Democrats in the Democratic party prior to the civil rights struggles of the 1960s, which finally drove the state parties closer to the national party.

It is therefore hardly surprising that political parties in Canada lack the cohesion usually associated with a parliamentary system. Partly for this reason, Canadian parties of the left have not always succeeded in effecting close alliances with national labor unions; and, in turn, Canadian unions were and still are weaker than those in Britain. Thus, while a hierarchical model of liberal democracy does exist in Canada, a model of social *class* hierarchy is not quite as evident.

The factor which most distinguishes the Canadian liberal democratic model is, of course, Anglophone/Francophone dualism. The importance of this dualism cannot be overestimated; consider, for example, that for many years French and English Canadians could not even agree on the same national anthem. The English version of the anthem envisaged the future expansion of Canada northward, with English-Canadian sentinels resolutely on guard. The French version apothesized the past, with French "forefathers" bringing the Cross to Canada and then protecting not an *expanding* Canada but, instead, the "hearths" of Quebec alone. As recently as 1965, Canadians remained at odds about a national flag; a compromise (maple leaf) design finally triumphed over a British insignia (the Union Jack) or a French insignia (the fleur-de-lis).

The dualism of Canadian politics is enshrined in law and custom. According to the Official Languages Act of 1969, French and English are co-equal languages of the two "founding peoples." Therefore, each language enjoys protected federal status. Furthermore, partly through provincial acts such as Quebec's Bill 101, partly through federal law, the French language enjoys legal protection within Canada's provinces.

Canadian conceptions of language and ethnicity differ markedly from such conceptions in the United States or Britain. The United States, despite its vaunted ethnic diversity, does not recognize minority cultures by law; as we will see in chapter 6, American bilingual education programs are meant to assist in the transition to the majority language — English. Paradoxically, the primary purpose of bicultural education is assimilation. By contrast, in Canada, the purpose of bilingual education is the rejuvenation of both French and English cultures, around which clusters a mosaic of "third force" cultures drawn from recent non-French, non-English immigrants (Harney 1988: 51–99). Meanwhile, the British extend no educational recognition at all to competing languages or cultures, except in purely symbolic ways.

How does the dualism of Canadian politics affect the possibilities of conflictive democratic participation in Canada? To be sure, the hierarchical features of Parliamentarianism in Canada do their usual sharpening of classification and conflict. For example, Landes found in a limited study that, "Canadian children indicate a higher level of partisan identification in all grades [4–8] than . . . American children" (1977: 75). In Canada early-learned partisanship may promote the party dialogue characteristic of a hierarchical, group-based model of politics. These tendencies are complemented by party solidarity in Parliament. By 1976, "only once in the history of Canada (had) a government been defeated in the House of Commons as a result of its own followers voting against it" (Matheson 1976: 187).

But, in Canada, in contrast to Britain, these party classifications lack strong social class roots. For example, "the portion of the electorate which supported the Liberals during the 1940s and the 1950s was not distinguished from the rest of the voters by significant social and economic characteristics" (Smiley 1967: 49; see also Meisel 1975). By contrast, in the United States of the 1930s, the New Deal coalitions had constructed a distinctive class base for America's loosely structured party system.

The chief reason for the lack of coordination between partisan identity and class in Canada is a disjunction between the Parliamentary, majoritarian model of liberal politics, and an alternative dualistic, regional, ethnic model. As Verney (1986) points out, the majoritarian model conflicts with Canada's adherence to co-equal, constitutionally protected French and English cultures. Were it permitted to run its natural course, the majoritarian model would erode the protections Francophones enjoy. Instead, however, there is tension not only between Parliamentary parties, but also between those who favor extending the majoritarian model throughout Canada and those who support a dualist or even multicultural model. The result of this tension is a more complicated system of political classification than we find in either Britain or the United States.

The Canadian dualistic model supports horizontal cultural tension between French- and British-Canadian identities. French Canada is Catholic; British Canada is Protestant, a superimposition of religious upon linguistic polarization which is a critical feature of Canadian life, particularly in the area of education. As Verney explains it, "public education in Canada was not as secular as in the United States, because in Canada there was no constitutional separation of church and state. At the same time, there was no Canadian Established Church as in Britain. . . . Certainly the educational system was not unreligious. As in England, it was secular only in the sense of being 'nondemonimational'" (1986: 272). The dangers felt by French Catholics under this system were somewhat mitigated by the Church's domination of Quebecois education, a domination which has only recently eroded. In any case, the superimposition of language, regionalism, religion, and education permits dualism in Canada to promote conflictive democratic participation.

Another factor that supports conflictive democratic participation in Canada is, of course, the continuing debate about the very survival of the nation. Although a referendum in 1980 decisively rejected "sovereignty association" (the proposition that Quebec should negotiate withdrawal from all but economic ties with the rest of Canada), the referendum did not signal satisfaction with existing political arrangements. Indeed, the abortive Meech Lake Accord would have ceded major new rights to Quebec as "a distinct society," a decision which promoted further conflictive democratic participation. The refusal to ratify Meech Lake has, in turn, stimulated new calls for a sovereign Quebec.

Thus, uniquely, the Canadian liberal democratic model is as much negative as positive. The cleavages that stimulate conflictive democratic participation in Canada emerge as much from the need Canadians feel to *defend* themselves as from any desire to advance common values. In no respect is this defensive posture more salient than in Canadian anti-Americanism.

Anti-Americanism in Canada is a natural consequence of geographical reality. Forced by an inclement climate to reside near the American border, many Canadians feel themselves at risk vis-à-vis their more populous and powerful neighbor. Many Canadians spend vacations and/or long periods of work in the United States. There is naturally a fear of permanent emigration, a fear supported by a long history of substantial Canadian emigration to the United States (Malcolm, 1986: 153). Moreover, the flight of American Loyalists to Canada created a lingering tradition of anti-American sentiment within Anglo Canada; as Americans moved away from the mother country toward independence, the Loyalists strengthened their ties with England. And in the 1960s French-Canadian nationalists singled out the United States for its economic imperialism in Quebec. Anti-Americanism thus fueled Quebecois separatism.

Anglo/French and Canadian/American cleavages are intertwined. For example, a fresh wave of anti-Americanism swept through Canadian politics during the 1970s, when Canadians themselves were at odds over the future of Quebec. In part, Canadians—newly insecure about their national unity—used the United States as a scapegoat to reinstate Canadian identity. Thus, nationalist definitions in multiple forms infuse Canadian culture and politics more pervasively than in Britain or the United States. The result is a complicated but strong pattern of conflictive democratic participation.

Conclusion

I have argued that in Britain, Canada, and the United States varying political histories and institutions have crystallized into three distinct blueprints of liberal democracy. These blueprints, or cultural models, demarcate the group classifications, conflict cleavages, group boundary properties, and normal modes of participation through which conflictive democratic participation may emerge.

In the United States, liberalism's unchallenged domination continually disrupts major group and institutional classifications. The American cultural blueprint is, therefore, fluid; few solidary groups find legitimate cultural footholds upon which to build conflictive democratic participation. The primacy of private life and of a market economy drains energy away from political activity centered on the state. Also, the cultural theme of individual success questions the legitimacy of group-based motives. Finally, the powerfully reproduced inequalities of market capitalism suppress political participation among the disadvantaged. In anthropological terms, therefore, the United States is a culture in which the legitimate domain of politics is narrow and individualistic even for newly mobilized groups, such as blacks and women. For all these reasons, participation in American politics has a sporadic, fluid, unpredictable quality, rarely fully conflictive or democratic.

By contrast, in Britain, a hierarchical model of liberal democracy has crystallized. The classificatory features of British politics remain comparatively clear and persistent (e.g., class, party, and—now—race). The legitimate resolution of conflict extends from socialism on the left to pure market capitalism on the right, all within a Parliamentary format. Perceived opportunities for individuals to escape group constraints are fewer in Britain than in the United States; traditional distinctions between leaders and led are strong; and the domain of legitimate political activity is broader than in the United States. These factors favor conflictive democratic participation.

Finally, a principal feature of Canadian politics is a conscious struggle over Canadian culture. Unlike the United States or Britain, Canada explicitly promotes or suppresses culture *as such* (whether French, British, or a mosaic of ethnic cultures) (Handler 1988). The appearance of culture as a legitimate political issue conveys to Canada a unique quality, provoking unusual horizontal and vertical classifications and a markedly dualistic cultural structure. Individualism is less common than in the United States; yet class consciousness is weaker than in Britain. However, the combination of religion, language, and region provides a sharp line of conflict in Canada. Moreover, French-Canadian clericalism and prairie socialism provide challenges to liberal individualism. Canadian culture thus consists of strong group classifications, a broad political domain, and a complex conflict between a hierarchical model of Parliamentary liberalism and a bifurcated model of race and region. It is hardly surprising that a stable Canadian national identity remains but a prospect, and that considerable fuel for conflictive democratic participation exists.

Our next task is to follow these blueprints of liberal democracy from their governmental to their nongovernmental manifestations. Culture describes a concentric circle of homologous classifications throughout a society. The aspects of politics we have just identified should, therefore, appear throughout the culture. Indeed, a principal hypothesis of this study is that these blueprints infuse popular culture. Popular culture thereby helps reproduce the institutions of liberal democracy. But culture can also alter or even undermine political institutions. This is because culture, in "making sense" of liberal democracy, sometimes encourages people to remake liberal democracy itself.

CHAPTER TWO

Popular Culture as Liberal Democratic Discourse

Culture's role in shaping conflictive democratic participation takes two forms. The first *— political culture as individual attitudes — is a surface manifestation of a deep cultural structure revealed in the* second *— popular culture narratives. The argument in this chapter borrows from Durkheim's ideas about collective representations and from recent research in symbolic anthropology. Questions of theory and method are addressed in preparation for the country analyses that follow.*

Liberal Democracy in Popular Culture

By what means do the cultural models of liberal democratic politics described in chapter 1 become diffused? After all, only a few people take an active part in the political process. How then does a cultural model of politics make its way from this elite of political actors to the larger, generally passive public?

One answer to this question is popular culture: the consciously contrived, deliberately produced media forms which abound in all three societies and reach a large audience. I shall argue that popular culture elaborates liberal democracy's cultural dimensions. Popular culture reproduces the group/individual; the static/dynamic; and the egalitarian/hierarchical elements of liberalism. Moreover, popular culture links all three dimensions together in accessible and attractive story forms or narratives (for an empirical investigation, see Riley 1983: 414–37). These narratives construe the lives of ordinary people within a liberal democratic culture (see also Douglas 1982b; Abramson, Arterton, and Orren, 1988; Nimmo and Combs, 1985).

Claims of this sort abound in anthropological studies of folk culture and high culture (Geertz 1983; DiMaggio 1987: 440–55; Bourdieu and Passeron 1977). But in Britain, Canada, and the United States neither folk culture nor high culture dominates cultural discourse. Instead, the mass media — not the oral folk tale or grand opera — tell our stories. A mass-mediated popular culture provides many of the socially validated cultural images by which we live, including the narrative of liberal democratic politics in everyday life.

Can there be a single popular culture in such heterogeneous societies as Britain, the United States, and Canada? In each country we find a complex pattern of ethnic and class distinctions, regional identities, and religious sectarianism. Surely description of a single popular culture — much less a unitary culture of politics descending from liberal democracy — must oversimplify this diversity.

To this question, let me offer three responses. First, liberal democracy in popular culture creates a system of discourse — a characteristic mode of conceiving and expressing social relationships (for a related approach to social relations, see Perin 1988). Although this system may not capture fully a group's particular experience, it does represent and interpret these feelings in a way that connects the group to other groups. Therefore, while systems of discourse never represent the experiential world comprehensively (Gardner 1985), they nevertheless restrain, constrain, and domesticate parochial perceptions. Indeed, culture as a system of discourse distinguishes the cosmopolitan from the parochial or the particular from the universal in the first place.

Second, as a system of discourse, culture helps every group *adapt* itself to the demands and opportunities which other groups present. The culture of a society is a lingua franca through which groups regulate their relationships with each other. Social interdependence forces even the most parochial group to share in partaking culture. Over time, group or individual survival requires the use of cultural discourse, even when a particular group would prefer to avoid the culture entirely.

Finally, cultural discourse describes the acceptable forms of political conflict in a society. Inevitably, therefore, such discourse construes both the experience of disadvantaged minorities and the experience of advantaged majorities. Every group contributes to conflict; therefore, if culture ignores any group, it loses its function of communication and regulation. Of course, no culture performs this function perfectly; one of the aims of this study is to understand the paradoxical combination of conflict representation and conflict suppression in liberal democratic cultural discourse.

Another aspect of cultural diversity involves the *production* of popular culture (Gans 1974). The book publishers who produce and disseminate social studies textbooks, for example, are different from the advertising agencies that produce and disseminate television commercials (Coser et al. 1982; Bensman 1967). The public relations departments which design and produce corporate publications are different from rock music producers — and so on.

But diversity in *production* should not be confused with diversity in a *system of discourse*. If culture is a form of discourse, then we must turn first to discourse itself rather than to its production. Moreover, if we examine forms of popular culture *seriatim*, a verdict of unlimited cultural diversity becomes foreordained. Yet just as a language consists of rules for combining parts of speech, so also does a culture consist of rules for combining individual spheres of popular culture: for example, advertising, corporate publications, television shows, and textbooks. No study can connect all spheres, but even an incomplete attempt distinguishes culture as *discourse* from culture as an unrelated, confusing sequence of illusions. The approach I pursue seeks the configurational "rules" of liberal democratic culture as a whole, rather than treating individual cultural forms as meaningful only in themselves. Culture is a system of relationships, not a set of compartments (see Leymore 1982: 421–34). It is a text, not a file cabinet.

Finally, what about audience diversity? There are different audiences for different forms of popular culture. Yet the pluralism of audiences is often overstated. For example, people who read magazines have usually been exposed to considerable amounts of textbook culture. Most such people also watch a good bit of television, and many receive — either as wage earners or as shareholders — one or more corporate publications. As a system of discourse, popular culture may not penetrate all segments of a society equally, but it does reach a large, potentially powerful segment of society.

Objections to studying popular culture as liberal democratic discourse also emerge from other directions (e.g., Williams 1981; Ewen 1988). In an effort to account for the failure of working-class and intelligentsia opposition to capitalism, some neo-Marxist theorists argue that the capitalist class has created a popular culture which preserves the class's hegemony (Williams 1981; Ewen 1988; Exoo 1987). The question, of course, is whether my formulations underplay the relationship of cultural discourse to the power of dominant economic classes.

I reject this argument. For one thing, in Britain, Canada, and the United States the liberal tradition took root before industrial capitalism flowered. Given this fact, we can readily wonder whether liberalism shaped capitalism, or whether capitalism reshaped liberalism, but it is certainly implausible that capitalism actually *submerged* liberal politics in the struggle over culture.

Moreover, capitalist ownership of the media does not assure a "dominant class *ideology*" (Abercrombie, Hill, and Turner 1980). The economic structure of popular culture no more determines cultural *content* than does diversity in the audience. We therefore must examine cultural content itself before drawing any conclusions.

Indeed, if they constitute an important part of popular culture, then liberal values might restrict procapitalist messages in popular culture. Though it is a *truncated* theory of conflictive democratic participation, liberalism is nevertheless a theory of democracy (Bowles and Gintis 1986; Carnoy and Levin 1985). Therefore, it constitutes a language that can be used to deny capitalists the full bounties of legitimacy. Paradoxically, if the dominant class actually *adopts* liberal democratic discourse for itself, it contrives to question its own power.

But if institutions are not free from liberal cultural values, neither is liberal culture free from institutional interests. Ultimately, institutions and cultures combine uneasily to produce and reproduce political life. This volume emphasizes the particular role culture plays, but culture is dialectically connected to institutional structures, both adapting to institutional change and promoting such change when institutions fall beneath liberal democratic cultural norms.

Finally, the hegemonic perspective unwarrantedly divides cultural "mystification" from economic "truth," assuming that culture is the tail which the economic dog wags, albeit "in the last instance [*sic*]" (Abercrombie, Hill, and Turner 1980). By contrast, the perspective I urge denies such a separation. Culture and economics cannot contradict each other completely if either is to endure. As a result, cultural discourse inevitably constrains dominant and subordinate classes alike.

How Not to Proceed: The Political Culture Approach

In 1984, according to Byron E. Shafer, "the rise of culture as the organizing issue in American politics was so fully realized that it did not so much dominate other issues as subsume them" (1984: 227). Shafer defines the cultural issue as a series of debates about "the basic values and patterns of preference by which individual citizens organize their daily lives" (1984: 221). Today cultural politics in Shafer's sense retains its importance in the United States; such issues as abortion, creationism, textbook censorship, prayer in the public schools, capital punishment, race in foreign policy (e.g., apartheid in South Africa), *inter alia*, remain at the top of the American political agenda.

Yet, welcome though it is, Shafer's piece underestimates the range of cultural politics in three ways: historical, sociological, and conceptual. As to history, Shafer does not recognize that the "traditional"/

"rational" divide which he believes to be the focus of cultural debate in America is very old indeed (Hofstadter 1965; Kelley 1977; Norton 1986). As to sociology, Shafer treats culture as an "output," or object, of politics. But though government ended slavery in 1863 and denied legal access to spirituous liquors in 1920, large numbers of Americans continued to imbibe spirituous liquors and to discriminate against blacks. Thus, culture constrains policy as effectively as politics alters culture. Finally, as to conceptualization, the "basic values" of culture are not confined to a few zealots, extremists, fundamentalists, and radicals who vex themselves over pornography, drug abuse, creationism, prayer in public schools, and abortion. The "real majority" also deploys basic values, but about other things—chiefly economics (see, for example, Wildavsky 1987: 3–21). Most Americans aspire to a rich mix of consumer goods, to a decent standard of living, and to satisfying work that pays well (Yankelovich 1974: 104; Carnoy and Levin 1985: 196; Inglehart 1977; Reinarman 1987). And these things people judge also by applying basic values (Douglas and Isherwood 1979; McClosky and Zaller 1984). Thus, economic choices do not escape culture.

The popular success of Allan Bloom's *The Closing of the American Mind* (1987) testifies to a hunger among many Americans for a broad-gauged analysis of American cultural and political conundrums. In this chapter I propose a strategy for addressing these conundrums—a strategy that is more comprehensive than Shafer's and most other mainstream political science investigations of these matters, less deterministic than hegemonic theory, and more anthropologically grounded than Bloom's effort. I will first use the American case to analyze the insufficiencies of the dominant mainstream political science approach to the study of political culture. Then I will offer my alternative.

Since the early 1960s, the concept of political culture has dominated the study of culture and politics. As a source of orientation, "political culture" has many virtues. For one thing, the concept is theoretically broad. Almond and Verba subdivide political culture into a large number of substantive orientations (i.e., attitudes toward the political regime, the political community, and the authorities; political participation; attitudes towards the self in politics; and, finally, attitudes toward policy outputs). Almond and Verba further subdivide individual dispositions toward these components into cognitions, affects, and evaluations (1980: 27–28).

The political culture approach also concentrates on the expressed attitudes of individuals responding to reliable survey questions. This feature permits sophisticated quantification and accurate description. In tandem, conceptual breadth and methodological refinement have made the political culture approach by far the most popular tool among political scientists interested in explaining culture and politics.

Despite these attractive qualities, however, the political culture approach has yet to deliver its full portion of riches (but see Ingelhart 1990). As a result, recent years have witnessed few attempts to synthesize its findings. Indeed, even in the volume from which I have drawn Almond and Verba's conceptualization, Alan Abramowitz's description of American political culture falls short of Almond and Verba's guidelines (Abramowitz 1980: 177–212). Abramowitz ignores political tolerance, orientations toward equality, and political ideology in America. He also overlooks American orientations toward religion and economic well-being, two topics which earlier analysts of culture and politics in America—most notably Tocqueville (whom Almond and Verba cite positively)—accorded a central political role.

What is wrong with the political culture approach represented by Shafer and Abramowitz? Is the difficulty solely a matter of inadequate coverage? If so, why not just extend political culture research methods to new subjects, and then add these investigations to extant findings? But to put the problem in this way is disingenuous. The real question is why this apparently straightforward task has yet to be attempted. Could it be that *existing* findings from the political culture tradition have become problematic, yielding too few firm conclusions to encourage fresh undertakings?

Indeed, as regards virtually every aspect of American political culture, there now exist sharp differences of opinion. Take, for example, the question of ideological conceptualization in the mass public. Does American political culture contain sizable percentages of ideologues? Yes, answer Verba, Nie, and Petrocik (1980); no, say John Sullivan and his associates (Sullivan et al. 1978: 233–49). Other observers hedge their bets, directing us to examine particular issue clusters. On questions related to capitalism, for example, we encounter a considerable amount of ideology (McClosky and Zaller 1985); and on issues of race, strong feelings anchor well-integrated belief systems (Carmines and Stimson 1982: 2–20). But as to the question of ideology *tout court*, researchers are as divided in their assessments as are the people whom they purport to describe.

Perhaps political ideology is cognitively too demanding ever to be a major component of political culture in America. How about partisanship? Partisanship lacks ideology's complexity. Moreover, American political parties are distinct, historically durable organizations. The two major parties have dominated the American political terrain for 120 years, a record unmatched in Western democracies. From the standpoint of simplicity, historical centrality, and institutional crystallization, we must surely expect partisanship to be an important component of American political culture.

But many observers now question the role of partisanship in American political culture. Just how partisan are Americans? Not very, according to Wattenberg (1984) and Dennis (1986); in fact, in a recent study of children, Moore et al. (1985) report that partisanship is a distinctly minor component of political learning in America. If so, an insidious question begins to emerge: Is it sensible to discuss political culture when so many of the concept's putative components disappear upon investigation?

There is even doubt about the few secure partisan attachments that do exist. It was once believed that people develop partisan attachments in childhood, keep them through the life cycle, and apply them to evaluate issues and candidates, and to make electoral choices (Campbell et al. 1960). But is this still true? Not necessarily. Many Americans apparently jettison their earlier partisan affiliations, while others discover that their issue opinions are not much influenced by their perception of parties (C. Franklin 1984: 459–78; Fiorina 1981).

Moreover, partisan allegiance does not prevent large numbers of Americans from behaving unpredictably at the polls (Axelrod 1986: 281–84). Thus, if we apply to partisanship such criteria as coherence, durability, and breadth, even this heretofore apparently secure component of American political culture does not hold up. Again we are led to ask the question: Is there an American political culture worth exploring?

Perhaps we should abandon this confused landscape and search for more promising terrain. Maybe the problem with ideology and partisanship is that they divide people against each other; to many observers, however, the unique quality of American politics resides in *consensual* norms. Consider the value of *tolerance*, which the Bill of Rights hallows, political rhetoric embeds, American education enshrines, and publications as different from each other as *The Progressive* and *Hustler* exuberantly exploit. Surely tolerance is a consistent, widely shared, durable belief which actually shapes political behavior. But again we encounter disagreement among observers. To McClosky and Brill (1983), tolerance is a central component of American political culture. Tolerance, they argue, is widespread, learned through formal education (particularly legal education), and regularly and reliably manifested in action. However, they admit that political tolerance is also stratified, with certain elites (especially lawyers) serving as its guardians. We are, therefore, tempted to inquire whether a set of beliefs so narrowly held can be a major element of political culture. By analogy, would we take seriously the claim that witchcraft is central to Azande culture if the witchdoctors are the only ones who avow the beliefs in question?

Even McClosky and Brill's modest case for tolerance has come under attack. Jackman and Muha argue that tolerance among the educated is mainly lipservice (1984: 751–70). Sullivan claims that not only is political *intolerance* the norm in American politics, but also that the few tolerant Americans are so not because of formal education, but rather because of certain personality characteristics (Sullivan et al. 1982). Can a society whose major vehicle for the dissemination of tolerance — the public school — apparently fails in this task actually be said to manifest the cultural norm in question? Again by analogy, wouldn't we question the centrality of paternalism and imperialism in Victorian Britain if the elite British public schools failed to transfer such norms (Wilkinson 1969)?

Some political attitudes do deserve inclusion as components of American political culture. For example, American beliefs about equality appear to be consistent, durable, and cohesive (McClosky and Zaller 1985; Verba and Orren 1985; Hochschild 1981; Sniderman and Tetlock 1986a: 62–97). Moreover, as befits a true cultural norm, sociologists and child psychologists have tracked beliefs about equality to their youthful origins (Leahy 1983: 111–25; Forgas 1983: 381–97). This efflorescence of convergent research is heartening; equality, after all, has a long and noble pedigree among students of American political culture. It is almost superfluous to recall the centrality with which Tocqueville himself endowed it in 1835 (Tocqueville, ed. Bradley 1969).

Yet research reveals that the concept of equality, like an image in a fun-house mirror, becomes fragmented when Americans attempt to situate it in their political culture. More precisely, Americans adjust their attitudes toward equality in deference to other, competing values, such as fairness, compassion, entitlement, efficiency, and obligation. As a result, there is no single meaning of equality in American political culture. Equality simply slips in and out of view (see also Wildavsky 1987: 3–21).

The problem is that Americans differentiate sharply between economic equality and equality in the domain of socialization (Hochschild 1981): they sternly reject the former and strongly endorse the latter (see also Dahl 1985). Indeed, the situation is even more complex, for these two forms of equality remain connected in the public mind. Americans apparently believe that the political system can balance social equality against economic inequality, thereby creating a moderately inegalitarian but still wholly legitimate cultural system. So equality appears to be *three*-dimensional in American political culture. What then have we learned about "the" role of equality in American political culture? A great deal perhaps, but nothing convincing enough to generate a theory of political culture.

To summarize, "political culture" has yielded few fruits for the investigator of culture and politics. Many candidates for inclusion in American political culture fail reasonable tests, such as durability, integration with other beliefs, internal consistency, logical cohesion, or secure relationship to behavior. Given these difficulties, it is hardly surprising that so many political scientists have abandoned the study of political culture (see also Dittmer 1976–77: 552–82; Elkins and Simeon 1979: 127–46; Szalay, Kelly, and Moon 1972: 151–74; Wildavsky 1987: 3–21).

To point out the inadequacies of political culture research in the United States is not to condemn such research, but rather to indicate the need for considering political culture within a broader theoretical framework. I offer such a framework in this study. To be sure, my framework contains its own inconsistencies and lacunae, but at least it moves the subject of culture and politics into fresh, if rough, terrain.

In pursuing the alternative put forth in this book, I take up suggestions that Dittmer, Elkins and Simeon, and Wildavsky have previously offered for the analysis of culture and politics. Although all three articles recommend applying structural anthropology to improve political culture research, only Wildavsky fully developed the anthropological aspects of his argument. But Wildavsky implies that an anthropological approach vitiates much of the research conducted within the mainstream political culture paradigm (Wildavsky 1987: 3–21). I disagree. Instead, I believe that traditional political culture research plays the same indispensable role in an anthropological approach to culture and politics as (to take a risky example) an analysand's free associations play in an analyst's therapeutic interpretations. Hence, I shall return to political culture in chapter 6. But in this particular chapter, I contrast my own anthropological approach to the study of culture and politics with the political culture approach.

An Anthropological Approach to Culture and Politics

Culture is the focus of anthropology. Therefore, if political scientists wish to talk about political culture, or popular culture, or the relationships between culture and politics, they should attend to anthropology, not out of some bogus impulse to mask the disciplinary familiar with the interdisciplinary esoteric, but out of sheer theoretical necessity.

As regards the study of culture, anthropologists are today divided into schools of phenomenologists, structuralists, functionalists, and materialists (Sass 1986: 49–58; Marcus and Fischer 1986). For exposition purposes, with due regard to the difficulty of so summary a division, we may classify anthropologists into two groups: those who proceed from materialist assumptions and those who proceed from idealist assumptions. The former argue that ultimately economic and ecological factors account for culture; the latter argue that culture is a set of cognitive maps which can never be reduced to material imperatives (Harris 1979; Sahlins 1976; Douglas 1982b: chap. 2).

Inevitably, I must choose between these approaches. As might be suspected, I rely principally on the idealist or, more properly, symbolic approach, particularly in its vision of culture as a system of discourse. The principal writers in this tradition are Durkheim, Victor Turner, Edmund Leach, Marshall Sahlins, Clifford Geertz, Mary Douglas, Gustav Jahoda, and (to a lesser degree) Lévi-Strauss (Durkheim 1965; Durkheim and Mauss 1963; Lévi-Strauss 1963; Sahlins 1976; Geertz 1973, 1983; Turner 1967; Douglas 1966, 1970, 1982b, chap. 9; Jahoda 1982). All agree that social behavior proceeds from and acts out symbolic systems, texts, or what I call, borrowing from Durkheim (1965), *collective representations*. I adopt the symbolic approach for essentially three reasons: first, it fits better than does its materialist competitor into an analysis of political culture and liberal politics; second, it captures popular culture in advanced industrial societies more effectively than does materialism; and third, it creatively reinterprets some apparently straightforward, materialistic features of modern cultures. Let me elaborate.

As traditionally studied, political culture consists mainly of subjective phenomena: ideologies, beliefs, attitudes, and opinions. Of actual behavior, only political participation typically finds its way into most accounts (Verba, Nie, and Kim 1978; Brody 1980: 287–325). Symbolic anthropology also directs itself to an understanding of subjective phenomena. Therefore, it is a more promising anthropological approach to political culture and liberal democratic politics than is its materialist competitor.

The symbolic approach is also especially appropriate to the study of advanced industrial societies. Even contemporary Marxists now admit that such societies permit considerable diversity and variety in forms of legitimation (Aronowitz 1981; Williams 1981). A combination of economic affluence, education-driven demand for culture, and legal safeguards for the creators of culture (e.g., copyright laws) permits modern culture to depart quite far from any economic "imperatives" (Goldfarb 1982). In Canada, Britain, and the United States it is ever more problematic to trace the content of culture back to an economic base.

Finally, the symbolic approach creatively reinterprets certain practices in modern societies that have for too long been assumed to be solely materialistic in origin and function. Take, for example, the phenomenon of modern economic exchange. Neoclassical economics treat exchange as a competitive struggle among self-interested parties motivated solely by the promise of unequal material rewards. By contrast, a reading of the anthropologist Lévi-Strauss (1963) suggests we treat modern economic exchange as equivalent to the exchange of women in primitive societies. Just as the traditional exchange of women bound together designated persons as kin while keeping others apart (Clarke 1981: 51), so markets today draw specific people together in the exchange of goods, not persons (Gregory 1982). The cash nexus thereby becomes a coordinated activity of *communication* in the form of buying and selling. The result is cultural cooperation in the midst of economic competition.

Of course, there are competitive, materialistic elements in both traditional wife exchange and modern economic exchange (Popkin 1979). The point, however, is that symbolic analysis adds richness and complexity to the analyses of both kinds of exchange processes. In particular, such an analysis helps explain how unequal material exchanges can still promote social integration as well as social alienation in modern societies.

As the above example suggests, symbolic anthropology encourages us to reconsider certain fundamental aspects of liberal democratic culture. Before utilizing the approach for this purpose, however, we must compare it with the political culture approach in eight principal respects:

1. Differences about the *form* of culture
2. Differences about the *structure of cognition*
3. Differences about *cultural processes*
4. Differences about the place of *individual persons* in culture

5. Differences about the *content* of culture
6. Differences about the place of *agencies* in cultural analysis
7. Differences about the *strategy of cultural explanation*
8. Differences about the *relationship between culture and conflictive democratic participation.*

Let me discuss each of these differences.

Cultural Form

Symbolic anthropologists argue that culture is constituted by sets of ideas. Lévi-Strauss (1963) conceptualizes these ideas in polarities, representing elaborations of the elemental bipolar distinction people make: the distinction between nature and society. Lévi-Strauss and Douglas argue that initially people divide their cognitive worlds into two sets: one composed of natural, unrefined objects, the other composed of civilized, refined objects. Foods, for example, are either natural (if not milled or cooked) or prepared (if altered prior to consumption) (Douglas 1984). Important social classifications—kinship groups, economic classes, religious communities, even political movements (Laponce 1981)—are transformations of the underlying nature/culture dichotomy. A further example may prove helpful: as Alan Jenkins (1979: 98–99) shows, Lévi-Strauss treats totemic insignia as binary systems of classification which represent social groups either as "natural" or as "civilized."

Binary opposition creates psychological contrasts that help people make sense of their worlds. Thus, black "makes sense" primarily because it stands out sharply against white. Citizenship is meaningful because we possess the concept of alien (Schutz 1944: 499–508). Our friends are precious to us because their helpfulness contrasts starkly with our enemies' hostility. Although few symbolic anthropologists rely upon social psychology for support, all could profitably do so, since Gestaltists, cognitive dissonance researchers, and social-identity theorists provide ample experimental support for the importance of contrast in social cognition (Tajfel 1982, 1978; Doise 1978; Lock 1981: 19–39; see also, Lanzetta and Orr 1986: 190–94).

The forms assumed by contrasts vary, depending upon social, political, and economic conditions. There is room for contrasts to be constituted by a range of loosely related phenomena. There is also room for hierarchy, with a dominant pole construed as morally superior to a subordinate pole (Dumont 1986; Schwartz 1981). And there is even room for fuzziness at the boundary between contrasting classifications.

In other words, evenly balanced, rigid binary oppositions are not the only forms that cultural contrasts assume.

There is a clear difference between the central role of contrast in symbolic anthropology and the emphasis upon consensus in studies of American political culture. Political culture theorists have generally argued that there must be a consensus on "fundamental" political values if a democratic political culture is to flourish (see Goldfarb 1982). The question then becomes how *much* agreement on political values is necessary before we can decide that a consensus — and thus, presumably, a democratic political culture — exists (for critiques, see Mann 1970: 422–39; Wright 1976). But by subordinating democratic cultural configurations to the theme of shared values, the political culture approach denies any positive role to cultural conflict. However, symbolic anthropology suggests that cultural conflict may stimulate conflictive democratic participation.

Symbolic anthropology also differs with Marxism about the subject of cultural form. Although Marxists argue that contrasts between political ideologies are normal, they assume that such contrasts produce transformative struggle, that the struggle itself is economically motivated, and that, should socialism triumph, cultural struggle — like the repressive forces of the state — would eventually wither away.

Symbolic anthropology denies this argument, claiming that cultural contrast is elemental and ubiquitous. Nor does such struggle necessarily promote transformative political conflict, as opposed to conflictive democratic participation. Although the relationship between cultural contrasts is dialectical (as Marxists argue), the transformation of existing cultural contrasts into a "superior" (socialist) form of harmony is unlikely. Moreover, even were this transformation effected, new cultural contrasts would soon emerge.

The Structure of Cognition

Symbolic anthropologists argue that cultures contain "deep structures," which, though inaccessible to direct observations, can be reconstructed through linguistic, mathematical, or textual analysis (Wuthnow et al. 1984: 137–39). Such analyses reveal formal or metaphorical equivalence between different spheres of substantive culture. For example, the configuration of eating habits in a society will parallel the configuration of social class. The two spheres express a common deep structure which expresses the elemental distinction between nature and civilization — between the wild and savage, on the one hand, and the refined and domesticated, on the other (Schwartz 1981; Goody 1977).

Does the search for deep cultural structures relegate the study of political attitudes and values to a secondary position? Not at all. Rather, the relationship between deep cultural structures and varied political attitudes and values is analogous to the relationship between grammar and speech act. Just as every grammar permits a constrained variety of meaningful sentences, so also does every deep cultural structure permit a constrained variety of attitudinal configurations. These delimited configurations crystallize into a unique political culture (Lidz 1982: 229–56; Varenne 1977).

Understanding the relationship between a deep cultural structure and the political expression of this structure presents three difficult problems. The first involves inference: How can we infer from surface indications, such as political attitudes and beliefs, the particular deep structure which underlies a political culture? Because deep structures are not directly accessible, Grafstein's critique of structuralism becomes apposite: "Structuralists must be particularly sensitive to the possibility that the structures they posit have no basis in fact." And, he adds, "One wonders to what extent structural analysis is empirically unconstrained projection onto the work in the manner of Disney nature stores" (1982: 620). By examining popular culture systematically as a vehicle for liberal democratic culture, I hope to allay Grafstein's concern.

But if there is a single underlying cultural structure, what explains synchronous and diachronous variations in political attitudes? Uniformity cannot explain variation. We must therefore create a theory which explains choice among "candidates" for attitudinal configurations, and then connect the configurations which actually emerge to the deep cultural structures they express (Oestereicher 1982: 668–89). We began this process in chapter 1; we resume it in chapters 6 and 7.

However, our efforts to this end confront a third problem. It is charged that symbolic anthropology cannot explain any particular deep-structure/political-attitude configuration without introducing materialistic considerations (Godelier 1982: 232–61). If culture is a system of discourse, then surely the institutions which produce discourse—such as schools and the mass media—must be considered. But, as Godelier argues, these institutions possess their own particular material interests. Too often, symbolic anthropology ignores this point and thus leaves "unposed the question of how different forms of discourse come to be materially produced and maintained as authoritative systems" (Asad 1979: 619). Again, we will return to this issue in chapters 6 and 7.

Cultural Processes

Deep structures of culture are essentially static. How does cultural form gain vitality, or, more directly, how do the formal qualities of liberal democratic culture combine into processes? Anthropologically, cultures are constituted by metaphor (a system of formal homologies) and metonymy (sequences of interactions). How can we get at metonymy and process?

Cultural processes appear in narratives which recount interactions between contrasting classifications within any cultural set (e.g., good and evil; black and white; North and South; Republican and Democrat). Such accounts take the form of myths, rituals, ceremonies, or stories, in which exemplary persons (heroes, villains, etc.) or designated role players act out components of the culture (for an ethnographic example, see Buker 1987). In Britain, Canada, and the United States, popular culture is replete with such narratives. Occasionally, in real life, fateful political events also reveal clearly these same narrative qualities. A recent example is the kidnapping and murder of the Italian Prime Minister, Aldo Moro (Wagner-Pacifici 1986).

Take as an illustration of cultural narrative the Christian myth. Leach argues that for Christians the story of Jesus makes sense in part because it complements but formally reverses the story of John the Baptist (1973: 55). Jesus begins life as a secular "King of the Jews" and ascends to supernatural status at death; *in contrast*, John begins life as God's spokesman (a hermit prophet) and ends his life a martyred king. The two stories are opposed role reversals, through which the protagonists explore their culture's formal limits and, in so doing, display the role classifications the culture offers (e.g., King, prophet, martyr, hermit), and the normatively preferred means of moving from one role to another (e.g., from hermit to martyr via salvation or illumination).

Victor Turner has provided the most complete analyses of cultural narratives. To Turner, the "root paradigms" of a culture consist of two phases: *structure* (civilization, hierarchy, fixed roles) and *communitas* (nature, equality, diffuse roles) (1969: chaps. 3–5). In the phase of *structure*, people encounter each other indirectly and partially through specialized social positions and limited functions. In the phase of *communitas*, people encounter each other directly and wholly through shared, often ecstatic, rituals. Metonymically, cultures constitute oscillations between these two types of human connection. Transition from one phase to another takes place through rites of passage, during which exemplary persons take leave of a demarcated, structured position, are symbolically stripped of their status insignia, and temporarily join a new category of status equals (Kishima 1987). They then engage in direct, egalitarian communion for a prescribed period (a phase of liminality). Finally, they either return to the position from which they departed or accept a new position (as in rites of initiation). Examples of such rites of passage include pilgrimages, ceremonies of initiation, and rituals of degradation which not only dramatize existing cultural contrasts, but which also become sources of new myth and legend (Turner and Turner 1978; Geertz 1983).

From the perspective of symbolic anthropology, political culture can change fundamentally only when new cultural narratives and new cultural classifications develop. By contrast, students of political culture assume that political culture changes when the distribution of political attitudes and opinions significantly alters. But this view does not inquire into whether the new distributions alter basic cultural forms or reflect new cultural narratives. Until they do so, they will be evanescent and superficial.

The Place of Individuals in Cultural Analysis

Students of political culture aggregate the opinions of individuals into frequency distributions. From these they draw inferences about political culture. By contrast, symbolic anthropologists insist that cultures are also composed of *collective representations*, and these the study of individual attitudes does not identify (Durkheim, 1965). At best, the "entities" of political culture are pale shadows of collective representations.

On this issue the differences between symbolic anthropologists and political culture researchers are essentially philosophical. Following Durkheim, the symbolic anthropological perspective denies that culture can be reduced to individual attitudes, not so much because culture possesses an *emergent* property (a position political culture analysts readily accept), but rather because culture possesses an *a priori* quality. Indeed, particular persons and even whole social groups appear and vanish without altering cultural forms or narratives in the least (Durkheim 1957b). Hence, culture must be analyzed in its own terms (see also Archer 1988).

Moreover, culture comprehends images of society as a whole, not just orientations toward particular groups or issues. No individual or group is so centrally located as to envisage clearly society as a whole; instead, people are unevenly dispersed throughout a society (Shils 1975). People, therefore, have at best partial, distorted views of society's inner workings. Aggregating people's views does not solve this problem; partiality and distortion added to partiality and distortion only yields further partiality and distortion.

Finally, the political culture approach misses the fact that culture is not a popularity contest in which people choose their favorite classifications and narratives; rather, culture is the set of collective representations which people feel bound to *respect*, if not always to obey. And this normative set of representations individuals do not invent. As Durkheim pointed out, individuals can not impose moral norms on themselves, for what they accept they can as easily forswear (Durkheim 1960). By contrast, culture is relentless; it never lets people escape. Consider an analogy: a person who wishes to communicate with English speakers in an English-speaking community will become both pragmatically and, eventually, morally disposed to use English; this disposition springs from the expectations and sanctions of the community, not from one's own will.

If individuals are not the source of culture, what is? Durkheim argued that only society itself has the power to create culture. Culture persists because individuals are vulnerable to—though surely not helpless before—the power of collectivities, such as educators, government officials, journalists, and television producers (Lane 1981; Aguirre 1984: 541–67). It follows that those who study culture must not only investigate the individual's images of *collectivities*, but also these collectivities' images of *individuals*. For example, to the student of political culture, it is important to understand whether the public respects its leaders; to the symbolic anthropologist, it is equally important to understand whether leaders respect the public. The question is not whether people are "individualistic," but whether there is a collective representation of *individualism* upon which people rely.

Collective representations in liberal democracies are not free of inconsistencies. To the contrary, insofar as they represent the struggle between public and private, individual and collectivity, they inevitably incorporate mixed messages. Moreover, as idealizations, they do not fully capture life as actually lived by real groups. For both these reasons, they not only permit political change, but are also internally dynamic themselves. Yet insofar as they keep political change within liberal democratic auspices, they continue to perform both a regulative and a legitimating function.

The Content of Culture—Discourse

Upon what should the analyst focus in order to describe culture? The answer is the self-referential discourse that all societies generate. Because culture consists of narratives involving collective representations, we must deal first and foremost with communication, for communication consists largely of these narratives (Leach 1976).

Students of traditional societies have long looked to media of communication in order to discover discourse involving collective representations. They find myth, ritual, and folklore to be filled with the collective representations of traditional societies (Leach and Aycock 1983; Muir 1981; Lévi-Strauss 1973).

The research problem is more complex in Western democracies, where there is greater diversity among communication media, and where such media escape from centralized direction or accountability. Modern communication is as subject to the division of labor as other spheres of contemporary society; consider just one new medium, cable television, which in the United States runs the gamut from music videos to quality drama. Moreover, in modern democracies, government is also an important communicator, disseminating collective representations in the form of advertising campaigns, informational pamphlets, and, of course, administrative directives. Finally, business corporations now produce numerous house organs, mass-market publications, and public-interest advertisements. These also contain collective representations.

Confronted by this flood of communication, the student of culture and politics in liberal democracies encounters formidable research problems. Does the cultural pluralism I have just described contain a common pattern? What discourse, if any, unites the rock lyric, the civics textbook, the popular magazine, the corporate house organ, and the dystopian novel (Marwick 1980)? All these narratives contain collective representations; none should be ignored. Yet each seems distinct, and together they are simply too many to investigate. What scheme of analysis can comprehend them as parts of a single cultural system? My response to this question comprises the analysis put forth in the next three chapters.

Nevertheless, the approach of the symbolic anthropologist is very different from that of the political culture researcher. The latter typically asks how communication influences audiences (Graber 1984; Clarke 1973). By contrast, the anthropologist does not depend initially on audience research. The first question is the nature of collective representations within communication media; only later does the question of audience effects arise.

The Analytic Role of Culture-Formation Agencies

Students of political culture usually analyze survey respondents' opinions by reference to such presumably formative agencies as social class, religion, family, and school (see, for example, Jackman and Muha 1984: 751–70). The symbolic anthropologist considers such a strategy incomplete. Because the agency classifications developed in the analysis are usually products of survey questions (respondents placing themselves in a predefined social class, for example; see Jackman and Jackman 1983), the "agencies" may be methodological artifacts, even reifications. Therefore, the analyst must always proceed so as to confirm the cultural significance of the "agencies" he or she claims to discover.

The argument may be put differently: the odds that any two respondents in a national survey actually know and interact with each other are minuscule. Therefore, the "social class" of any political culture analysis is not a self-conscious, cohesive collectivity capable of generating or disseminating its own collective representations. It is an analytic convenience, not a social fact. It becomes real partly because the analyst constructs it and writes about it. Beyond this point, its reality is conjectural.

An important lesson may be drawn from these observations: all accounts of cultural agencies should include descriptions of the collective representations such agencies create (see Runciman 1966; Cawelti 1984; Gitlin 1983; Marchand 1985). For example, if our purpose is to understand the attitudes of working-class people, we must locate these attitudes in collective representations of the working class and in the media which communicate these representations—such as the "penny dreadfuls" of Hoggart's turn-of-the-century British working class or the rock music lyrics of contemporary working-class American teenagers (Williams 1961). In short, we must search out the *correspondence* between attitudes and collective representations (Noelle-Neumann 1981).

Studying Cultures as Wholes

Most investigators distinguish between the study of political culture and the study of culture and politics. The anthropological approach rejects this distinction, holding that collective representations within the political realm are connected to collective representations beyond. For example, the moderately egalitarian political position Americans adopt is comprehensible only in relation to two nonpolitical positions—one highly inegalitarian (as regards economics), the other highly egalitarian

(as regards social intercourse). Political equality attempts to mediate between these cultural opponents; alone, however, political equality lacks
a sensible cultural logic (for a relevant comparative study, see Greenstein and Tarrow 1970).

Thus, the approach taken in this study is holistic, partaking of three
assumptions, the first being the principle of contrast. Just as an individual's cognitions become meaningful through contrast, so also do
entire social spheres — including the realm of politics itself — make cultural sense only when juxtaposed against contrasting realms. It follows
that the cultural shape of any particular social sphere can be identified
only by locating its position within a larger pattern of discourse.

Second, the collective representation of any particular social sphere
finds echoes in other social spheres. Metaphor is a powerful instrument
of cultural reproduction; by metaphor, I denote the repetition of form
from one cultural sphere to another, so that substantively different
narratives, stories, or practices embody similar formal configurations
(Schwartz 1981). Substantive contrast between and formal equivalence
among cultural spheres is the configuration cultures tend to develop.

Consider an example. The symbolic anthropologist expects the compromise that often characterizes two competitive political parties in liberal democracies to reemerge in market negotiations between buyer and
seller, and in family dialogues between parent and child. Of course,
the polity, the economy, and the family are substantively different spheres,
but the cultural theme of compromise helps to counterbalance this fact.
Formal commonalities thus temper substantive differences.

Third, the reproduction of form amidst substantive contrasts depends
upon equilibration, which Piaget defines as the "self-regulation" of
structures (1971: 62). Just as equilibration of cognitive structures proceeds via specific psychological mechanisms such as reversibility and
compensation, so do cultures develop analogous mechanisms to equil-
ibrate their structures. Equilibration extracts order from the fruitful tension between similarity and contrast; therefore, "order" itself is a concept best applied to whole structures, not to parts.

The Relationship between Culture and Conflictive
Democratic Participation

From the anthropological perspective, culture consists of collective representations which eventually influence people's subjective dispositions towards conflictive democratic participation. These dispositions display
themselves in political language and public opinion, the topics of chapter 6.

How is this influence accomplished? Existing research on mass-media effects suggests at least three likely processes at work: agenda setting; third-person effects; and priming. Agenda setting is the well-known tendency for the media to cue individuals about what is important in politics (Iyengar and Kinder 1987). Third-person effects refer to people's disposition to consider media representations indicative of the state of public opinion, and to respond accordingly (Davison 1983: 1–15; Mutz 1989: 3–23). Priming is the tendency for people to employ media standards in judging political performance and political character (Iyengar and Kinder 1987).

I hypothesize that collective representations in liberal democracies set the agenda for people either to "perceive" conflict or to avoid it. I also hypothesize that collective representations persuade people that conflict is "on the minds" of others (and is therefore important), or that it is not. Finally, I hypothesize that collective representations prime people either to judge politics by reference to conflict or not to do so.

These hypothesized processes remain speculative; I do not identify them empirically in this study. However, they are consistent with existing research in the political culture tradition. But whereas that research is content to probe media impacts on surface structures (attitudes, values, issue positions, etc.), this study investigates basic political classifications, sch as the liberal democratic categories of the individual and the collectivity, and the public and the private. These classifications are embedded in and dramatized by collective representations.

Nevertheless, because these processes of influence remain hypothetical, the actual relationship between culture and conflictive democratic participation remains conjectural in what follows. I hope to demonstrate in chapter 6 that cultural configurations are *consistent* with the political language and structures of public opinion in Britain, Canada, and the United States. Moreover, patterns of culture, language, and public opinion are consistent with different amounts of conflictive democratic participation. But in no sense do I argue that culture is alone causally responsible for conflictive democratic participation. To the contrary, as the historical analysis in chapter 1 suggested, culture itself responds to historical and institutional circumstances. Ultimately, I suspect that collective representations and conflictive democratic participation are mutually causative. Attempting to disentangle the two is fruitless and, in any case, unnecessary for the argument I shall make.

Liberal Democracy as Narrative

As a narrative, liberal democracy conceives of politics largely as a matter of legally and politically equal individuals dealing with each other in a dynamic, unpredictable social context. Elsewhere I designated the contemporary American version of this narrative a *loosely bounded* culture (Merelman 1984). I believe that this narrative is basic to all cultures with strong doses of liberalism, such as Britain and Canada; however, for reasons already discussed, I do not expect to find this configuration as strongly displayed in the latter two societies.

Liberal democratic narrative nevertheless suffuses the social life of these three societies, constituting a legitimate form of discourse from families to jobs, churches, sports teams, and singles bars. Why devote the next few chapters to popular culture, rather than to these more "organic" spheres of social life? In part, we have already addressed this question; searching for culture at the behavioral level should follow rather than precede a search for cultural discourse in narratively powerful collective representations. Popular culture specializes in such collective representations, which—unlike social behavior—not only reduce liberal democracy to its essentials, but also insert liberal democracy into widely viewed, and therefore potentially unifying, dramatic frameworks. Popular culture therefore mythologizes liberal democracy, and also fuses the abstract principles of liberal democracy with the "everydayness" of mundane life, thus creating didactic and emotionally engaging comedies, tragedies, and melodramas.

A good illustration of the mythological possibilities latent in liberal democracy may be found in American civil religion. Bellah argues that many Americans consider the United States the secular embodiment of a transcendent, predestined sacred truth (1967: 1–21). This civil religion is a narrative of American history as the unfolding of God's plan.

Certainly we need not search far to discover collective representations of civil religion in the United States (Diggins 1984). For example, some traditional ceremonies (e.g., Inauguration Days and Memorial Days) present such depictions (Warner 1959). During the 1960s, the funerals of martyred leaders provided unforeseen occasions for Americans to rededicate themselves to a newly expanded civil religion. Recently, television has developed "parasocial," or vicarious, civic rituals, such as the Statue of Liberty extravaganza, which managed to construe immigration simultaneously as a fertility myth and a myth of national foundation. In addition, newly created awards ceremonies, such as the Kennedy Center Awards, allow national leaders to celebrate deserving creators of artistic culture. Although some of these artists have vigorously criticized aspects of American life, by ignoring this fact, awards ceremonies demonstrate the power of the civil religion to win over and domesticate dissidents. The producers of culture thus become cultural productions, cranky outsiders metamorphosed into fellow communicants.

Of course, contemporary popular culture in Britain, the United States, and Canada contains few narratives comparable in power and intensity to a civil religion. A television sitcom is to civil religion as Mantovani is to Mozart. Yet paradoxically its very innocuousness makes popular culture an effective cultural vehicle of liberal democracy. Just dramatic enough to retain its audience, yet not messianic, partisan, divisive, or exclusionary, popular culture allows *all* people—no matter how lethargic or "nonpolitical"—to take part. Contemporary popular culture cajoles politically; it is the culture of a mature liberal democracy, not of a liberal democracy in the bloom of youth. The question, of course, is whether the stories it tells promote or inhibit conflictive democratic participation, a question to which we now turn.

CHAPTER THREE

American Culture:
The Institutionalization Of Individualism

After discussing the methods this study employs to uncover collective representations, I describe the dominant pattern of American culture: institutionalized individualism. *Institutionalized individualism is an uneasy merger of individualism with institutional collectivism. Because this merger manages to circumvent group conflict, institutionalized individualism limits conflictive democratic participation.*

On Method and Theory

The perspective on culture and politics which informs the next three chapters is *configurational*. I explore popular culture in an effort to reveal dominant cultural configurations in Britain, Canada, and the United States. The question I address is how these cultural configurations shape conflictive democratic participation. My approach is holistic, for a culture is a particular arrangement of several collective representations. Therefore, I investigate representations of the four most prominent collectivities in the popular culture of liberal democracies: the family, the corporation, the polity, and the world of consumption. Each of these collective representations also depicts a corresponding social role — the ideal family member, citizen, employee, and consumer. Conjunctions among these four collective representations create the configuration of a culture and, through the conjunction, either foster or retard conflictive democratic participation.

I direct my attention to four media, each of which specializes in one collective representation and its corresponding ideal role. First, I analyze television situation comedies and prime-time soap operas, which specialize in depictions of the family (Esslin 1982: 46). In this chapter I draw upon eighty relevant programs that were among the most popular American series in the 1985–1987 seasons.

I then turn to magazine advertisements, which specialize in the depiction of consumption, and in how consumers ought to behave (Gold 1987). I analyze all product advertisements drawn both from a large sample of the most widely read American magazines and from a small group of "elite" magazines. The total number of American magazines examined comes to forty-one for the 1986–1987 period.

High school social studies textbooks specialize in collective representations of the polity and of the ideal citizen. Therefore, I focus upon fifteen high school American history and civic textbooks (for comparison, see Gagnon November 1988: 43–74). These texts enjoy wide distribution in leading textbook adoption states (Texas, Illinois, California), as well as broad national usage. I concentrate on text material related to the roles of democratic citizens—particularly participatory roles. These include depictions of individual rights (e.g., the Bill of Rights), of movements to regulate corporations (the Progressive period), of democratization in the Jacksonian period, and of citizens as conflict group members (the treatment of labor unions). I also focus on images of political parties, for parties are the primary devices through which citizens engage in conflictive democratic participation.

Finally, I analyze a sizable group of house organs published by the ten largest American corporations during the 1985–1987 period. Corporate house organs not only enjoy wide distribution inside and outside the corporation, but also specialize in depicting the corporation as both a productive unit and as a collectivity of ideal employees (Ewen 1988: 260).

I utilized a combination of qualitative and quantitative approaches to analyze this material. Collective representations are rhetorically complex; therefore, no purely quantitative content analysis can capture the whole (Rowland and Watkins 1984; Kaminsky and Mahan 1985). After all, the four collective representations tell *stories* about citizens, consumers, family members, and employees. These stories emerge through qualitative and quantitative analysis. Therefore, for television programs I developed plot summaries, describing the apparent moral of each story for family well-being (a different approach is Fiske 1987b). For other media, sometimes I employed rudimentary quantitative methods—for example, I used content analysis techniques to count particular product appeals—in order to construct a profile of magazine advertising's ideal consumer. Similarly, I report content-analyzed quantitative data on citizen images in social studies texts. But I also offer qualitative reconstructions of the story lines that particular appeals and images convey; inevitably, these interpretations go beyond statistically supportable findings. (For further details, see the Methodological Appendix.)

In trying to isolate particular configurational patterns that promote conflictive democratic participation, I have, of course, been much influenced by symbolic anthropology. To the symbolic anthropologist, tension is a normal and persistent component of culture, springing from the distinction between *nature* (the spontaneous, the wild, the dangerous, the alluring), and *civilization* (the artificial, the domesticated, the predictable, the secure). Collective representations of all social spheres, from the family to the polity, symbolically reproduce this tension in terms appropriate to the particular collectivity being represented. Ultimately, each such representation mediates the nature/civilization cultural tension.

From the standpoint of symbolic anthropology, liberal democracy's conflicts between public and private, between the individual and the state, and between rich and poor could be transformed into popular culture narratives which promote conflictive democratic participation. But to do so, popular culture must represent these conflicts clearly and sharply, making use of the nature/culture dialectic (for comparison, see Bell 1976). Similarly, when ethnic, racial, religious, and regional differences are inserted into the dialectic between nature and civilization, these differences too might generate conflictive democratic participation.

The configurations of popular culture which promote conflictive democratic participation in Britain, Canada, and the United States, therefore, consist initially of clear classifications within each collective representation. For example, in television sitcoms, the role of child is clearly distinguished from the role of parent; in social studies texts, the role of the citizen is clearly distinguished from that of the political institution; in corporate publications, the role of employer is clearly distinguished from that of employee; in magazine advertisements the product is clearly distinguished from the consumer. If popular culture sharply defines collectivities and roles, then productive tension between and debate among these aggregates may well emerge.

Each of the four collective representations must also turn its particular tensions into actual conflict. For example, if textbooks do not depict citizens in conflict with each other or with the state, then the legitimacy of political conflict itself declines. If corporate publications do not depict useful debates between employers and employees, such publications cannot contribute to conflictive democratic participation.

Promising cultural configurations consist also of specific relationships *between* as well as *within* collective representations. For example, the family is a predominantly *private* component of liberal democracy; the polity is, of course, *public*. Does popular culture portray conflict between the role of family member and the role of citizen? If so, a debate between the two spheres becomes urgent and legitimate. Similarly, the consumer is a private person who purchases goods for his or her own use. The corporation, however, is a publicly chartered entity which is subject to state regulations as it carries out the function of economic production. Is there tension between consumption and production, between the roles of consumer and employee, and between the world of consumption and the corporate world? In short, might cleavages between the corporation and the consumer promote conflictive democratic participation?

Consider also the dichotomy between collective and partial interests. Although the state and the corporation are both public entities, the state's goals are collective, while the corporation's goals are partial and self-interested. The state allocates values for an entire society, while the corporation aims primarily to make profits for its stockholders (Dahl 1985). To its employees and owners, the corporation's impact on society as a whole is a secondary concern. By contrast, to politicians and citizens, the state's social impact is of primary concern. Does this goal-related cleavage between the corporation and the state appear in collective representations of the two realms, thus supporting conflictive democratic participation (see also Lane 1983: 445–82)?

A similar division separates the family from the consumer. Like the polity, the family pursues collective ends; therefore, it subordinates the desires of its individual members to the interest of the family unit. By contrast, the consumer attempts to mainly satisfy himself or herself first. Even though women specialize in consumption *within* families, consumerism itself remains essentially a matter of personal priorities (but see Douglas and Isherwood 1979), a fact that unites the consumer with the corporation. Is this opposition between family selflessness and consumer self-interest made clear in popular culture, so as to stimulate conflictive democratic participation?

Figure 3.1 summarizes the cultural relationships between polity, corporation, family, and consumption that liberal democracy describes.

Finally, if a cultural configuration is to promote conflictive democratic participation, it must show how people can join together to address cultural conflicts. Symbolic anthropologists have uncovered many such narratives in traditional mythology (Lévi-Strauss 1963, 1973a), where heroes typically arise to overcome cultural oppositions. By identifying with such heroes, ordinary people vicariously come to terms with the cultural tensions that permeate their lives.

But this sort of narrative is, in the end, undemocratic, for it relegates ordinary people to the role of passive spectators, an audience mesmerized by the cultural gymnastics of a few charismatic leaders. Democra-

	Collective Ends	Partial Ends
Public Entity	Polity	Corporation
Private Entity	Family	Consumption

Figure 3.1. Cultural Spheres in Liberal Democratic Theory

cies, however, consist of *popular* rule, not rule by heroes; though heroes may initiate change and conflict, the people themselves must ultimately become the heroes of democratic narratives. Thus, we must seek out a cultural configuration in which the people attempt to control their own lives. Do the collective representations of American, British, and Canadian popular culture provide scenarios of *democratic* heroism in the midst of cultural conflict? Does conflictive democratic participation become not merely one among many possibilities, but a preferred reality through which conflict serves democratic control, rather than promoting passivity, hero worship, or stalemate?

There are several methodological issues my approach must confront. How can we draw sweeping conclusions from what is essentially a time-bound sample of collective representations? Fortunately for the analysis, the period from which these collective representations are drawn was one of conservative resurgence in all three countries. Therefore, any national differences which emerge in the analysis are likely to be truly *cultural* in character, rather than products of a particular historical period. Of course, a longer historical examination would reveal different cultural configurations, for culture is dynamic, as chapter 7 makes clear. However, the *relationships* within and between the cultural representations of each country are unique to that country; therefore, cultural change too almost certainly follows paths consistent with the relationships described in this analysis.

In addition, we focus on four collective representations in each country, not just on one. The odds are long that the cultural configuration these four *together* produce is misleading or accidental.

A related issue is whether these cultural configurations represent the "collective conscience" of a people rather than simply projections of the mass media. For example, generations of high school students have managed to forget, ignore, or deride their civics texts, often because such texts do not reflect accurately individuals' personal circumstances. Moreover, the four media I examine are not the only ones I might have used. Unions publish magazines which also contain collective representations of the firm; television is full of ads for consumer products. Why not focus on these particular collective representations?

The four collective representations I have chosen specialize most completely in the respective cultural spheres they depict. Moreover, they do so with particular clarity. For example, television advertisements run so closely together and are so swamped by television entertainment offerings as to be impossible to analyze in isolation (Williams 1974). By contrast, magazine advertisements are more clearly separated from other magazine content.

I do not claim that public consciousness resembles in every detail these cultural configurations. But media research, referred to in chapter 2, suggests that these configurations become the raw materials of public discourse. They provide the grammar and vocabulary through which people attempt to articulate their political interests. Insofar as these collective representations misrepresent or marginalize some citizens, they promote what Durkheim called "anomie," the withdrawal from public life that produces incomplete democracy and helps motivate my calling these cultural visions *partial*. Indeed, these representations *do* serve some groups more than others and so sometimes bring partial visions close to Gramscian hegemony.

Finally, is the pattern of collective representations I describe in each country a *reification*? What is the relationship exactly between the pattern I construct and the way ordinary persons think? Of course, the mass media consist of vicarious experience and fantasized situations, not "real life." But these fantasies and projections spring from actual spheres of society—the corporation, the family, the polity, and market. *These* are not fantasies, but real institutions in which people live their lives.

If the media create projections of these realities in the form of collective representations, how do they do so? Why, as I will argue, do so many American television sitcoms depict the family as a team of equals? I share Rupert Wilkinson's view that the media adopt "folk conceptions. . . . In doing this, they make concessions to popular attitudes; they do not simply invent them" (1984: 124). Collective representations of particular cultural domains crystallize popular beliefs, aspirations, and attitudes. Therefore, to describe these representations is not to reify them.

Connections *between* the domains, as depicted in Figure 3.1, seemingly enhance the danger of reification. After all, ordinary people do not usually divide their world consciously into public/private or collective/individual categories. But *liberal democracy* is the dominant political theory of the Anglo-American world. People therefore learn to consider liberal democratic categories "normal." Though they may not apply such categories *consciously*, they "make sense" of popular culture in terms of liberal democracy, and, in so doing, reproduce liberal democracy itself.

Finally, any social analysis, even a straightforward account of survey results, creates abstractions from public consciousness. Some reification is unavoidable; the question is whether the analyst creates reifications which illuminate the social terrain. I believe the cultures I describe pass this test.

The Collective Representation of American Families

According to Jane Feuer, "Every genre of American Television is based on some kind of family structure" (1984: 56). This generalization takes on greater significance when we recognize that, in Todd Gitlin's words, "Television's images are extraordinary at the same time that they appear in our most ordinary settings. They come from afar, but they loom up right there in our own living room and bedroom" (1983: 333). Should it therefore be surprising that television, which reaches to the very bosom of the family, should take the family to its own bosom?

Consider the 1985–1986 season, for example. Of the top ten rated series week in and week out, five (*The Cosby Show, Family Ties, Who's the Boss?, Dynasty,* and *Kate and Allie*) were about families, and another three (*The Golden Girls, Cheers,* and *Highway to Heaven*) were about quasi families, that is, non-kin who form an intimate unit based on sentiment (see Feuer, Kerr, and Vahimagi, 1984). In the 1986–1987 season, the list of most popular programs remained much the same, except for the reemergence of *Dallas* and the entrance of two new series: *Night Court* and *Moonlighting*. The latter two series portrayed quasi families in workplaces (a courtroom, a detective agency); *Dallas*, of course, portrayed the Ewings, a family bound painfully together both by kinship and occupational ties.

As we can see, these television families do not display a uniform set of role classifications. *The Golden Girls* are widows and divorcees. *Night Court, Cheers,* and *Moonlighting* consist of intimate friends drawn together through common recreation and/or work. *Who's the*

Boss? consists of two single parents and their children—the former being not only man and woman but housekeeper and employer. *Kate and Allie* are single mothers who, with their children, share a house. *Newhart* consists of a core married couple who are quasi parents to an "extended family" of friends and workers. As for *Dynasty* and *Dallas*, an entire chapter would be required to sketch the genealogy of the characters in these two prime-time soap operas.

Do a family's defining characteristics then lie in a sort of undifferentiated eroticism, a conception of kinship favored by some contemporary family analysts? Certainly such a characterization would explain why television families do not contain stable role differentiations. Erotic connections are labile and unpredictable; a conception of family predicated upon such connections would, therefore, not promote role classifications and, by extension, would discourage conflictive democratic participation. Yet, aside from the occasional clinch between the Cosby parents, the erotic denouement of Sam and Diane's relationship on *Cheers*, and the long-awaited emergence of an affair between Maddie and David in *Moonlighting*, eroticism was largely absent from the 1985–1987 seasons. Of the top ten series featuring families of kinship, only *Dynasty* and *Dallas* regularly highlighted eroticism. And, significantly, in both instances eroticism proves destructive.

What then does hold the family together? The simplest answer to this question is friendship, but friendship does not do justice to the depiction. The *engine* of friendship—what makes friendship succeed—is *teamwork* in the provision of care. The television family is a team of flexible role players who offer each other affection and support while respecting each other's individuality.

However, teamwork alone cannot assure family survival. The family team can operate effectively only if it respects a norm of choice and legitimate withdrawal for its individual members. This norm permits each family member to quit the team if circumstances warrant. To illustrate, in one *Kate and Allie* episode (2/9/87), Kate, fearing her daughter will attend a college far from her New York home, tries to undermine the girl's confidence in her capacity to strike out alone. Her daughter, therefore, decides to enter Columbia. But this decision troubles Kate, who gradually realizes that she has allowed her own illegitimate desire for control to overcome her daughter's legitimate need for independence. So Kate reverses herself, and encourages her daughter to attend UCLA. As she explains, "You're supposed to want to go," thereby suggesting—albeit grudgingly—that a primary, if paradoxical, function of the American family team is to prepare its members to depart.

Television's family team thus depends upon the consent and emotional well-being of its members, not on traditional claims of parental priority or kin solidarity. But consent can always be withdrawn. Therefore, the family is constantly at risk, vulnerable to the seductions of the outside world.

From a political perspective, the internal structure of the family is primarily liberal, despite the somewhat subordinate position of women (see Fiske 1987b: chap. 10). Nevertheless, the family aims toward a contractarian conception of unity and organization. Paradoxically, however, the result is a social institution which is often on the defensive against an invasive public world. A family strong enough to win this struggle might well contribute to the goal of conflictive democratic participation. But does the family win?

Most of the time the family manages to remain intact as a working team, mainly because it successfully balances group constraint against individual freedom. Defection from the family team — a common source of conflict in family programs — is usually transient. Typically, other family members intervene to lure the putative rebel back to the fold, often by demonstrating that, rather than hindering individuality, the family helps each member to become a fuller person. In this way, the family unit surmounts the dangers of unrestrained individualism while continuing to respect each member.

Maintaining family unity is critically important, because the family is often sharply demarcated from a hostile public world (Tunstall and Walker 1981: 26–27). For example, family programs often distinguish clearly between business and politics — the public realm, with its qualities of efficiency and competition — and the relaxed, cooperative practices of family life.

Family life succeeds only when efficiency and competition give way to flexible, changeable, emotionally satisfying relationships. To illustrate, in the series *Family Ties*, Alex, the teenage son, is the continual butt of other family members' jokes. Why? Because Alex's worship of the corporate world encourages him to import inappropriate, futile business practices into the family. In one episode, for example, Alex announces that he has selected a new girl friend on the basis of student pictures and biographies in his college directory. In other words, Alex intends to make courtship rational, efficient, and thoroughly sexist. But while he is busy pursuing his mail-order Ms. Right, he falls in love with Ms. Right's roommate, Ms. Wrong. Ms. Right is blond, beautiful, and gregarious; Ms. Wrong is slight, dark, and introverted. Worse yet, Ms. Wrong, an artist, displays unlimited indifference to Alex's beloved business world. Alex is bewildered: how could he have fallen for Ms. Wrong? The story demonstrates that trying to run a romance like a business is a doomed enterprise, and that Alex's brand of sexism is quite outmoded.

However, the reverse of this argument does not hold. Television situation comedies and prime-time soap operas often intimate that running a corporation like a family *is* a good idea. For example, in another episode of *Family Ties*, Alex accompanies his prim female boss to a business convention, where she hopes to make a good impression on *her* boss at the convention's cocktail party. Instead, in her anxiety to do well she imbibes too much and actually insults her boss. Later, still under the influence, she propositions Alex. Do these twin breakthroughs of impulse against cold-hearted efficiency damage her career? Not at all. Instead, they prove that she is a "real human being," not a one-dimensional "professional." If she "lightens up" both personally and professionally, her career will flourish. In short, being "human" is good business.

Families also protect themselves from the public world by rejecting inequalities of power which permit some family members to impede the development of other family members. (For a different interpretation, see Rogin 1987: chap. 8). Again a *Family Ties* episode provides a good example. In this case the father (Michael) complains to his wife that their teenage daughter has become cold to him. His wife explains that the girl is growing up and needs more freedom. Michael rejects his wife's diagnosis, and instead embarrasses the girl by accompanying her to a meeting of an all-female social club to which she belongs. At the meeting, he blurts out that as an adolescent he had been preoccupied with sex. His daughter's distressed reaction to this heavy-handed parenting finally convinces him that his wife is correct; he must respect his daughter's autonomy if he is to retain her love. He must let go in order to stay connected. Michael apologizes, and father and daughter begin to redefine their relationship. The family team survives because roles alter (see also Bellah et al. 1985).

The chief dynamic in this depiction is a transition from the family as a fixed hierarchy of age and status to the family as a team of comparative equals, each of whom is bent on personal growth. The resulting collective representation cannot serve easily as a model of classification or conflict for viewers, for all classifications and conflicts are subordinated to a common, but individualized goal: namely, personal growth. And because growth is measured by reference to future accomplishments, traditional family patterns—much less intransigent family divisions—need not be endured as "normal." When present hierarchies and fixed roles are but waystations on the road to a freely cooperative future, the family must be able to alter its form without losing its cohesion. Its capacity to transmit the idea of classification and conflict therefore declines, and its contribution to conflictive democratic participation also lessens.

Because of their loose structure, quasi families are uniquely vulnerable to disruptive outside forces, especially the force of ambition. For example, in a *Cheers* episode, one of the bar's *habitués*, the quintessential plodder Norm, loses out to a rival on a job promotion. However, Norm knows that his rival is having an affair with the boss's wife. He is tempted to pass this information to his boss, get the rival fired, and win the job. But Norm's quasi family at *Cheers* discourages him from playing this card; it is clear that if Norm succumbs to ambition he will forfeit the respect of his friends. So Norm restrains himself. No job is worth destroying *two* families: the boss's and his own at *Cheers*.

Politics also presents dangers to families, as illustrated in a *Highway to Heaven* episode. *Highway to Heaven* features a quasi family composed of an angel and his buddy who travel around the United States doing good deeds for people. In this episode, the two bring a Soviet leader to the bedside of his long-lost mother, who is dying in Cleveland. At first, the Soviet is suspicious; he believes the woman to be a CIA agent. After he finally becomes convinced she is in fact his mother, politics again rears its ugly head. Mama begs him to strike an arms deal with the Americans; he refuses, explaining that as a responsible leader, he simply cannot. On this depressing note, she expires. Later, however, the leader relents, and in memory of his mother takes a first step toward detente. When politics intrudes into families, families always deteriorate; however, when family love somehow is restored, politics may actually be redeemed. (For a related image of political power, see Gans 1980; Paletz and Entman 1981.)

Television depictions of the besieged family reach their zenith in *Dynasty* and *Dallas*, which are in fact cautionary tales, repetitious warnings about how the convergence of two properly distinct social spheres—that of the corporation and that of the family—invariably releases powerful destructive forces (see Inglis 1988: 120; Mander 1983: 44–51). *Dynasty* and *Dallas* make this argument effectively because their characters are simultaneously related as family members and as corporate moguls. *Dynasty* conveys its message of warning by paralleling good and evil characters, who represent the delicate balance of evil and good which resides within all families, and which the intrusion of corporate ambitions invariably upsets. In the 1985–1986 season Blake Carrington, the good, family-loving brother, encountered his double— villainous brother Ben, long lost in Australia but now back to cheat his way into a share of Blake's fortune. Ben and Blake represent polar facets of the same character and the same family, as symbolized not only by their similar names, but also by Ben's confronting Blake at a masquer- ade ball, where he dramatically rips off his mask to reveal himself to his dumbfounded brother.

Likewise, the arch-good girl of the series, Krystle, Blake's present wife, finds her hated double in evil, greedy Alexis, Blake's previous wife. Krystle's deepest fear, however, is of her own barely suppressed desires, which she projects outward in distorted form. Several episodes detail her kidnapping by greedy characters who put in her place a golem—a double who intends to deceive and rob Blake (see also Kracauer 1947). Meanwhile, the real Krystle is imprisoned by the proverbial tall, dark, handsome—but evil—stranger, a sort of Heathcliff in Gucci's. Here we see Krystle in thrall to her unconscious fears—first, the fear that she actually married Blake for money, not for love; and second, the fear that she would happily commit adultery. Appropriately, it is Alexis who snidely interprets Krystle's imprisonment to her in precisely these terms. Alexis, after all, is Krystle's *Doppelgänger*.

Dynasty repeatedly warns that a family which becomes engulfed in the pursuit of riches inevitably disintegrates, not only because money itself corrupts, but also because money liberates promiscuous sexuality, sibling rivalry, and parental abuse of power. Indeed, *Dynasty's* hyperex- tension of the soap opera form—for example, its frequent, poorly moti- vated role reversals and its endlessly fluid cast of characters—represents a formal complement to its narrative content (Cantor and Pingree 1983). When we actually try to unite business and family, we fragment the family itself.

The same argument appears in *Dallas*, the other top ten program in which family members are simultaneously united by corporate ties. For example, in a two-part sequence during the 1986–1987 season, *Dallas* told about a soldier of fortune whom J. R. Ewing hired to sabotage oil refineries in the Middle East, and whom Ewing then betrayed. Bitter and desiring vengeance, the man kidnaps J. R.'s wife and young son, holding the latter hostage in order to lure J. R. into a fatal gunfight. Not surprisingly, J. R. becomes wholly preoccupied with providing security for his beleaguered family, who do not realize that it is J. R.'s business machinations which have brought this calamity upon them. Ultimately J. R. and his brother Bobby shoot the man dead and rescue

J. R.'s son. But, once again, J. R.'s overweening ambition in the public world has jeopardized the private world of his family (for reactions to *Dallas*, see Ang 1985).

To summarize, American television's image of the family divides the private from the public sphere; in so doing, television contributes to a dialogue between public and private in the United States. *Between* public and private there is tension and the defense of social boundaries; *within* the family, however, classification and conflict largely dissolve, save for residual hierarchy involving gender. While there remains an opportunity for the family team to stimulate conflictive democratic participation, all depends upon whether the public/private conflict generates collective action by the family. If families are able not only to *defend* themselves, but also to *affect* the public hierarchies that threaten them, then they might help reconcile public and private, and a truly democratic outcome could be envisaged. But do such story lines emerge?

The short answer to this rhetorical question is "not usually." The family rarely succeeds in influencing positively either the political or the corporate realm. Further, when the family does occasionally become effective, it is only through the impulsive, unpredictable power of love, not through either the controlled, stable power of kinship ties or of democratic teamwork. But, in a paradoxical inversion, erotic love — the tie that supposedly binds together husbands and wives — is actually more common to *ersatz* families, who are in closer contact with the public world than are families of kin. Television depicts little passion among married couples or even domesticated lovers; instead, passion flowers in *public* settings. Sexual passion is unnecessary and dangerous at home, but becomes the flawed tool by which the family attempts to gain control of the public world. Let me provide two examples of these contradictory and paradoxical tendencies.

The fear of domestic passion appears graphically in *Who's the Boss?* One episode juxtaposes Angela and Tony — as platonic lovers in a family team relationship — against Emily and Ernie, two friends of Angela and Tony who meet, quickly have an affair, and equally quickly separate. The two males — Ernie in particular, but also Tony — are crude, working-class, macho stereotypes, whom middle-class Emily describes as "simple, but exciting." Even the chaste suburbanite Angela observes of Tony that "opposites do attract." The deeper message, however, is that sexual relationships which cross class lines are fleeting. Ernie states that his fling with Emily "ain't natural," and retreats to Brooklyn, while Emily flies back to her job as — of all things — a college professor. By contrast, Angela and Tony remain together; they make it as a team because they don't make it as a couple.

On one level, this episode reinforces bourgeois domination in television sitcoms (Parenti 1986; Butsch and Glennon 1983: 77–81). Forcing working-class characters to defer to the midle-class characters with whom they sleep is an especially subtle example of hegemonic craft (Gitlin 1980). But more significant for our purposes is the rejection of family passion itself, a rejection which *transcends* class. Indeed, in *Who's the Boss?* even *intraclass* sexuality threatens the family team. A different episode of the series depicts a rich suburban woman whose reputation for promiscuity disqualifies her as a potential PTA President. Instead, working-class Tony gets the job, though only after Angela disavows rumors about her relationship with him. Sexual propriety is more important than class background when it comes to the construction of a family team or, in this case, a familylike association of parents and teachers.

The denial of family passion in *Who's the Boss?* contrasts vividly with the pursuit of quasi-family passion in *Moonlighting*. *Moonlighting* features a quite public male/female quasi family—two attractive private detectives. But, unlike Angela and Tony, Maddie and David are constantly rancorous; the habitual mode of interaction between the two is mordant, snarling, and ego-deflating. The source of the tension is their unresolved passion for each other. By the time David finally admits his passion, he discovers that Maddie is about to marry a glamorous, high-status competitor (Sam). The central issue in *Moonlighting* is the conflict between the required efficiency of any successful business—even a detective agency—and the establishment of a sexual relationship between David and Maddie.

In *Moonlighting* the the private world does gain temporary control over the public world, but only through the consummation of passion. David finally seduces Maddie and sleeps with her; their newfound private happiness temporarily reduces the disharmonies of their public life. Thus, the family may overcome the outside world, but only by exporting its most exclusive quality—passion—into the public sphere. However, the victory of private over public, though real, is unstable and pyrrhic. Even after they have become lovers, the public and the private worlds of David and Maddie remain spartan and unsatisfying. Soon the public quarreling resumes, destroying their private lives. In one scene near the climax of David's pursuit of Maddie, the audience is admitted for the first time into David's apartment. There is nothing at all in the place except a bed. David's private life is a vaccuum, just as his public life is a failure. Only romance can temporarily bridge the two.

Interestingly, *Moonlighting* calls attention to its own artifice. Indeed, it even mocks itself through such devices as freeze frames, asides addressed by characters to the audience, comments about the writing or the plot, and—most startlingly—a concluding episode for the 1985–1986 season in which the "characters" leave the set with the crew, thereby directing attention both to the artificiality of *Moonlighting* and, by extension, to the artificiality and fragility of the television family itself.

Moonlighting contrives to explore its contrivances and thus satirizes television itself as a cultural form. In so doing, however, *Moonlighting* *stylizes* the sitcom's split between public and private, hierarchy and equality, efficiency and romance, personal ambition and family connection (Ewen 1988). But neither passion nor artifice nor the stylish send-up represent real democratic control by the family. Passion is only a temporary escape from, not a reshaping of, reality. Artifice vainly attempts to turn reality into illusion. Stylization places quotation marks around the concept of "struggle." None of these strategems creates conflictive democratic participation in the real world.

Undifferentiated Consumers/Unequal Goods

In his study of American magazine advertisements between the wars, Roland Marchand (1985) argues that advertisements pictured a new world in which, as consumers, people might play a commanding role (Marchand 1985). Magazine advertising thus implied that products embodied standards of quality, value, and propriety through which people could participate in a progressive community. Advertisers also regularly employed guilt appeals, which assumed that consumers shared a common morality each person felt obligated to respect—and promote—through product purchases. Finally, advertisers regularly depicted "high society" in mass-market magazines, although they knew most consumers had no connection to any social elite. Still, advertisers believed that readers not only deferred to elite values, but also used their purchases to embody elite values in practice.

Contemporary American magazine advertisements reveal a quite different set of assumptions. No longer do advertisements expect readers to connect product choices to shared values, common standards of quality, or approved ways of life. Instead, contemporary magazine advertisements content themselves mainly with *utilitarian* or *hedonistic* appeals, neither of which assumes consumers share any values as a group. Contemporary magazine advertising is thus a more privatizing collective representation than was the magazine advertising of the interwar years.

The withdrawal of product advertising from the world of politics and business does promote the liberal democratic distinction between the public and the private. However, like television, advertising does not conceive of the private world as mounting effective opposition to the public world. For example, in interwar magazine advertising, products almost always appeared in social or family gatherings. By contrast, in today's magazine advertising, one sees mainly the product; the reader must *infer* the sort of people who use the product. It is as if products have colonized the private space, banishing families and individual consumers alike. The delicate balance between products and people has vanished.

The disappearance of consumers from magazine advertisements is puzzling in view of the family-oriented content of most popular American magazines. These magazines include *Time, Family Circle, Better Homes and Gardens, McCall's, Cosmopolitan, Reader's Digest,* and *Ladies' Home Journal,* four numbers of each of which I investigated from 1986–1987. Yet the "family circle" is uniquely absent in magazine advertising.

In part, of course, today's concentration on products rather than persons in family magazine advertisements reflects alterations in the American family. The traditional nuclear family has become simply one among many family types, and no other intimate association has fully taken its place. Yet, this cannot be the entire explanation, for even a *non*-family magazine such as *Ms.*—which caters to young, single, professional women—rarely allocates to such women a visible role in its advertising copy.

We appear therefore to have encountered a fundamental reordering of cultural assumptions (for comparison, see Foucault 1972). Contemporary advertisers perhaps feel the private world has become so fragmented readers no longer share a common way of life. As a result, advertisers concentrate on products, hoping that the qualities of products will define the persons who use them. To extend Michael Schudson's analysis, while interwar advertising constituted capitalist *idealism*, an embodiment of American consumers impressing their *own* purposes on capitalist production, today's advertising constitutes capitalist *realism*, in which the production of *goods* creates American as consumers.

Consider, for example, the classificatory structure of advertisements (Leymore 1975). A simple, direct, and usable method for describing this structure is to look first at specific product comparisons, for such comparisons rank products by reference to inferior and superior qualities (for relevant research, see Garfinkel 1983: 175–95). In this way, product comparisons expose consumers to the concept of hierarchy and to product dimensions which allow for hierarchical judgments against some shared public standards. These qualities thus draw the reader towards public life.

It is significant and politically promising, then, that product comparison is the most frequent advertising appeal in my sample of ads. In many cases, the comparison is made on technological grounds. Automobiles, for example, are most often represented technologically, the usual claim being that unique design or performance features make the advertised brand superior to its competitors. By implication, such advertisements assume the automobile buyer to be capable of making informed, complex comparisons.

Other sorts of comparison involve vague references to the advertised product's presumed superiority in some nontechnical way, that is, by virtue of high sales, general popularity, or customer satisfaction. Typically these claims impute no particular attributes to the *product*, and therefore, make no claims about superior quality. Instead, the implicit argument is that popularity alone indicates worth.

Of the total number of appeals in the advertisements I examined, claims of superior quality appear more than twice as frequently as any other. But on what grounds is quality asserted? There are several quite specific claims, which together reveal a view of the consumer as not really a *private citizen* able to act on his or her own, but in fact a dependent *isolate*. To begin with, in approximately half of the quality appeals *convenience* is the main appeal. For example, microwave ovens are often praised for their time-saving qualities. A related appeal celebrates ease of use or lack of physical effort; in other cases, the sheer physical comfort associated with the product (e.g., chairs) becomes the principal element of quality comparison. What is striking about all these appeals is the absence of any notion of initiative, effort, or performance on the part of the consumer, hardly an image conducive to conflictive democratic participation.

Strikingly, most advertising appeals pretend that products alone create quality performance. The intelligence or effort of the consumer matters not at all. Products vary in quality; consumers do not. Goods are ranked; people are equal. The economic logic of this presentation is obvious: to admit that consumers differ in capacity to use the product might alienate some potential buyers. But there is also a cultural logic implicit in the presentation: consumers should discriminate only between objects, and never evaluate each other (compare Cusick 1983). The result is a kind of cultural leveling that surely discourages conflictive democratic participation.

A ubiquitous appeal which differentiates products in terms of both quality and convenience is that of progress or innovation. Half the advertisements which claim to be "progressive" are quite vague about what they mean — referring solely to "new," usually unspecified model characteristics. In other instances specific innovations are named, especially where the product is in fact technologically novel and sophisticated. For example, many advertisements for computers read as if they were computer user manuals. Significantly, the names given the novel technological features are often neologisms or acronyms which convey little factual information. Such appeals, therefore, transform product innovation into mythology, not consumer rationality. And only rarely does an advertisement couple a claimed innovation with a specific company's reputation for product leadership. *Companies* do not create innovations; instead, new products spring out of an apparent technological vacuum or emerge from breakthroughs by small, anonymous groups of scientists *within* companies. The promise of progress is thus sundered from corporate images, reducing consumer awareness of the corporation as a unit of production.

A significant difference between progress appeals in contemporary magazine advertising and the earlier progress appeals examined by Marchand is the decline of any clear vision of the future. In the interwar years product appeals often tied technical innovations to a depicted family's or consumer's long-range goals (Marchand 1985). Technological progress thus had a humanly defined and controlled purpose. By contrast, progress appeals in contemporary magazine advertising avoid the consumer's own aspirations or values. General Electric, for example, changed its motto from "Progress is our most important product" to "We bring good things to life." Technological innovation apparently is worthwhile solely for its own sake. Again, conflictive democratic participation suffers.

A final quality claim in magazine advertising also restricts the consumer. This is a claim about consumer choice, often connected to arguments about innovation. Specifically, many advertisements judge a product to be of high quality if it permits a wide choice among optional uses. For example, advertisements for cameras offer many attachments which produce different sizes of pictures, different picture textures, and so on. Similarly, many small-truck advertisements claim the product serves during the day as a work vehicle and at night as a perfectly acceptable family automobile.

Appeals of this sort appear to offer consumers power within a clearly defined, apparently inviolate private sphere. Yet there are inherent limitations on this power. Choice is defined by the capacities of the product itself (Ewen 1988), not by the autonomous desires of consumers; significantly, few advertisements envision the product helping the consumer toward a wholly new, self-defined vision of life. Although a camera can take many different sorts of pictures, it cannot—at least as depicted—help the photographer to transform his or her life. Contemporary advertisements usually confine their attention to the product alone; consumer choice is limited to a fixed range of product uses, which assume that the consumer's own interests are equally fixed.

Of course, nothing prevents magazine advertising from making more far-reaching claims; yet such appeals rarely appear. For example, my sample of advertisements includes only 77 appeals that promise to free the consumer from stultifying constrictions. Most, such as *VISA* ads, appear in magazines like the *National Geographic*, which reach a select audience. But this figure of 77 may be compared to 310 "limited choice" appeals. The disparity indicates that just as television sitcoms construe personal growth to be consistent with family unity, so also do magazine ads construe consumer satisfaction to be consistent with a limited range of product choice. Both messages portray the citizen as satisfied with the basic structure of values society presents. Hence, there is no need for more democratic ways of life (for a more extreme view, see Graebner 1987).

Only one personal change emerges often in magazine advertisements: change in personal appearance, which appears four times more often than appeals to social liberation. Strikingly, however, the alterations in personal appearance which such advertisements promise occur almost entirely in private. Rarely do we see "beautiful people" engaged in any social activity at all. This advertisement slant appears to sharpen the public/private dichotomy of liberal democracy; however, as pictured, the private world consists of attractive but isolated people who belong to no groups and therefore lack the power to oppose the public world. Such persons exist in a value vacuum; so far as magazine advertising is concerned, the self is literally skin deep.

Even when the public world does appear in contemporary American magazine advertisements, it does so only in a profoundly antiparticipatory fashion. Of the appeals which link the consumer to a world beyond the product itself, the most frequent is the "popularity contest." Popularity appeals consist of the public's testimonials to product worth. As such, the popularity contest legitimizes not only the product, but also, implicitly, consumers who purchase the product.

Popularity contests are either populist or expert. Populist ads claim that a product enjoys widespread acceptance in the general public, implying that consumers should consider such acceptance a sign of worth. For example, "Tone" is "preferred . . . overwhelmingly over the leading beauty soap. That's what women say after trying New Formula Tone" (*Ladies' Home Journal*, October 1986: 67). Populist ads connect the consumer to a mass of anonymous peers, thus suggesting that the consumer might share at least some standards with a larger public. But the standards themselves are never stated. Popularity alone is enough. Moreover, such ads never suggest that consumers might operate as a group to exert their collective preferences on *producers*, rather than on each other. Instead, consumers are an anonymous, privatized, atomized "group."

Expert "popularity contests," which appear as frequently as populist appeals, report the favorable judgments scientists, researchers, or other specialists make about the product. For example, because actresses presumably bring an expert's perspective to haircoloring, Clairol has *Dynasty's* Linda Evans endorse their product. Significantly, a picture of a German palace — a symbol of rank which complements Evans' own claim to expertise — helps Evans argue that Clairol's shades are as "lustrous" as anything in Europe (*Family Circle*, 11 November 1986: 106–7).

Expert appeals assume that consumers need assistance in deciding what to purchase. Therefore, even though such advertisements do reveal a publicly validated hierarchy of competence, they too relegate consumers to a dependent, inferior position. Thus, not only do consumers choose in isolation, they also choose in a context of vulnerability to power.

Expert testimonials also couple presumed authority with political neutrality. The expert is apparently offering an unbiased opinion about the product (but see Czitron 1982: 190–91). The advertisement thus portrays a publicly sanctioned, benign world of legitimate hierarchy beyond the private sphere. Therefore, the consumer need not fear being misled. In sum, the most frequent relations between the private and the public world in magazine advertising either endorse the existing public hierarchy or portray a world of unconnectd, anonymous, dependent consumer equals. Neither image promotes conflictive democratic participation.

Interestingly, although American magazine advertisements elaborately classify products, they rarely classify or rank consumers. Products and public life are graded and differentiated, but consumers are undifferentiated and equal. For example, prestige advertisements which state that the product will improve the consumer's social position (e.g., make him or her more refined, discriminating, interesting, etc.) are less than half as common as product popularity contests. To the advertiser, the world of consumers is one of uniformity; but the world of goods is one of variety. Between the two worlds lies a gulf which cannot and not not be bridged.

Prestige appeals are frequent only in magazines directed to a wealthy, refined readership. In my sample, these include the *New Yorker, Ms., The Atlantic,* and *National Geographic,* four copies of each of which I investigated from 1986–1987.

The greater frequency of prestige appeals in "quality" magazines perhaps reflects the advertisers' belief that depictions of consumer hierarchy flatter those who command society's heights. Readers of *Ladies' Home Journal, Cosmopolitan,* and *The Reader's Digest,* by contrast, might not appreciate being reminded they don't quite measure up. By confining the revelation of a prestige hierarchy mainly to the privileged, the latter are commended for their "inside" knowledge of how society actually works. Yet even magazines which cater to the educated and powerful feature privacy and individualism in their consumer depictions. Such magazines are replete with mail-order catalog offerings of expensive goods. By definition, these goods are unavailable to the general public in popular retail stores. Catalog advertising thus portrays an exclusive and exclusionary relationship between a wealthy individual consumer and a selective mail-order firm. The import of this depiction is clear: to be able from one's study to order a personally monogrammed china set or a goose-down comforter—and thus avoid the *hoi polloi* in department stores—is the ultimate in power. The advertisement thus defines power as the *denial* of the public world. Even at the apex of the social structure, magazine advertisements equate power not with collective action against a resistant public world, but with private bonding with a nurturant public world.

If magazine advertisements do not attend to contemporary social values, neither do they connect consumers to a value-laden past. In magazine advertising the past may surface by reference to a valued practice or to a company's well-earned reputation for quality. More forceful appeals to tradition claim that not only has the company long produced excellent goods, but also that it preserves valuable pre-industrial practices, such as craftsmanship or small-town friendship. An example of such an ad is that for Jack Daniels bourbon, which portrays Lynchburg, Tennessee (pop. 600), where whiskey is still aged in hand-crafted, oaken, weathered barrels, and where local "characters"—who are themselves appropriately aged and weathered—continue to provide a benign presence in American life.

Yet there are three times fewer appeals to tradition than there are invocations of a hazy future in American ads. Most often, the consumer inhabits an eternal present which offers much product choice, but little historical guidance to shape choice. The consumer therefore appears *free*, yet is subtly constrained by the technical features of the product itself. And the consumer is separated from traditional values that might fuel conflictive democratic participation.

Surprisingly, in magazine ads, consumers apparently pay little attention to financial considerations in deciding whether to purchase. A product is rarely lauded for its economy; moreover, the few money-saving appeals usually take the form of "introductory offers," confined to a brief time period. In addition, the argument that a product's durability will save the consumer money is conspicuously absent. So just as the consumer's future is ill-defined, so also is the future of the product.

Money-saving was once a major appeal in magazine advertising (Marchand 1985). Why have things changed? Partly, no doubt, because a large proportion of contemporary goods are discretionary. Home computers and microwave ovens are not necessities; they sell only because the consumer has surplus funds available. But today even ads for necessities rarely emphasize price or durability. Could it be that advertisers assume consumers no longer are influenced by the *concept* of "necessity?" If so, the image of discretionary and luxury goods now defines the *ordinary* consumer, who is urged to ignore monetary constraints in favor of self-expression. But monetary constraints often stimulate group action and conflictive democratic participation.

Only one appeal in magazine advertisements attempts directly to raise consumer anxiety in order to sell a product. These are health appeals, which are 3.5 times as frequent as safety or security appeals. Typical examples are ads for low-calorie foods, like the "Wish-Bone Lite Italian Dressing" ad which invites us to "live the Wish-Bone Lite [*sic*] Style" depicted by the healthy family splashing in the ad's backyard pool (*Better Homes and Gardens*, April 1986: 139). Paradoxically, even ads for products which harm the consumer often appeal to health. Thus, advertisements for low-tar cigarettes claim that, while the product doesn't actually improve health, at least it isn't dangerous.

The dominance of health over security appeals reinforces the privatizing quality of magazine advertisements. The experience of health is, for the most part, self-referential. Disease arises from within the individual; therefore, appeals to health focus the consumer's attention inward, rather than outward to a public world.

Finally, more than twice as many ads portray people using the product alone as in groups. The relationship between the consumer and the product is generally solitary, even when, as in the case of formal apparel, the product is apparently meant for public display. Moreover, in the advertisements which *do* depict groups, most of the action takes place in the private sphere — among family members, friends, lovers, and so on. Few advertisements depict persons in public settings (offices, streets), or in public roles (workers, citizens). The consumer's world is a world away from politics and society.

To summarize, magazine advertisements reinforce liberal democracy's distinction between public and private. Magazines thus endorse the boundary between the two realms as necessary and proper. But by restricting consumption mainly to private use, by highlighting only the qualities the *product* defines, by isolating consumers from each other, and by eliminating both a valuable past and a defined future, magazine advertising discourages people from using products to pursue conflictive democratic participation. Moreover, mass-magazine advertising conveys the illusion of an undifferentiated, egalitarian private world. Such a picture removes any private motives for public action, and therefore deprives consumers of the sense that they need to participate in public life.

The Corporate Machine Humanized

Families cannot project their own collective representations very far; for this purpose, they depend upon the mass media. Similarly, products and consumers do not advertise themselves, but must be constructed as collective representations by advertising agencies. However, the large corporation constructs its *own* collective representation through house organs, recruitment brochures, orientation pamphlets for new employees, and so on. And, given their goal of profit, their history of labor-management conflict, their struggles against government regulation, and their marked internal inequalities, corporations are naturally motivated to present quite misleading representations of themselves (see also Burawoy 1979).

Do such deceptive, self-serving collective representations deserve our attention? Of course. Although corporate self-representations are flattering, they are not necessarily fabrications; persuasion and deception work best when perpetrators truly believe what they are saying. As Deal and Kennedy put it, a "strong corporate culture" presents values more praiseworthy than profits alone (1982: 7). Corporate publications propound ideals and performance standards, which, mouthed often enough, are accepted as much by their creators as by their audiences (Sutton et al. 1956). Indeed, even crudely designed propaganda may turn upon its creators, becoming unwitting claims which the public uses to judge the corporation (see also Scott 1985: chap. 8).

A related question is whether a single unified image emerges from the welter of corporate literature. Concluding his provocative historical study of General Electric's photographic archives, David Nye claims that no unified General Electric image emerges. General Electric directed one publication to scientists; another to assembly line workers; a third (*The Monogram*) to managers, and so on. According to Nye, "these . . . did not embody a unified system of beliefs that one group imposed on another but rather were a discontinuous system—a series of mutually contradictory statements made to a number of groups. These photographic forms served as an effective vehicle for communication . . . but analysis reveals no overarching ideology, no conscious attempt at class domination, and no awareness that any code was being employed" (Nye 1985: 152–53).

There are several reasons for disputing Nye's conclusion, the first of which he suggests himself: "General Electric created multiple legitimations of itself, addressing each to an appropriate group. Large corporations generate not a hegemonic ideology, but plural identities" (1985: 159; see also Susman 1984: chap. 13; Abercrombie, Hill, and Turner 1980). But, if legitimation does occur through "plural identities," this is because corporate pluralism has become a collective representation of great force. Put differently, plural corporate identities fit American culture's deep structure of liberal democracy, where impulses to power dispersion are strong. For this reason, corporate self-images which appear inconsistent become important objects of analysis.

Whatever the case in the past, today's GE *Monogram* is highly synthetic. It contains articles about GE consumers, GE blue-collar workers, managers, and engineers. It includes stories about community involvement and leisure activities among General Electric employees, as well as stories about GE's internal organization. True, it retains a managerial emphasis, but only because managers epitomize the ethos of GE, as they do in most large corporations.

Finally, the themes which Nye discerns historically in GE's specialized publications combine in today's expanded *Monogram*. Contemporary corporate house organs synthesize themes that earlier appeared in separate publications. Curiously enough, the economic specialization of American corporate life—the refined division of labor in production—

is reversed in American corporate culture. The productive unity which the assembly line and the computer have torn asunder, the corporate house organ repairs.

Our task, therefore, is to describe the particular collective representations corporations develop in their house organs. Do representations of the corporation contrast sharply with representations of the family and the consumer? How do executives differ from parents or purchasers? Do house organs depict tension between corporate roles? Is democratic participation a viable means of responding to such tension? Finally, do we encounter democratic participation both *within* the corporation and between the corporation and its public and private audiences — the government, the family, and the consumer?

From the outset, corporations flatter themselves in many ways. For example, some corporations depict themselves as a collection of specialized teams engaged in friendly, productive, nonconflictive competition, all for the good of the enterprise as a whole (Hirszowicz 1982: 67, 69). Here, for example, is Exxon's version of a team image:

> What will it be like to work at Exxon? You'll find a good deal of independence, and plenty of personal responsibility. You'll find a great deal of freedom to do a job as you think it should be done — once you earn that franchise.
>
> But you'll also find a great deal of help from your manager, your peers, your associates. It's a supportive, goal-oriented, team-play atmosphere. Other people need your work and your input and your success. (*Exxon and the MBA*, 4)

Corporations also present themselves as heirs to a distinguished past. Mobil, for example, publishes a glossy "Brief History," which traces the company from 1866 to the present; the publication begins, "Mobil and its predecessors have been serving America for more than a century." The language of national service frames Mobil as a contributor to America's progress towards world economic superiority (Parenti 1986). The implication is clear: why tamper with an enterprise that has served so well for so long?

Another self-congratulatory image corporations adopt is that of the good citizen. Since the 1950s, American corporations have sharply increased their "public interest" endeavors; today, new priorities such as affirmative action, environmental protection, and urban revival provide many opportunities for corporations to picture themselves as disinterested patrons of the community (for comparison, see Bunce 1976). To read the General Electric *Monogram* is to confront story after story about GE's community programs. For example, the lead article in the Winter 1985 issue describes how GE helped renovate dilapidated subway cars on the Boston Red Line. In depicting the project supervisor, the article skillfully invokes patriotism, localism, and heroism:

> Leo Flanagan is a beefy Boston native. A former merchant marine officer and 17 year GE veteran, his enthusiasm is contagious. To Flanagan there are no problems, just opportunities. (6)

The dominant collective representation in American corporate literature, however, is that of machine enterprise — a vision of ambitious individuals whose personal drive for success creates efficient teamwork, which, in turn, produces goods of high quality that create profits *and* serve the public interest. These three elements (individual, team, and organization) of the corporate representation are inextricably intertwined. When completely assembled, they initially convey a harsh, even forbidding picture, wholly opposed to the family (see also Sennett 1970). Initially, therefore, the distinction between family and corporation creates some possibility for fruitful dialogue between the public and private spheres of American liberal democracy.

The individualistic aspect of the corporate representation appears most prominently in personnel recruitment literature, which is designed to attract aggressive, ambitious executives. Here is Xerox's version of corporate individualism:

> We have found that successful salespeople tend to have certain personal qualities: energy, confidence, motivation — and yes — ambition. People who sell for Xerox must also be independent, mature, self-motivated, tenacious and well-organized. (*Xerox Career Opportunities*, 4)

Corporate literature carefully disentangles healthy ambition from destructive competition. The corporation argues that personal ambition never creates a "xero"(x)-sum game, where the success of one employee is purchased by another's failure. The reason why ambition and competition can peacefully coexist is that the organization is always *growing*. Therefore, success is *general* to all hardworking employees. There is considerable similarity between this image and that of the sitcom family; the ambitious family member can be accommodated within a flexible family role structure. Thus, there is no conflict between the individual and the "team."

The team element of the corporate representation appears often in house organ stories about specialized divisions in the company. *Mobil*

World, for example, describes, "A day in the life of lube problem-solver" Frank Muelbauer, who likens himself to an "old-fashioned general practitioner." But although Muelbauer may view himself as a generalist, the article emphasizes his specialized function in a national team of Mobil technical experts. Although Muelbauer's generalist self-image reduces the possible danger of cultural fragmentation through excessive specialization, the story itself carefully places Muelbauer in a specialized team setting.

Images of the corporation as a productive monolith also appear often in house organs. Here, for example, is the way Texaco begins a story about its computers:

> Walk into a control room at Texaco's refinery in Anacortes, Washington, and the colorful panels and flashing lights you see may conjure up images of a *Star Wars* sequel. The latest in computer technology here will not put unknown galaxies within your reach, but it will give you total control over one of the most modern, efficient, and productive petroleum refineries in the world. (*Texaco Today*, no. 1, 1986, 6)

Though different from each other, all three of these corporate images endorse challenge, effort, ambition, efficiency, and legitimate technical authority—qualities which are at odds with the relaxed sociability of the television family and the isolated, dependent acquisitiveness of the consumer. However, American corporate literature ultimately reduces tension between the image of the corporation and that of these two private spheres.

For one thing, the corporation likes to portray itself as a congenial environment for unlimited personal development (Bellah et al. 1985). Here are two examples of this "growth metaphor":

> [From a Texaco recruitment brochure] In summary, at Texaco we invest substantial time and resources in the development of our people. We recognize the importance of total resource development both for the individual and the corporation, enabling you to grow as we do. (*Texaco: Careers for Today and Tomorrow*, 21)

> [From a DuPont recruitment brochure] Du Pont is an organization of professionals . . . more than 160,000 people working together and enjoying the benefit of productive careers. We are a company that provides the individual with prestige and responsibility and the opportunity to grow and mature in a professional environment. (*What Chemical Engineers Do at DuPont*, 3)

The corporation assumes that income inequality among employees is compatible with personal development; yet among high-powered, ambitious executives, even small inequalities undermine self-esteem, destroy dignity, and decrease psychological well-being (Sofer 1970; Howarth 1984). Still, note how IBM runs personal growth and competitive success together in a recruitment brochure:

> IBM is a demanding, competitive place to work, offering challenging career opportunities. If you welcome this kind of environment, IBM gives you plenty of room to grow both personally and professionally and every chance to stand out, be recognized — and be rewarded. One of IBM's most abiding beliefs is respect for the individual — respect for the dignity and rights of each person. (*IBM: The People and the Company*, 1)

If, as Deal and Kennedy claim (1982: 60), IBM enjoys a strong corporate culture, its good fortune cannot be traced to a logically coherent corporate image. But culture, not logic, is the point. The growth metaphor connects the image of the corporation to television's image of the family. In the process, clear distinctions between cultural spheres diminish, and conflictive democratic participation suffers.

The growth metaphor promotes related softening images of the corporation. One such image envisages corporations *empowering* their employees to accomplish worthwhile public goals. Again I draw on the *GE Monogram* (Spring 1985), which constructs a homology between GE's contributions to one employee, and the employee's contribution to his hometown:

> Bernard Chartrand is mayor of Fitchburg. His roots run deep in this city. He remembers when he was a kid at St. Bernard's elementary school and for one day he was acting mayor. He remembers World War II and the years after when the mills began to play out and the buildings took on that run-down look, and unemployment started going up. In those days — and for the next 36 years, he worked for GE.

This passage implies that, through Chartand, GE is reinfusing life into Fitchburg. GE has transmitted energy and good sense to Mayor Chartrand; he can now do the same for his native city. Or as Jack Morrisy, Mayor of Merchantville, N.J., puts it in a related story, "I've been working for General Electric for 20 years, and because of the training and experiences I've gained on the job I can honestly say it has helped me better my community . . . the transition for me from GE to the community is a natural one" (*GE Monogram*, Spring 1985, 20).

The empowerment motif de-emphasizes conflictive democratic participation as a way of resolving culturally induced tensions. Conflictive democratic participation makes *ordinary people* the heroes of political conflict. By contrast, corporate literature portrays the *corporation* as hero, and the citizen/worker as a dependent beneficiary. When workers, citizens, family members, and consumers are divided, the corporation sweeps to the rescue, supplying wisdom to overcome all difficulties. Thus, in a sense, corporations, not people, exert sovereignty (Walzer 1980).

The empowerment motif assumes several forms. For example, some stories highlight the hobbies of employees; others describe the corporation contributing facilities to enhance the leisure activities of its employees. Still others describe contests between employee teams within the corporation and against rival firms. Safety competitions in particular are popular.

Articles of this kind comprise fully 25 percent of the stories in corporate house organs. By describing the interesting, unusual, and talented people who work for the company, such articles indirectly claim credit for employee achievements. In addition, these stories foster "employee consumerism." Because the corporation promotes leisure among its employees, consumption, which occupies leisure time, becomes an expression of corporate power. The empowerment motif thereby receives enhancement, as the corporation invades the private sphere of the consumer. Meanwhile, the harsher side of corporate life—production, with its hierarchy, its competition, its specialization, and its steely efficiency—recedes from view.

Corporations also attempt to blur their image by claiming that they serve "public needs" (compare Edelman 1984: 44–61), thus becoming more like nurturant parents than like impersonal monoliths pursuing profits. Corporate literature often makes this argument by yoking together stories about products which undeniably *do* meet basic needs with stories about products which clearly do not (compare Williams 1974). For example, in its November/December 1985 issue, *DuPont Magazine* sandwiches a story about DuPont's new "Pediatric Radiograph System" ("Treating Tiny Lives") between a story about Thermax, a fabric for skiers, and Imron, a paint used to refurbish the Houston Astrodome. By symbolically equating paint and skiwear with critical medical care, this three-story sequence creates the illusion of a virtually inexhaustible reservoir of genuine public needs to which DuPont responds.

But public needs are not confined to market expression. Sometimes corporations reinterpret political programs which they initially resisted as newfound opportunities to display "good citizenship." Affirmative action policies in employment provide a good example. Most corporate literature contains at least a few favorable references to such programs, and some corporations spotlight their affirmative action accomplishments. For example, *Xerox World* (Summer 1985) contains an eleven-page insert on affirmative action, which begins with the following statement from Xerox's Chairman:

> At a time when equal opportunity and affirmative action are once again the subjects of broad nationwide debate, Xerox unreservedly reaffirms its commitment to these goals. However national trends may fluctuate, this company's stance is unwavering.
>
> Critical to Team Xerox is the full participation of women and minorities in every organization and at every level of the company. Our record is already among the best in American industry. Yet, our efforts on behalf of a balanced workforce and heightened advancement opportunities for minorities and women are unceasing. (1)

Stories of this kind create an impression of corporate responsiveness to those public needs the market cannot register effectively. Again the corporation appears as more than just a soulless machine in quest of profits and power. Such stories also direct attention away from the structural inequalities of the corporate enterprise, and towards the corporation's openness to the outside world. For Xerox "achieving balance" (*Xerox World*, Summer 1985) thus becomes as important as making money; the competitive demands Xerox puts upon its employees become justified by Xerox's worthy public pursuits (for a related historical perspective, see De Brizzi 1983).

This portrayal fudges the distinction between collective aims and private aims. The corporation pursues private profit; the government pursues the public good. But by appearing to embrace programs such as affirmative action, the corporation portrays itself as a selfless, quasi-public entity (for a related argument, see Lowi 1969). This portrayal, of course, ignores the often antagonistic relationship between government and corporations. Thus, conflictive democratic participation is poorly served.

Corporate publications also use "visual obfuscation" to soften the corporate image. Over half of the pictures in these publications are of twosomes or individuals—usually managers, occasionally workers. These pictures typically portray employees in earnest conversations or solitary moments of reflection. The process of production usually appears only indirectly—in photographs of shiny but unmanned machines or in panoramic displays of massive production sites, such as off-shore oil rigs. Less than 15 percent of these pictures portray the actual work of production itself. Goods, therefore, appear as if by magic, rather than by human labor (see also Nye 1985: 128).

Of course, this presentation is deceptive. After all, General Motors admits (1985 General Motors Public Interest Report, 60) to being four-fifths blue-collar, a class ratio hardly evident in its self-portrait (compare Parenti 1986). A Marxist interpretation would emphasize how this depiction weakens workers. But an anthropological perspective attempts to interpret the form of this ideological bias. In the pictures, managers appear primarily as freely cooperating individuals rather than as a struggling group of anonymous organization men. We usually view managers in personal vignettes, in biographies of individual success, and in friendly one-on-one conversations; we never glimpse the tense sales meeting, the anxious board of directors, or the faceless work group in the massive office. From boardroom to assembly line, from the executive's volunteer job to the factory worker's glass-blowing hobby, it is personalization which above all softens the corporation's collective representation (Merelman 1984: chap. 3).

Does the conjunction of family, corporate, and consumer collective representations promote conflictive democratic participation? Certainly there is friction between the warm, spontaneous teamwork of the television family and the house organ's cold, efficient, business machine. And television series such as Dynasty and Dallas demonstrate that families whose members are business partners or competitors must always struggle to survive. Such depictions imply real conflict between a fragile, shrinking private world and an expansive, aggrandizing world of corporate enterprise. At times, therefore, these collective representations do promote political struggle and democratic enlightenment.

But the corporation also absorbs into its self-image many aspects of family life. The growth metaphor, for example, draws corporations close to the healthy families we see on television. Likewise the family team reappears as the corporate team. Family norms thus humanize and sustain corporate life.

Equally flimsy is the boundary between the apparently hermetic insularity of the magazine ad's consumer and the spontaneous collaboration of managers in corporate literature. After all, the consumer and the corporation both depend upon technological innovation to symbolize product quality and personal well-being. Product innovation therefore serves as a metaphor for human progress; as goods develop technologically, so also do consumers and producers.

Moreover, both the corporate employee and the consumer accept constrained choices. The consumer's definition of pleasure is largely dictated by available products, not by any autonomous "vision of life." Likewise, the many choices the corporation offers its managers must ultimately contribute to corporate profits.

Collective representations clearly divide corporations from consumers only along the public/private border. Corporations propel employees into many outside social and political activities; moreover, within the corporation, managers interact in many leisure activities. By contrast, *consumers* inhabit an insular world bereft of a public life. Although consumption may be a social process (Douglas and Isherwood 1979), neither magazine advertisements nor corporate publications recognize this fact.

But this difference is less important politically than it seems. After all, corporate literature claims that managers do not occupy positions in rigid hierarchies; instead, each manager freely develops to his or her full potential. Similarly, although magazine advertisements elaborately differentiate *products*, they rarely rank *consumers*, except in magazines pitched to a wealthy, minority audience. American popular culture's general refusal to rank people thus reduces the distinctiveness of different cultural spheres. Tension between public and private thus diminishes, draining away motivation for conflictive democratic participation.

Textbook Citizens/Uneasy Democrats

Unlike magazine advertisements, corporate publications, and television sitcoms, school textbooks have as their first order of business presenting *facts*. Is it appropriate to treat texts as collective representations along the same lines as these other media? Moreover, if texts *do* present facts, are they not simply reproducing, rather than reconstructing, reality?

Textbooks can devote only brief attention to historically and socially complex subjects. Inevitably, writers select from the factual record particular events and persons to highlight. They must therefore construct their own interpretation of these events and persons. It follows, therefore, that texts create subjective realities, even as they relate facts. Moreover, textbook writers must win the acceptance of political authorities for textbook adoption. Therefore, they must select facts which illustrate the best aspirations of American politics. In this sense, too, they resemble the other collective representations we have already examined, which also represent subjects not as they *typically* are, but as they are at their *best*. Thus, textbooks extract ideals which help reproduce the culture, just as do magazine ads, sitcoms, and corporate publications.

Do American history and social studies textbooks promote conflictive democratic participation? Do they delineate citizenship roles clearly, seeing the citizen as distinct from the consumer, the family member, and the employee? Do they visualize tension not only within the polity, but also between the polity and other cultural spheres? Do they envisage conflictive democratic participation addressing these tensions?

There is ample reason to expect at best equivocal answers to each of these questions. Investigators charge that textbooks are biased, defuse conflict, and unduly personalize political issues (Gagnon 1988: 43–74; Carroll et al. 1987; Davis et al. 1986; Fitzgerald 1979). If so, they can hardly promote conflictive democratic participation.

Jean Anyon and Michael Parenti have charged that disadvantaged groups in America receive unfair treatment in history and social studies texts (Anyon 1979: 361–86; Parenti 1986; see also Davis et al. 1986). Bias allegedly includes stereotypical depictions, under-representation, or selective interpretation. Bias may even extend to statistical data; for example, after surveying high school economic textbooks, Ellington reports that "only one-half of the books contained even descriptive data about black and Hispanic poverty, and only one-third included descriptive data about unemployment among these groups. Virtually none addressed three topics of great national attention and controversy: illegal immigration, the effects of government antipoverty programs upon blacks and Hispanics, and urban economic problems faced by blacks and Hispanics" (1986: 66; see also Leming 1985).

A second charge leveled against high school social studies and history texts is that they de-emphasize conflict. Critics on the left have often claimed, for example, that texts depict strikes as divisive and unsuccessful, never as helpful or just (Anyon 1981: 31–43). Recently similar charges of blandness, distortion, and resistance to conflict have appeared among conservatives. For example, Paul C. Vitz argues that history textbooks ignore Protestant dissent and religious struggle as a stimulant to American democratic politics (1986: 79–90). Vitz implies that an honest discussion of religion in American democracy would create useful debate among students, just as would an honest depiction of unions and strikes. Instead, the treatment of both topics restricts student interest in conflictive democratic participation.

Finally, Frances Fitzgerald (1979) has argued that American history textbooks reduce complex historical movements to instances of "great men" shaping history to their own purposes. From the worshipful portrayal of the Founding Fathers to the contemporary iconography of John Kennedy, American history becomes a parade of charismatic leaders. Similarly, Progressivism lives mainly in the inspired visions of Presidents Roosevelt and Wilson, who somehow singlehandedly "solved" the social problems Progressivism only identified. By framing American history through particular leaders (e.g., "The Age of Roosevelt"), or through the problems major leaders "solved," (e.g., "Dealing with the Trusts"), social studies and history textbooks further reproduce personalization (Anyon 1978: 40–55).

Because it suggests that extraordinary leaders always appear to right social wrongs, fight good wars, and quiet social turmoil, a personalized social history weakens conflictive democratic participation. Such narratives disregard people's contribution to their own defense. Therefore, a democratic public does not emerge, and conflictive democratic participation suffers.

We thus have an idea of what to expect from these collective representations, but what in fact do we find? We begin our analysis with depictions of the Bill of Rights. Conflictive democratic participation requires citizens who can distinguish clearly between public and private, seeing the two as legitimate cultural domains in tension with each other. A promising place for young citizens to learn such lessons is in treatments of the Bill of Rights. Do American history texts describe the Bill of Rights as a symbolic boundary between opposed public and private realms?

Given a commonly accepted view of Americans as "individualists," we would predict a positive answer to this question (Levin 1987: 69–70). But textbook treatments of the Bill of Rights are disappointing on this score. Not one of the eight high school American history texts I examined distinguished explicitly between the public and private spheres in connection with the Bill of Rights. Most simply listed *particular* rights the Bill protects. Conspicuously absent also was any situating of rights within a larger concept of American citizenship. Thus, the student encounters American individualism not as a bounded, coherent, philosophical whole, but as a fragmented collection of rights lacking any unifying political or anthropological logic.

Of course, a philosophical rationale for the Bill of Rights need not restrict itself to the public/private dichotomy. There are other justifications for rights, such as the necessity for popular consent to authority, protections against tyranny, or evocations of a Lockean state of nature.

Although these permeate scholarly discussions of American politics, five of the eight texts mentioned not a single such justification in connection with the Bill of Rights. The student, therefore, leaves the Bill of Rights without a clear philosophical justification even for the particular freedoms the Bill proclaims, much less for freedom itself.

A minority of texts attempts to connect the Bill of Rights to liberal political theory. For example, Berkin and Wood's *Land of Promise* (1983) relates the Bill of Rights to earlier English legal innovations. Berkin and Wood also discuss the delicate balance between freedom and responsibility in the Bill of Rights, thereby implying that rights, while real, are open to reinterpretation, discussion, and struggle. But this sophisticated conception of the Bill of Rights is conspicuous mainly because it deviates markedly from those of other texts.

Treatment of the Bill of Rights could promote conflictive democratic participation by recognizing that rights are fluid, contextual, and open to interpretation (Wildes, Ludlum, and Brown, 1983: 255). Rights then become living things in need of public vigilance and nurturance, rather than static, given, and implemented automatically by far-seeing leaders, an interpretation which obviously inhibits conflictive democratic participation. But here again most texts fall short. Five texts mention the struggle to *attain* a Bill of Rights, but then simply stop dead. None of these texts argues that *after* the Bill of Rights appeared, different interpretations of specific rights have decisively shaped American politics. By implication, political struggle over rights ceased with the Bill of Rights itself. One is left to wonder, therefore, what all the contemporary fuss about abortion or the death penalty is all about.

Textbook authors also seem unsure about the relationship between the Bill of Rights and American liberties. For example, Conlin in *Our Land, Our Time: A History of the United States* (1985) sees the Bill of Rights as protecting "basic American liberties," a formulation which suggests that liberties exist apart from the *practice* of rights described by the Bill. Other writers imply that the mere existence of the Bill proves that rights *now* enjoy protection. For example, Wildes, Ludlum, and Brown (*This is America's Story* [1983]) write, "Because there is a Bill of Rights in our Constitution, you are not in danger of losing your freedom" (255). This is reassuring, but hardly true.

The texts also underestimate the Bill's changing shape over time. Authors could picture the Bill either as crystal clear and nondebatable today or as the subject of continuing interpretation and change. The former interpretation suggests that political conflict has left the Bill of Rights untouched, and, further, that the Bill cannot help resolve continuing contemporary conflicts. By contrast, the latter interpretation suggests that long-established rights must always respond to contemporary struggles, and, in the process, generate conflictive democratic participation.

Of the eight texts examined, only two describe a process of continuing rights interpretation. The more adequate of the two is Jordan's *The Americans: The History of a People and a Nation* (1985), which notes that the Bill of Rights regularly undergoes legal reconstruction. In fact, Jordan visualizes the entire Constitution as an evolving instrument. Most texts, however, ignore the question of change and interpretation entirely; this avoidance reaches an apotheosis in Wildes, Ludlum, and Brown's contention that not only are rights generally uncontested, but the Bill of Rights is so complicated that only lawyers can understand it (1983: 255)!

To summarize, considering the prominence of the rights tradition in American politics, major high school American history texts pay surprisingly little attention to the Bill of Rights. Moreover, most texts do not attempt to justify individual rights philosophically or to portray an engaged public continuing to debate rights. Rights are simply not the object of fundamental political struggle. For these reasons, discussion of the Bill of Rights does not confront the public/private dichotomy, nor does it envisage tension between the two realms animating American political life.

Portrayals of the citizen as political actor appear prominently in text treatments of the Jacksonian era. "Jacksonian democracy" broadened electoral suffrage, fostered mass political parties, and, most important, stimulated class struggle in America (Benson 1961). Therefore, treatments of the Jacksonian period illustrate the way American textbooks describe historical episodes of conflictive democratic participation. Moreover, the treatment of Jackson himself also invites attention. Is the Jackson of the texts a *charismatic* hero or a *representative* of the people? The latter image, of course, provides a populist stimulus to conflictive democratic participation, while the former casts Jackson as an extraordinary figure beyond the reasonable ambitions of his followers. Which of these images of Jackson do the texts develop?

The texts disagree about whether Jacksonian democracy depended more upon Jackson himself or upon social forces. Most of the texts discuss the struggle between rich and poor during the Jacksonian period; the conflict between Jackson and the Bank of the United States serves as the lens which focuses these class tensions. But the severity of the struggle differs from text to text; moreover, some texts, after first em-

phasizing class struggle, confusingly deny it. For example, Wildes, Ludlum, and Brown (1983) initially describe a struggle between the forces
of democracy (represented by Jackson) and the "wealthy few," (embodied in the Bank). Most often, however, Wildes, Ludlum, and Brown
disparage this image by referring to what "Americans" did or wanted.
This rhetorical device implies that, despite the appearance of conflict,
Americans basically agreed with each other during the Jacksonian era.
The authors write, for example, that during the Jacksonian period,
"Americans . . . became more concerned with people who were less fortunate than themselves" (347). One wonders what country these less
fortunate "non"-Americans inhabited.

But six of the eight texts do explicitly and clearly refer to social class
struggle during the Jacksonian period. Some even employ such terms
as "rich" and "poor" to characterize the struggle. Others call Jackson's
supporters "ordinary people," but then rely upon class terminology to
describe the struggle (e.g., Todd and Curti, *Rise of the American Nation*, 1986). Davidson and Lytle (*The United States: A History of the
Republic*, 1986) describe a struggle between the "common people" and
the "aristocracy," but then observe that many cross-cutting cleavages,
particularly regional cleavages, divided the common people. Although
the texts accept the presence of social class and political struggle during
the Jacksonian period, the principles which they use to delineate social
class remain obscure and confusing. Thus, no agreed-upon theory of
class emerges.

Uncertainty also attends the portrayal of political participation during the Jacksonian period. Most of the texts discuss several modes of
participation, and emphasize that Jacksonian democracy increased all
these forms. However, the two most frequently cited forms of participation, voting and the Presidential nomination process, are intermittent,
and therefore do not constitute sustained conflictive democratic participation. The texts also discuss Jackson's use of patronage to open office-
holding to ordinary citizens. Although patronage promotes conflictive
democratic participation by removing office-holding from a narrow social elite, most of the texts decry the corruption and incompetence
fostered by the spoils system. Many texts also refer derisively to the
way the "common people" conducted themselves at Jackson's inauguration; the texts picture Jackson's supporters as an unruly mob who
stormed the White House and then drank excessive amounts of punch
at the President's reception.

Significantly, the texts say little about the one form of political action
that reliably fosters conflictive democratic participation: mass political

parties, a major legacy of the Jacksonian period. Of the four texts which discuss this significant Jacksonian accomplishment, one — Berkin and Wood (1983) — pictures Jacksonian parties not only as conflict-making creations, but also as instruments which held the Union together after the Jacksonian period. The other three relevant texts, however, treat parties solely as electoral vehicles or voluntary organizations, not as permanent organizations of mobilized citizens. Jacksonian parties therefore do not continually stimulate conflictive democratic participation.

A similar ambivalence characterizes the treatment of Jackson himself. Every text devotes considerable attention to Jackson's personality. But what is the relationship between Jackson's persona and the political forces of his time? Is Jackson cause or effect? The majority of the texts treat Jackson as ambiguously "symbolic" of his followers. To a few writers (e.g., Berkin and Wood), Jackson also symbolizes basic American myths, such as the myth of the "self-made man" (Cawelti 1965; Cook 1988: 39–61). The problem, however, is that the texts wish to have it all ways. Although they treat Jackson as "just" a man of his times, they also ascribe to him charismatic qualities which are quite atypical of his followers. Some texts, for example, emphasize that Jackson was a "born leader" (Wildes, Ludlum, and Brown 1983). Others describe particular personality characteristics which permitted Jackson — and Jackson alone — to be heroic. For example, Boorstin and Kelly (1986: 191–92) suggest that Jackson's unusual courage prevented the Nullification controversy from taking a disastrous course. Most of the texts picture Jackson as uniquely strong and decisive; for example, several claim that Jackson's force of will created the Bank War and the Nullification struggle.

How can we reconcile these conflicting images of the typical and the heroic? The texts aim toward an image of *representation* and *response*; Jackson emerges as neither a passive instrument of turbulent social forces nor an autonomous leader. Instead, Jackson initially responds to political forces, and then uses his own unique qualities to push history through critical decision points. History is neither socially determined nor the plaything of "great men." Rather, history is a stream of events which calls forth extraordinary individuals to make crucial choices (see also Wilkinson 1984: 104–105). This complex image is as close as history texts come to describing *democratic* heroism and, with it, conflictive democratic participation.

But textbook treatments of Progressivism modify these themes. As with the Jacksonian period, so also with the Progressives: again we can imagine one treatment which promotes conflictive democratic participation and another which inhibits it. The former treats Progressivism as a fundamental reconsideration of uncontrolled corporate capitalism. In this version Progressivism is a social movement with class characteristics. New ideologies of organization appear (e.g., scientific management), and the party primary, the initiative, referendum, and reform restructure the political landscape. The problems of capitalism appear deep and abiding, incurable simply by removing a few corrupt politicians or greedy corporate magnates. The problems are *structural*, involving a convergence of interests between the large corporation and the party machine, both of which resist popular democratic forces. Business greed and government corruption thus become symptoms of more serious underlying problems. Major Progressive political leaders, especially Presidents Theodore Roosevelt and Woodrow Wilson, are vehicles of reform, rather than autonomous players in the Progressive equation of forces (an influential study is Hofstadter 1955).

By contrast, a reading of Progressivism less favorable to conflictive democratic participation emphasizes the centrality of charismatic leaders and the "purifying" elements of Progressive reform. Progressivism appears mainly as a prophylactic movement intended to cure a few transient ills in a basically healthy social corpus. In this treatment, Progressivism succeeds, and tensions between democracy and capitalism succumb to wise elites who need not appeal to popular movements of protest and change.

Of these two interpretations, history texts fall closer to the second. On the positive side, the texts do acknowledge that the Progressives confronted problems that were consequences of capitalist development, and that political corruption itself was only a by-product of corporate growth. While all of the texts devote attention to business abuses during the Progressive period, none features governmental reform prominently. Only two texts equate political corruption with business corruption during the Progressive period. One of these, Clark and Rimini's *We the People: A History of the United States* (1975), is the weakest text in the sample. Indeed, Clark and Rimini claim that reading Upton Sinclair's *The Jungle* immediately turned Theodore Roosevelt into a Progressive, so shocked was he at the corruption Sinclair describes. Fortunately, most of the writers avoid such simplistic analyses and recognize that Progressivism involved more than corruption and individual "conversion experiences."

Yet, despite this promising beginning, the texts ultimately draw back from a conflictive interpretation of Progressivism. Five of the eight emphasize that Progressives did not wish to end free enterprise or introduce socialism. Several emphasize Roosevelt's distinction between "good" and "bad" trusts, implying that Progressivism only wished to eradicate a few "bad" trusts. Only one text reports the compromising fact that corporate monopolies actually increased during the Progressive period. Most of the texts carefully separate Progressivism from socialism, pointing out that, unlike socialists, Progressives favored free enterprise under government regulation. Indeed, socialism emerges only as a negative "other" for Progressivism. For example, although Conlin in *Our Land, Our Time* (1985) treats Debs and the socialists sympathetically (pointing out that the Haymarket riot was not the work of socialists), he also characterizes Theodore Roosevelt as "the Radical's Enemy" and thus, by implication, the moderate, Progressive reformer's friend.

If the texts agree that Progressivism was not socialism, they disagree about what the movement actually *was*. Some treat Progressivism as a movement of intellectuals and the middle class (Clark and Rimini 1975). By contrast, Todd and Curti (1986) characterize Progressivism as a movement of "ordinary people" completing *Populism*. Most texts treat the movement narrowly, preferring to see it targeting a few extreme abuses in government and business. Only one book characterizes Progressivism as directed toward remaking the whole of society. This is Clark and Rimini (1975), who discuss the urban settlement movement and immigrant education, *inter alia*. But all the other texts ignore the broad range of Progressivism and thus diminish Progressivism as a stimulus to conflictive democratic participation.

Given these diverse interpretations, it is not surprising that the texts turn to Teddy Roosevelt in almost palpable relief. Some texts offer a quite simplistic portrait of Roosevelt; for example, Clark and Rimini claim that Roosevelt himself "settled" the 1902 coal strike. Wildes, Ludlum, and Brown describe how "Roosevelt tackles problems in American life," implying that Roosevelt dragged the Progressive movement along after him. But other writers are more subtle. Interestingly, Berkin and Wood see Presidents Roosevelt and Wilson exemplifying the new *controls* over leaders which Progressives demanded. By contrast, Davidson and Lytle argue that Progressivism depended upon charismatic leaders to accomplish reforms which exceeded the power of the movement itself.

On balance, the treatment of Progressivism is ambivalent and uncertain. The texts do not actually deceive, but neither do they promote conflictive democratic participation. Certainly they say conspicuously little about the outcomes of Progressivism. When all is said and done, the texts are silent about whether broad-scale social reform is worth the public's effort.

We turn next to the texts' treatments of labor and managment during the 1930s. Do the texts treat labor unions as legitimate manifestations of labor/management strife? Do they picture union/management struggles not only over specific economic issues, but also over social philosophy? Or are unions only transient responses to minor tiffs between normally cooperative economic partners? The first of these portrayals obviously favors more conflictive democratic participation than does the second.

On unions, the texts again search for a middle ground. Five of the eight texts do use the language of class to describe the rise of unionism. More telling is the fact that the texts ascribe unionism to a lost sense of community between owners and workers, not to economic inequalities. Thus, unions become a symptom of disarray, rather than a progressive development toward conflictive democratic participation.

The texts all admit that the relationship between workers and managers is inherently one of conflict, but most writers lament this situation. Indeed, the texts generally equate unionism with strikes, and strikes with violence. For example, after describing the "bitter" strike of 1877, Wildes, Ludlum, and Brown conclude that most major strikes provoke violence. Less common is the view that unions often function as peaceful but powerful expressions of working-class interests.

The texts' recognition of conflict between workers and management represents a small step toward conflictive democratic participation. However, familiar tendencies soften the texts' position on this point. For example, unions appear mainly as one among many other comparable voluntary organizations. Frequently the texts discuss the CIO strategy of actively recruiting members from unskilled, noncraft occupations. Readers thus discover that many workers must rely upon the assistance of professional organizers to realize the interest of labor. Unions thus resemble other organizations, such as the United Way, which also depend upon membership campaigns. The distinctive interest base of unions thus diminishes.

In addition, the texts personalize unions by concentrating upon leaders such as John L. Lewis and David Dubinsky. Again we see that people depend upon enlightened, energetic leaders to organize them and lack the ability to organize themselves. Ultimately, unionization becomes yet another instance of charismatic leadership, rather than of conflictive democratic participation.

Finally, none of the texts treats unionism as embodying any particular ideas or ideals. Beliefs about fraternity, workplace democracy, or socialism simply never appear. Rather, the texts confine philosophical challenges to capitalism to "radical" groups, such as the IWW. The texts thus imply that normative ojections to the existing economic order are unnecessary and unpopular. Just as treatments of the Bill of Rights ignore the philosophy of individual rights, so also do discussions of unions ignore the philosophy of class action. The texts thus marginalize intellectual perspectives that would foster conflictive democratic participation.

Analysis of eight widely used high school American government texts reveals similar patterns. Consider, for example, text treatments of political parties. Of the five texts which can be characterized appropriately, four picture American political parties as builders of consensus rather than as possible mobilizers of conflictive democratic participation. *Macgruder's American Government*, for example, depicts parties as "bringing conflicting groups together" and as "soften(ing) the impact of extremists" (McGlenehan 1983: 166). The texts connect this consensus-building role to party decentralization and to competitive elections. Decentralization, winner-take-all elections, ethnic diversity, and widespread one-party dominance at the state level push parties towards the moderate center. Parties thus reject the politics of "extremism" and conflict.

Like unions, political parties emerge as unstable voluntary organizations, rather than as durable conflictive institutions which control their own fate. Only two texts (McGlenehan 1983; Rosencranz and Chapin 1982) devote attention to national and local party organization, while all the others concentrate on how parties expand in size during electoral campaigns. Between elections, however, the parties apparently cease to exist.

The texts are evenly divided in their treatment of party and issues. Three suggest that American political parties promote issue debate, a function central to conflictive democratic participation. But all three confine debate to narrow issues. Indeed Kownslar and Smart (1980) argue that major parties often leave *important* issues untouched. Therefore, *third* parties must emerge to stimulate issue discussion. Third parties, however, are a "safety valve," a term which implies that conflict over issues of substance is more dangerous than helpful. Elsewhere, Rosencranz and Chapin argue that the two major parties are outgrowths of liberalism, which "claims not to be an ideology. Instead, it stresses the right of individual choice (1982: 189)." Apparently, individual choice is not ideological; therefore, only third parties are ideological and conflictive.

The texts generally picture parties as loose coalitions which share few issue preferences or ideologies. Jantzen et al. (1977: 552–53) are typical; they resort to a sales analogy to explain partisan behavior. As these authors see it, competing parties attempt to market similar policy "brands" to a mass public. This characterization compares the relation between parties and citizens to the relationship between consumers and products. In so doing, it diminishes the significance of political choice itself.

Three texts envisage American parties appealing to cross-cutting cleavages, while two see parties poised along a single dominant cleavage. Jantzen et al. specifically contrast American parties to British parties on just this point. First they argue that British parties fall along a single cleavage: class. Then, without a supporting argument, they claim that American parties contribute more to democracy than do British parties. The implication is that parties which mobilize single, historically embedded cleavages harm democracy (1977: 552–53). Only two texts report statistical data on social cleavages in party support, and neither expands upon or explains these differences.

Not surprisingly, the texts emphasize the electoral role of parties to the detriment of parties as instruments of democratic governance. For example, Rosencranz and Chapin (1982) state flatly that Americans lack party governance. Only one text envisions American parties possibly setting government policy, but the text then separates party governance from majority rule. This treatment gives readers a reason to *fear* party governance, rather than to pursue it. Some texts are even ambivalent about the electoral role of parties. Richard Gross's *American Citizenship: The Way We Govern* (1979), for example, does not even mention political parties in an entire chapter devoted to political participation.

Most of the texts argue that parties in America blur rather than sharpen issues. Although some devote equal attention to consensus among and conflict between parties, more emphasize consensus. The texts also *prefer* consensus. For example, Kownslar and Smart cite the elections of 1964 and 1972 as harmful examples of party conflict. But they never explain exactly what *was* harmful about 1964 and 1972 (1980: 425–26). Treatments of this sort obviously discourage conflictive democratic participation.

Perhaps the most telling dismissal of political parties occurs in Jenkins and Speigel's *Excel in Civics: Lessons in Citizenship* (1985). The authors devote two chapters to voting and lobbying, but not one to political parties. Jenkins and Speigel apparently believe Americans vote and lobby effectively as unattached individuals. No greater testimony could be offered for the withdrawal of party democracy from American popular culture.

Conclusion: Institutionalized Individualism as American Culture

In a previous study, I termed American political culture *loosely-bounded*. I argued that Americans represent themselves as flexible, impulsive, and egalitarian individuals willing to alter traditional roles, yet fearful of the freedom such alterations create (Merelman 1984). The present analysis supports this characterization in certain respects. The textbook's emphasis upon charisma in politics; the house organ's emphasis upon personal ambition overcoming corporate hierarchy; the sitcom's emphasis on the flexible family team; and the advertisement's privatized chooser — all these can be seen as variants of loose-boundedness.

Yet the four collective representations we have investigated also portray severe institutional constraints on individual action. Social studies texts emphasize the need for charismatic leaders to organize a reluctant public. Corporate publications argue that managers depend for their personal development upon the corporation's institutionalized power. In these collective representations power does not flow upward from alert citizens to representative leaders; instead, power flows downward from wise institutions to dependent subjects.

The sitcom family at first appears to contradict this argument. However, the family can deploy its power against polity or corporation only in the often-ineffective form of eroticism. The family therefore is not an effective, stable mechanism of positive democratic action.

The starkest portrayal of institutionalized constraints on the individual lies in advertising's depiction of the consumer. In magazine ads, the insulated consumer is dominated by products (but see Pope 1983: 289). Although consumers choose rationally, their range of choice is limited by the available products. By contrast, according to corporate publications, the corporation — which *produces* goods — combines collective action with dynamic personal growth. The world of the consumer is isolated and static; the world of the manager throbs with life. There are no institutions to nourish the consumer, whereas the manager almost literally imbibes institutionalized power.

Ultimately, institutionalized individualism does not yield a fully democratic culture. Between the individual and the institution, little effective group action emerges. As a result, even autonomous, self-directed *individuals* rarely appear in these collective representations. True, images of personal "growth," "change," and "choice" abound, but the *purposes* of change — the *goals* toward which the citizen aspires — remain either obscure or under institutional controls. The consumer, for example, does not choose a vision of individual freedom, but only a product from an institutionally fixed product mix. The manager "grows" and "develops," but only within terms the corporation sets. In neither case is the actual *framework* of choice an issue.

Thus, the American cultural system is neither fully democratic in a conflictive sense nor fully liberal in an individualistic sense. It lacks the intermediate groups to mobilize democratic conflict, and it lacks the autonomous individuals of true liberalism. The principal choice institutionalized individualism provides is between personal isolation and institutional domination. Conflictive democratic participation fades from view.

CHAPTER FOUR

Canadian Culture: The Unfolding of Restrained Conflict

After defending Canadian popular culture as divergent from American and British influences, the chapter hypothesizes an imbalance between a weak and fragmented private sphere and a strong, conflictive public sphere in Canadian culture. Examination of Canadian popular culture reveals a pattern of public struggle which lacks intense private underpinnings. This public/private imbalance — coupled with residual uncertainty about Canada's independent national and cultural status — helps account for Canada's limited conflictive democratic participation, despite the presence of an otherwise favorable cultural template of restrained group conflict.

On the Problems of Comparison

Canadian popular culture is strongly influenced by the country's proximity to the United States (Audley 1983). The television programs which anglophone Canadians watch in greatest number are American (BBM [Bureau of Measurement] 1987). Canadian magazine advertising depicts many products made by subsidiaries of American firms, and Canadian corporate publications often portray Canadian branches of American enterprises. Even many Canadian textbook publishers are American subsidiaries.

We are naturally led to ask whether Canadian popular culture is simply an extension of the American presence in Canada. Are the "Canadian" images we hope to discover really American projections, or is there a "real" Canada in these collective representations (see also Jaenen 1977: 77–97)?

This version of Galton's problem actually works to our methodological advantage. Canada becomes a conservative case for comparative analysis. Because there appears to be little reason at the outset to expect sharp differences between American and Canadian collective representations, any marked differences we *do* find probably distinguish truly the two countries from each other. Hence, although there are drawbacks in the situation we face, there are also advantages.

Moreover, even should convergence between the United States and Canada appear in the material, interesting questions will remain. For example, do some cultural sectors converge more than others? If so, what are the likely consequences for the development of conflictive democratic participation? In addition, might the Americanization of Canadian popular culture trigger attention to cultural identity among Canadians, an issue which is generally absent from American political and cultural debate (see, for example, Bell and Tepperman 1979)? Finally, attempts to "protect Canadian culture" may make Canada quite different culturally from the United States, a country which seems less self-conscious about defining its cultural "identity." Put differently, perhaps Canadian culture is uniquely reflexive.

In any case, Canadian popular culture takes as its targets *Canadians*, not Americans. Therefore, at least indirectly, Canadians influence those images they don't actually create. Moreover, despite the strong American presence, most of the writers, producers, and artists who create Canadian popular culture are Canadian. Therefore, though problematic, Canada remains a methodologically valid case for comparative cultural analysis.

There is also reason to believe that the model of unstable group solidarity may be deeply embedded in Canadian popular culture. For example, consider Canadian spatial metaphors. Reflecting on Canadian literature and art, McGregor writes, "Canadians . . . express their sense of their existential condition in the static terms of figure/ground rather than the linear dynamic presupposed by the American vision of an ever-receding frontier" (1986: 531–43). Canadians, she argues, are preoccupied with the need to protect themselves from a hostile northern frontier. While Americans expanded easily and naturally into a beckoning West, Canadians struggled to survive a forbidding North (Hare 1988: 31–51; see also Atwood 1972; Lipset 1989: chap. 4). In McGregor's rendering, Canada becomes a psychological garrison state preoccupied with distinctions between individuals, social groups, and regions. If this is so, Canadian popular culture should embody a more clearly defined set of cultural boundaries than American popular culture. And, if Canadian popular culture does highlight group solidarity, this fact should promote conflictive democratic participation.

Canadian preoccupation with unified cultural groups emerges visibly with regard to Quebec. Raymond Morris found that images of family disintegration dominate mass media depictions of Quebec separatism (Morris 1984: 181–201). In media portrayals, Anglo-Canadians are bewildered, hurt, vengeful—jealous suitors scorned by the Quebecois coquette. The prominence of familial imagery perhaps symbolizes the bitterness of the regional struggle. No unit is more "naturally" solidary than is the family; no solidary group causes greater pain when it disintegrates. How can Anglo-Canadians distance themselves emotionally from the political struggle over Quebec when they portray the issue as akin to men unjustly spurned by their women? More to the point, how can such imagery not contribute to unstable group solidarity?

It will be noted that the materials examined in this chapter are not in French and, for the most part, do not reach Francophones. The absence of French materials, though clearly a limitation, again reduces the likely cleavage in the cross-national comparison; therefore, differences between the anglophonic and American materials probably provide a conservative estimate of the actual cleavage throughout the entirety of Canadian popular culture.

Also, treating the anglophonic materials as a single entity does not do justice to the provincial regionalism within Anglo-Canada. For example, Alberta, the most "American" of the Western provinces in settlement patterns, is well represented in the materials examined. By contrast, the more "British" Atlantic provinces are not well represented. However, the same conclusion again follows: by treating anglophonic Canada as homogeneous *and* "like" the United States, without a heavily "British" component, we again load the dice *against* conflict themes. Therefore, should such themes emerge, they would signify significant differences from both the United States and Britain.

For the reasons chapter 1 articulated, the cleavages in Canadian politics regionally and linguistically should be expected to emerge clearly as images of conflict in social studies texts. Similarly, given American penetration of the Canadian economy, fear of American domination might well permeate the culture of Canadian business, thus creating images of conflict in corporate publications. By contrast, the Canadian private sphere of television and magazine advertising may be less given to clear images of conflict and, therefore, more similar to American-style images of flexibility, individualism, consensus, and compromise.

We can explain this argument best by beginning with liberal political theory. Liberalism attempts to separate public from private, state from society, and the individual from the community; liberalism thus envisages a shield of privacy behind which families make their decisions freely and consumers pursue diverse "lifestyles." By contrast, the liberal polity and economy are public arenas, where collective decisions often take precedence over the preferences of dissenting minorities, who must accept their losses in deference to majority rule, political equality, and consumer sovereignty. In theory, therefore, the liberal world opens politics and economics to collectively chosen regulation, while freeing the private world to grow and change without coordinated direction.

Yet as the American case has already shown, popular culture deeply penetrates into liberalism's private world. The public institutions of mass advertising and television depict families and consumers in detail and, in so doing, invent new images of private life. Indeed, precisely because television and advertising lack explicit political designs — being interested mainly in entertainment or sales — they enjoy ready entrée into the home. As a result, American television sitcoms have come to dominate Anglo-Canadian collective representations of the family, despite the fact that Canadian families are in many ways quite different historically from American families. The Canadian family descends from Catholic and Anglican models; the American family descends from evangelical Protestantism. No matter; ironically enough, the private world of Canadian fashion, personal choice, and family cooperation proves considerably more vulnerable to American popular culture than liberal theory might have envisaged.

We can therefore anticipate a real gap between the Canadian family's own traditions and the collective representations of families and consumers which American sitcoms and advertisements present to Canadians. What Americans take in stride as idealized versions of the private world, Canadians may find intrusive, uncomfortable, and unsettling. Caught between their own traditionally solidary, hierarchical family models and American individualistic family values, Canadians may find themselves ill-at-ease. They may, therefore, wish to abandon such private typifications in favor of a public world where traditional ethnic and regional conflicts serve as vehicles of self-realization. If so, Canadians may seek out conflictive democratic participation more avidly than Americans.

Are Canadian political and corporate institutions really promising settings for expressing such culturally induced private dissatisfaction? I believe so. Surely Canadian parliamentarianism and regionalism provide more effective channels for group struggle than does the American "separation of powers" amidst an increasingly homogeneous national electoral system. In addition, the mosaic model of Canadian ethnicity, the historical tension between the two founding peoples, the recent emergence of *multi*culturalism as a goal of public policy, and the existence of a sizeable socialist party — all these phenomena facilitate the translation of private dissatisfaction into conflictive democratic participation in Canada.

To sum up, in the United States, the gap between private reality and collective representations of families and consumers is probably narrower than it is in Canada. Moreover, as the previous chapter showed, Americans have developed many institutionalized controls over private fluidity. Therefore, there is little opportunity for private dissatisfactions to fuel public action. Also, the fusion of family motifs (such as the growth syndrome) with corporate equivalents prevents the public world from presenting itself as a distinctly satisfying, distinct, or even appealing alternative to Americans.

By contrast, there may be a gap in Canada between a traditional, hierarchical world of family solidarity and American-influenced collective representations of egalitarian, flexible, and individualistic families. This gap may make Canadians uncomfortable. To learn that one's traditional private institutions are "old-fashioned" cannot be entirely pleasant; two natural reactions are to repel the American messenger or to adopt his point of view. Each of these reactions, however, somewhat discomforts the private sphere. As a result, Canadians may flee to the polity and the economy, where there exist many opportunities for useful action in the form of conflictive democratic participation. Whether these hypotheses are warranted, however, depends on the cultural materials themselves, to which we now turn.

A House Divided: The Canadian Private World

As already noted, the numerically dominant collective representation of families on Anglo-Canadian television is the American sitcom family. The American series that are popular south of the border are also popular in Canada. For example, during the 1986–1987 viewing year, the only American television series which regularly attained the top ten in Canada but not in the United States was *Matlock*, a lawyer-adventure program (BBM [Bureau of Measurement] 1987). By contrast, French Canadians do not watch most American television sitcoms. Instead, they prefer French-language programs developed both inside and outside the Canadian Broadcasting Corporation. These programs are mainly a mixture of music shows, quiz programs, soaps, and comedies. The only programs which comparable numbers of French and Anglo-Canadians watch are *Dynasty, Dallas,* and *Hockey Night in Canada* (BBM [Bureau of Measurement] 1987).

The greater popularity of American programs among Anglo-Canadians than among French Canadians is probably not only a matter of language, but also a matter of culture—the culture of the family itself. As we have seen, American situation comedies idealize fluidity, flexibility, individualism, and egalitarianism. Anglo-Canadians somewhat share with Americans the liberal political tradition which generates these collective representations. By contrast, French Canadians are more distant from the liberal tradition; American versions of family life are, therefore, perhaps quite unappealing.

Despite American domination, there does exist a significant domestic television industry in Canada. Under Canadian law, the CBC must carry predominantly Canadian content (Glen Luff, CBC, personal communication 12/30/88). In fact, approximately 75 percent of CBC programs derive from Canadian sources; moreover, CBC programs now comprise approximately 23 percent of all anglophone viewing and 45 percent of francophone viewing (Canadian Broadcasting Corporation, August 1986). Canadian domestic productions can therefore be seen as a kind of national "counterprogramming" to American television. In order to attract its audience, the CBC must provide a distinct alternative to American television. After all, it makes no sense for the CBC to imitate American program formulae at which Americans excel. Perhaps for this reason, Canadian sitcoms are quite different from American sitcoms and are therefore quite revealing.

In fact, Canadian sitcoms display a distinctly Canadian cultural theme: bifurcation. Canadian sitcoms construe the domestic world as a series of intertwined, nested dichotomies in which struggle first establishes a private sphere and then displays the fragility, limitations, and disappointments of family life (Atwood 1972). For Canadians, unlike Americans, television's collective representation of the family embodies conflict unleavened by flexibility, growth, reconciliation, or romantic mediation. However, though family conflict ultimately turns family members toward politics, family conflict also reduces the emotional force behind political action.

These observations must remain tentative, for I do not have a large sample of Canadian series and programs from which to generalize. I examined four programs from each of three popular CBC family series (*Danger Bay, The Beachcombers,* and *He Shoots, He Scores*), as well as two CBC series which have not only been highly successful in Canada, but have also appeared in the United States. One of these two, *De Grassi Junior High*, focuses on teenagers, and is at this writing appearing on the American Public Broadcasting System; the other, *Anne of Green Gables*, is a legend in Canadian television. *Anne* is by far the most successful miniseries production in CBC history.

Though limited in number, this group of programs nevertheless proves quite revealing. For one thing, every program contains family problems as a central theme. In addition, obvious contrasts with the American family model emerge, contrasts which not only link Canadian television tightly to the larger corpus of Canadian popular culture, but also carry interesting implications for conflictive democratic participation in Canada. Finally, symbolic anthropology demonstrates its utility as a tool of cultural analysis. Thus, the quality of this small group of programs exceeds its size.

The traditional Canadian model of stable family authority emerges clearly in some of these series. An example is the series *Danger Bay*, which features a single father and his two teenage children who live in British Columbia. The chief theme of this series is the adolescents' conflict between their desire to chart their own course and their need to defer to parental authority. When they must choose between those needs, *Danger Bay* is clear about what they should do: defer to father. For example, in "Roots and Wings," the teenage son Jonah becomes infatuated with a wealthy, irresponsible girl. The girl teases Jonah for being "square"; so, in order to please her and assert himself, he steals money from his father to take her to a rock concert. After the concert, there is drinking, and then an automobile accident. Needless to say, Jonah's father is mortified both by the theft and its aftermath. He punishes Jonah, while the girl escapes unpunished. This dichotomy between punishment and escape is only one of multiple bifurcations in the program. As further punishment, Jonah loses his place on the school track team.

The cultural significance of this tale lies in its denouement. Jonah, chastened by his experience, apologizes to his father and breaks off with the girl, explaining that he and she are "too different" from each other. Jonah's father eventually forgives him, observing that Jonah is basically level-headed, and was only "trying to fit in." His father reminds Jonah to resist peer pressure and "be himself," which, in context, paradoxically translates into an injunction to obey his father. As if this paternal triumph is not enough to drive home the message of paternalism, the girl also admits her error, and actually commends Jonah's submission to his father. Jonah's father concedes only that the boy needs more "space;" however, he warns Jonah not to grow up "too fast," and Jonah agrees not to do so.

Should we dismiss this depiction as only a sort of cultural lag, a temporary Canadian throwback to American television during the 1950s, when even the American Father knew best? I think not. After all, the plethora of American sitcoms on Canada television has given Canadians ample opportunity to embrace the contemporary American family model if they so desired. I suspect that *Danger Bay* endures in Canada precisely because it provides a clear rejoinder to the American version of family egalitarianism. For example, though the father recognizes the need to accommodate Jonah's growth, he never places himself on an equal footing with Jonah (*contra* Michael on *Family Ties*, who joins his daughter at a teenage soiree). Generational conflict in *Danger Bay* takes place within a set of values which the father embodies, and which the son can only aspire to possess. Although there is conflict, the value hierarchy itself is never in question.

The same conclusion applies to family disagreements about politics. In another *Danger Bay* episode, "Tangled Web," Jonah must choose among three alternative strategies to eradicate harmful fish poaching. He may cut the suspected poachers' nets, knowing this would be an illegal act. He may join forces with a female friend of his father's, whose photographs of wounded baby seals enmeshed in the poachers' net may stimulate a popular outcry against poaching. Or he may emulate his father, who protests poaching by lobbying his political representatives. Jonah rejects his father's advice not to "confuse commitment with common sense," and chooses the direct action alternative. Significantly, he himself becomes entangled in the net, and his father must save him. The moral is obvious: obey the law, and struggle within *its* limits.

"Tangled Web" does not favor political passivity. To the contrary, Jonah takes a significant step towards conflictive democratic participation. Nor is the failure of his act a retreat from political engagement. He simply evolves toward a different style of politics, one which resembles that of his father. But though his political views may eventually resemble those of his father, his act of protest made these views his *own*, not just his father's. Failed protest both restores the family and stimulates further political action. By contrast, Jonah's American television counterparts lack familial stimulus to political engagement at all.

As suggested by Jonah's experience, Canadian sitcoms equate support for parental authority with the rejection of radical politics. For example, in *The Beachcombers* we encounter a quasi family of friends who run a boat-rental and grocery store business. In one program the friends help an elderly curmudgeon to locate his long-lost son. The Canadian oldster is no lovable, cuddly American "senior citizen"; rather, he is a bitter, querulous and unappealing man. Father and son have been estranged for many years. Their disagreement stems from a clash of values. The son is an aging hippie, while the father remains an un-regenerate traditionalist. The son has taken his family to a remote wilderness area, where he attempts to avoid the corruptions of modern civilization. Characteristically, as soon as he finds his son, the father provokes a new quarrel. Still, it is the son, not the father, who loses the fight. The son's conversion occurs when his wife tells him she is sick of living from hand to mouth, that he ought to "grow up," and that until he does so she is returning to Vancouver with her father-in-law. The son then gives up his radicalism and accepts a conventional way of life.

A similarly conservative message emerges from "Dispensable People," another episode of *The Beachcombers*. One of the female characters befriends a homeless woman, whom she believes to possess mystical wisdom. But, unlike many American "outsider" characters, the woman turns out to be quite unlovable and defiant. She proclaims proudly that she chooses to be a scavenger; she gives no quarter, and she is quite inflexible. Does this proud assertion of difference ingratiate her to the quasi family that takes her in? Do they alter their roles in order to accommodate her idiosyncracies? Does she herself soften? Do they all "grow" into a team as they probably would in an American version of the story (but see Wolfe 1985: 55)? Hardly. Instead, the quasi family finds her repellent, and they force her benefactor to turn her out. Neither side in the conflict apologizes to the other. Although the girl herself remains friends with the outcast, she concludes that she "can't be a Mother Teresa," at least not if she wishes to remain part of her quasi family.

In "Dispensable People," rigidity not only forces the quasi family and the outcast to dwell apart from each other, but also creates mutual respect between the two quite divergent ways of life. Faced with the quasi family's rejection, the homeless woman refuses to yield. As a consequence, her benefactor admires the woman even more. This is a particularly subtle illustration of a recurrent Canadian cultural narrative: the construction of personal identity through group difference; the preservation of the domestic world through the reinforcement of public convention; the preference for "realism" over idealism; and the separation of equally legitimate but basically incompatible ways of life (for a possible historical illustration, see Prentice 1975: 110–33). Thus, Canadians separate, while Americans incorporate.

This Canadian pattern presents two dangers to family integrity. First, there may exist a crippling incongruity between the family's rigid structure and the demands of an insistent outside world. Second, the hierarchical family may separate affection from authority, turning those in power austere and unloving. Such a pattern may force children to search for love outside the family, thereby destroying the family unit. Making family authority more affectionate is, in fact, the theme of *Anne of Green Gables*. The great success of this miniseries lies in its aesthetically pleasing reconciliation of tensions within the culture of the Canadian family.

At first glance, *Anne of Green Gables* seems a fairly conventional combination of *Little House on the Prairie* and *David Copperfield*. Like David, Anne is an orphan; though mistreated, she stays plucky, romantic, idealistic, wholly charming. She is adopted, reluctantly, by a dour old brother and sister on remote Prince Edward Island. In the idyllic beauty of this pastoral setting, she comes to maturity; publishes a somewhat bathetic short story; wins a scholarship to a Charlotte-town secondary school; becomes a teacher; publishes a second, more substantial book about her home village of Avonlea; marries her boy-hood scholastic rival; and eventually settles down in Prince Edward Island. Like a standard American heroine, Anne succeeds through her enterprise and charm. However, she never mistakes the trappings of wealth and urbanity for true success, which she knows resides in establishing her own family, and becoming a local teacher and celebrator of rural virtues.

Looked at carefully, however, *Anne* is not an "American" story of freedom and escape, but rather a story about reconciling love with family authority and tradition. As a naive romantic and an orphan to boot, Anne repeatedly encounters hostility, cruelty, and suspicion from most of her elders, who deride her aspirations to become a writer or to direct plays. Some of the few adults who come to love her are inhibited by a rigid Christianity, while others hate and envy her vivacity as compared with their own emotional barrenness. Anne's task is to demonstrate to her elders that duty, tradition, and Christianity can be leavened with affection. Unlike many American heroines, Anne never really leaves home; instead, she embraces the conventional values of her elders. But she does so with characteristic warmth and impulsiveness, and, in so doing, demonstrates that emotion and reason, love and authority, need not be enemies to each other.

Significantly, Anne chooses not to defy, but rather to seduce her elders; she never openly attacks those upon whom she depends, and whom, for the most part, she truly respects. She knows that the sheer rootedness of hierarchy and family tradition will not countenance outright rebellion; therefore, Anne practices a sort of disingenuous guerilla warfare, sprinkled with a little deceit. She believes that her elders are basically correct but lack the demonstration that love and impulse can promote, rather than subvert, traditional values. So she takes it upon herself to demonstrate this fact time after time.

But if Anne has much to offer, so also does she have much to learn. Like Jonah in "Tangled Web," she must become "realistic." She must abandon her youthful dreams of marrying the Prince on the White Horse and settle instead for the boy next door. She must stop writing imitations of "The Lady of Chaillot," and instead chronicle the homely ways of Avonlea. She must return to the farm when her adoptive mother needs her, rather than remain in the city. Most important, Anne must learn that her affections can be fulfilled within a family of tradition. Once Anne and her elders have learned from each other, generational continuity can proceed. Anne marries the "right person," the domestic sphere thrives, traditional values reverberate, roles change slightly, but distinctions between acceptable and proscribed behaviors remain clear. But now love, not fear, has become the principal buttress of the family structure (see also Galbraith 1964).

Of course, not all families succeed as well as Anne's. Indeed, in Canadian sitcoms, the family often fails terribly, total collapse ensues, and there exists no hope for healing. In Canadian collective representations, the sole possibilities are traditional family authority or family anarchy; there is no flexible, egalitarian, spontaneously effective family "team USA." The traditional Canadian family thus contains an Achilles heel. Intact, it helps prepare Canadians for conflictive democratic participation; impaired, however, it not only frustrates its members, but also reduces their political capacities.

The negative side of the Canadian family appears vividly in De Grassi Junior High, a series which invites comparison to its American predecessor, Fame. The comparison is not exact; after all, Fame portrayed a high school for gifted—if often deprived—students, while De Grassi Junior High is an ordinary Canadian school. Nevertheless, the stark differences between the two series cannot be attributed entirely to their different settings. Instead, the "realism" of De Grassi and the "romanticism" of Fame represent and help reproduce two quite different cultural models.

In De Grassi, in contrast to Fame, there is a noticeable absence of effective, helpful adults to assist the teenagers through the trials of adolescence. Authority is distant, impersonal, uncomprehending, and unhelpful, a fact that is symbolized by the classroom loudspeaker, which continually barks unheeded directions to students from an unseen administration source. Moreover, most of the teachers at De Grassi are mediocre time-servers, hardly the inspiring role models of *Fame*. In fact, some of De Grassi's teachers are downright venal, such as the substitute English teacher in the ironically titled "A Helping Hand," who attempts to seduce one of his students.

The students' parents do not come off much better. One mother is an alcoholic who continually embarrasses her daughter. Another's parents consist of a minister and his dutiful wife, whose priggishness forces their son to conceal the fact that he has impregnated a classmate. A third set of parents is continually away from home, a fact which drives their teenage daughter to shoplift in order to get their attention. Even the few parents who try to help prove ineffectual. Her mother's sermons don't prevent Spike from getting pregnant. Katherine's parents cannot prevail upon her to take her epilepsy medicine, so the girl suffers repeated seizures. No family team emerges in this domestic desert. Instead, there is recurrent conflict and isolation between the generations; the difference from *Fame* is palpable.

Thrown on their own resources, how do the youngsters cope? In American sitcoms, teenagers, sometimes bereft of adult assistance, often cooperate spontaneously, forging their own family teams, establishing minidemocracies of self-help, and, in so doing, showing adults how things really should be done. But at De Grassi, coping is sporadic. For example, Shawn, who has impregnated Spike, allows his friends to entice him to a party where he acts irresponsibly, forcing Spike to run home in tears. In another episode, the friends of a smallish boy tell him that unless he accepts a bully's challenge to fight, he will have shown himself a coward. So, reluctantly, the boy fights and is viciously beaten to the ground. To be sure, there are instances of solidarity and altruism among the students, but one can never expect an automatically positive response, as so often occurs in American versions of teenage tribulations.

Lacking the support of adults and peers, the young people at De Grassi truly suffer. Pregnancy, child abuse, shyness, serious illness, theft—the list of problems is long. The children fight back gamely, but only to survive, not to "develop," as in American family sitcoms. In the absence of a cohesive, traditional family structure, the Canadian child's world collapses, anarchy sets in, and effective preparation for conflictive democratic participation evaporates.

Canadian magazine advertising also diverges from American advertising. I examined four numbers of six popular magazines: *Select Homes, Canadian Living, Equinox, Outdoor Canada, Saturday Night,* and *MacLean's.* Although there are more political and cultural stories in these magazines than in their American counterparts, Canadian magazine advertising leads the reader away from the public world; in fact, advertising is even more isolating in Canadian magazines than in American magazines.

I also compared several elite Canadian magazines to their American cousins. I investigated *Canadian Business* and *Canadian Geographic*, both of which reach a well-educated, upper-middle-class readership. Significantly, other Canadian elite publications, such as the Canadian equivalents of *The New Republic* or *The Nation*, carry no advertising at all. By contrast, even the most elite American magazines usually contain some advertising.

As this observation implies, Canadian magazines generally contain fewer advertisements than do American magazines. A rough comparison indicates the considerable dimensions of difference: for twenty-eight numbers of the seven most popular American magazines, the total number of separate product appeals equaled 3,262; the comparable figure for twenty-six numbers of the seven most popular Canadian magazines was only 965. Although there are more appeals than ads (since most ads employ mutliple appeals), even a generous estimate suggests that Canadian magazines are no more than half as "commercial" as American magazines.

The Canadian image of the consumer is thus less developed than the American image (see Malcolm 1985: 292). *A fortiori*, the same conclusion applies to products: products simply do not play as great a role in the Canadian private sphere as they do into the private lives of Americans.

Within this somewhat truncated world, what sorts of appeals do we encounter, and what sorts of consumers appear? Many of the appeals which dominate American magazine advertisements also predominate in Canada. These especially include appeals to quality, particularly in the form of brand comparisons. Seventeen percent of the Canadian advertisements make direct quality comparisons, virtually identical to the 18 percent figure in American advertisements.

Similarly, technological appeals are as frequent in Canadian magazine ads as in American magazines. The magic of computer graphics, cellular phones, state-of-the-art audio systems—in short, the promise of cutting-edge technology—composes 11 percent of the appeals in Canadian magazines, as opposed to the 9 percent figure in American magazines. Like her American counterpart, the Canadian consumer not only makes sound quality judgments, but also appreciates (or is at least awed by) technological advances.

Also equally appealing to Canadians and Americans is the promise of ease, convenience, and choice. The Canadian consumer, like his or her American counterpart, emerges as a rational chooser attracted to high quality, technically innovative products that are convenient, easy to use, and versatile (for related theory, see Leymore 1982: 421–34; Ewen and Ewen 1982: chap. 6).

But the world of the consumer is even more socially barren in Canadian magazine advertising than in American advertising. In the United States only 19 percent of the advertisements placed the product in social contexts. As we discovered, most advertisements depicted the product in a reified, iconic, solitary form, infinitely desirable for itself, lacking any broader social reference. This isolation is even more common in Canadian magazine ads, only 12 percent of which place the product in a social context.

But isolation is not complete, for magazine advertisements in Canada are more group-oriented than advertisements in American magazines. In almost half of the Canadian "social" ads, groups of people employ the product as a part of social intercourse. For example, we regularly encounter couples smoking cigarettes in an outdoor setting, such as a beach. By contrast, in American magazines there are almost twice as many individuals as there are social groups using products. Put differently, in Canadian magazine ads, consumers evidence a modicum of collective identity; products help to bring people together. In the United States, products promote solitude; people use products to quit society.

The group emphasis in Canadian advertisements is perhaps connected to the slightly greater frequency of Canadian appeals to tradition. American magazines rarely depict products as the fruits of traditional craftsmanship. In Canada, such appeals remain uncommon, but are still more frequent than comparable American ads: 5 percent of Canadian ads employ appeals to tradition, as compared to only 2 percent of American ads. The difference in part reflects residual British influences. For example, Scotch whiskeys often appear in Canada as high-quality goods which revered British companies have lovingly nurtured. In the United States, the absence of a continuing political connection to Britain perhaps erodes the appeal to tradition.

References to tradition fortify Canadian group consciousness. Today's consumers become a link in a long historical chain of satisfied purchasers. The past therefore becomes a story of group formation. Appeals to tradition in Canadian advertising thus reinforce and reproduce a more hierarchically solid Canadian domestic sphere.

Canadian advertisements also refer directly to history more often and more favorably than do American advertisements. For example, in *Mac-*

Lean's (5 January 1987: 64), we encounter something entirely absent from American magazine advertising, namely, a reference to the life cycle. This ad compares IBM personal computers to *Roget's Thesaurus*. IBM, like *Roget's Thesaurus*, is one of "very few things to go through life with. That grow as we grow, as our needs grow. Through school, through college, and into our working lives." Life cycle depictions place products within enduring, worthwhile, group-based *ways* of life, rather than within transient individual life *styles* that yield only temporary satisfaction. Such appeals therefore also reinforce a traditional, solid domestic sphere capable of supporting conflictive democratic participation.

Canadian advertising also appeals less often to nature and health than does American advertising (9 percent in Canadian magazines vs. 16 percent in American). The comparative absence of these appeals in Canadian magazines perhaps reflects Canadian acceptance of social boundaries and personal limitations. As McGregor (1986) and Atwood (1972) earlier indicated, Canadians do not romanticize nature as do Americans. The Canadian consumer thus accepts closure within a protective, if somewhat stifling, family group; the American consumer attempts to explore the unbounded terrain of personal choice. Indirectly, this Canadian tendency reinforces group solidarity. Symbolically deprived of fantasized escapes into nature, health, and an anonymous frontier, the Canadian consumer turns to solidary social groups — and to politics — for survival. Meanwhile, the American consumer, seeking unending personal development, escapes to nature when the going gets rough at home. Like Huck Finn, the American consumer can always "light out for the territory." Therefore, group action may appear less necessary for the American than for the Canadian (see also Smith 1950).

In summary, the private sphere appears less prominent or nourishing in Canadian popular culture than in American popular culture. Not only do Canadian television series oppose the American family model but, in so doing, they also buttress a bifurcated cultural template which displaces private conflict outward to politics. In addition, because French Canadians watch few American or Anglo-Canadian programs, different viewing habits in the two Canadas also reinforce a bifurcated Canadian culture. Widely viewed American sitcom families diverge from Canadian models, and Canadian sitcom families are often bitterly divided or ineffectual if they are not traditional. Therefore, Canadians may focus their attention outward, escaping familial conflicts for the political world.

The private world is further overshadowed by the paucity of Canadian magazine advertising. Within this diminished sphere, Canadians experience the same major appeals as Americans; most ads picture

Canadians as rational, technologically sophisticated, quality-seeking persons, anxious to maximize choice and convenience. However, the ads temper this predominantly individualist image with peculiarly Canadian subthemes. Canadians appear more often in groups than do Americans, and they do not pursue individual freedom through improved health regimes or continued escapes to nature, as do Americans. Canadians also more often respect tradition. Thus, the truncated private world of Canadian popular culture at least retains some group solidarity. But unstable group solidarity, cultural bifurcation, and embedded conflict do not entirely blossom in the Canadian domestic sphere. Instead, the private sphere pushes these themes outward to politics and the economy. Therefore, for the full embodiment of these Canadian themes—so critical to conflictive democratic participation—we must enter the public world.

The Emergence of Conflict: The Canadian Corporation

Basing his conclusions on interviews with Canadian corporation executives, Michael Ornstein writes, "the Canadian business community opposes virtually all efforts at further social reform and given the power would roll back many present programs" (1986:204). Whatever the views of individual executives, however, collective representations of Canadian corporations, in the form of house organs, depict a varied, somewhat troubled world, in which room exists for welfare-state reforms, worker power, and even group conflict (for related policy evidence, see Evans 1988: 155–90). As a result, one wonders whether the further extension of welfare-state measures in Canada than in the United States owes something to the collective representation of the corporation in Canada. Although there may be little to choose between the American and Canadian business executive (Ornstein 1986: 182–209), corporate self-images may restrain the Canadians from acting on the basis of their mercenary impulses.

At first glance, there appears little difference between Canadian and American house organs. For example, competitive themes are even more common in Canadian corporate publications than in American publications. These themes runs the gamut from the individual to the group to entire companies, all competing viciously against each other. And, as in the American corporate literature, individual competition always promotes the corporate good. An illustration is the article about George Craig in the *Maple Leaf*, the house organ of Canadian Packers:

George Craig is pleased but not surprised that a selection of
Chemicals Division hotel amenities products won a first place
award in a recent North America wide contest. George, who is
product manager for the division's hotel amenities products,
says the Top of the Vanity Awards win is a feather in the company's cap. "This was a very competitive event. Having our products in the winner's circle . . . is valuable recognition," he
said . . . (11, no. 2, 1985: 5)

This example equates intercorporate competition between specialty
groups (the Chemicals Division against its counterparts in other corporations) with the success of Canadian Packers in its competition
against other corporations. The competitive theme thus receives double
reinforcement, as it often does in American corporate literature.

Images of group competition for symbolic rewards (e.g., safety records, production quotas, etc.) are also somewhat more salient in Canadian than in American corporate literature. For example, in *B. C. Hydro News* (October 1985), a story about David Adams is headlined,
"A world badminton champion — after he retired." As the article explains, "Adams' personal motto is 'never give up', and it's paid off for
this lean, fluid-moving competitor who walks like a lanky teenager
rather than a member of the geritol set." The theme of endless, productive competition surfaces especially clearly when the article observes,
"He has always been a competitor and always will be" (5).

One factor that perhaps promotes these strong competitive themes
in Canadian corporate publications is the prominence of the international market (*New York Times*, 20 November 1988: 1). Lacking a
large internal market and facing severe competition from American
firms, Canadian corporations must compete against bigger international
rivals. The chairman of B. C. Hydro, for example, devotes an entire
page in one newsletter to the prices Americans pay for B. C.'s energy.
Sensitive to claims that B. C. Hydro charges its American customers less
than its Canadian customers, he writes, "The export sale of surplus
electricity produces revenue for Hydro which reflects to the advantage
of all our BC customers" (*B. C. Hydro News*, 2, no. 27 [August 1985]).
B. C. Hydro thus remains competitive both in the international market
and within Canada itself (see also Frank and Schanz 1978). Moreover,
the corporation resists American domination.

The clearest single illustration of the competitive theme in Canadian
corporate publications appears in *Ford of Canada's 1985 Report*, which
begins:

The competition is intense. Never before has the Canadian automotive industry faced such a crucial challenge for successful participation in not only the global market, but, more importantly, in its own home market.

Later the report notes:

A strategy based on competition, cooperation, and customer satisfaction is the key to our success. Ford of Canada's 1986 objectives are to: obtain quality and customer satisfaction leadership; continue market share improvements; implement our 'Guiding Principles'; improve the quality and efficiency of our marketing effort; reduce nonproductive workload; and become more cost-efficient.

The report reiterates the competitive theme in its conclusion:

We must be prepared to meet any eventuality. This will demand fostering the entrepreneurial spirit by creating a work environment that facilitates change, motivates and maximizes employee capacity, job satisfaction, and teamwork, and stresses excellence in everything we do. We welcome the challenge. (2)

The Canadian version of severe corporate competition embodies a unique sense of personal challenge. Although this emphasis sometimes combines with the growth and development themes that soften American recruitment brochures, more often it comes without the American gloss. For example, "The Ford Commitment and Your Career Future" begins:

Ford offers graduates an atmosphere of challenge in which they can develop profitably their talents and abilities. This challenge continues to grow in line with individual progress.(2)

Nothing in this statement so far distinguishes it from many comparable American publications, save perhaps the slightly ominous "in line with individual progress." What identifies the statement as peculiarly Canadian is the following:

The complex problems, together with the highly competitive nature of the automobile industry, present substantial challenge to the university graduate. The satisfactions, both material and personal, are also worthwhile and rewarding.(2)

The latter statement marries industry-wide competition to individual challenge. True, at the end of the statement there is brief mention of personal satisfaction, but this is a secondary theme in comparison with the emphasis upon material rewards. The priority of material over psychological rewards reverses American motifs and thus keeps the corporation sharply apart from the private world.

Like American corporations, Canadian corporations also place a strong emphasis on technological improvements. But Canadians use this technological theme to reinforce competition, mainly through the use of machine imagery. The best example of this coupling appears in *General Motors 1985 in Review*. Most noteworthy initially are the pictures, which are highly stylized, colorful renderings of advanced machinery (e.g., a computer-controlled stamping process; new transportation systems; computers (in violet); GM's futuristic pavilion at the Vancouver Expo '86). These pictures complement the President's Message, which emphasizes competition:

> 1985 reflects our ongoing commitment to provide leadership in new product styling and innovative vehicle technology.(3)

Breakthroughs in technology improve competitiveness, as befits a successful corporate machine:

> The introduction of the new SD60 series locomotive, a new generation computer-controlled locomotive with three microprocessors on board, represents a major product advancement.(4)

In addition to machine innovation, the magazine describes complementary managerial innovations which will increase competitiveness:

> The improvement of customer satisfaction remains a driving force throughout our organization as we strive to achieve world-class products and services. GM of Canada ranks highest within the Corporation in customer satisfaction and is dedicated to improvement in the years ahead. Several new programs in customer and dealer services were developed in 1985 and still others are planned.(4)

To summarize, the machine image of the corporation is even stronger in Canadian corporate literature than in the United States. But the Canadian machine image also differs slightly in content from its American counterpart; Canadians de-emphasize teamwork and group cooperation in favor of pervasive conflict. Canadians picture corporate life as a multifaceted struggle: corporation against corporation; team against team; manager against manager. Few of the leavening themes one encounters in American corporate images appear in Canada. Canadians idealize *realism*, not romance in their corporate images; they do not hide the starkness of corporate life behind a veil of self-improvement (Merquior 1979).

So far, the sizable gap between collective representations of the private world and of the corporation in Canada fits the theoretical perspective we earlier offered, whereby culturally represented conflict might stimulate conflictive democratic participation. However, the themes we have so far discussed are common to both the United States and Canada; only the emphasis differs. Now, however, we encounter uniquely *Canadian* corporate themes which depict historically rooted, group-generating struggles. Similar themes do not appear at all in the American materials. These themes obviously promote conflictive democratic participation in Canada.

A hint of these themes first appears in the strong Canadian emphasis upon corporate history. Every Canadian corporation studied, save B. C. Hydro, publishes a history of its organization. GM of Canada's "History of the Automobile," for example, is a substantial essay that runs to twenty-eight double-column pages. "Landmarks of Alcan's Worldwide History" is an attractive, brief history of both Alcan and aluminum. Even Canadian Life Insurance distributes a history to its new employees, a practice few American life insurance companies emulate.

This Canadian tendency not only legitimizes current operations by reference to the past, but also suggests that the corporation retains continuity despite dramatic innovations. Most important, the historical emphasis also records themes of struggle. Consider "A Profile of Bell," which states in its historical section:

> Bell Canada was incorporated in 1880 as The Bell Telephone Company of Canada. Contrary to popular belief, Bell Canada was never a subsidiary controlled by AT&T. At most, the two were once close cousins enjoying a strong relationship.(2)

Later the article reports that since the 1950s Canadian Bell has become more independent of its American "cousin." Both technologically and financially, therefore, Canadian Bell pictures itself struggling to become an autonomous entity, not a servant to the United States' AT&T.

Two kinds of group-generating struggle surface in Canadian corporate publications: struggles of class and struggles of region. As to class, Canadian corporate publications recognize the reality of blue-collar work more than do American publications. For example, "The Ford

Commitment and Your Career Future" offers graduates opportunities in "industrial relations," a specialty conspicuously absent from comparable American recruitment literature. The brochure comments:

> Due to the labor intensive manufacturing operations, labor relations play a large and vital role within the Industrial Relations function. . . . These assignments emphasize a traditional and pragmatic approach to problem solving.(11)

To be sure, this passage camouflages labor strife under an ugly neologism ("Industrial Relations"). But at least the passage demonstrates awareness of class struggle, as compared to the total absence of the subject in American corporate literature (Gutman 1987). Moreover, a "traditional and pragmatic approach" does not sanitize the topic. Canadian corporate publications also occasionally reveal the less pleasant aspects of blue-collar work. *Ford in Canada* actually shows pictures of blue-collar workers assembling automobiles on production lines.

Canadian publications also hint at sporadic conflicts of interest between workers and managers. For example, a series of *Ford in Canada* articles discusses ways of incorporating automobile workers into the design process, an indirect suggestion that exclusion of workers from automobile design perhaps causes friction. *Ford in Canada* reports there is a new disposition among Ford designers to include workers in the design process:

> A good example of this new attitude was the opportunity Oakville employees had — two years before production began — to study clay models and hand-built prototypes of the 1984 Tempo and Topaz. They made 202 suggestions affecting product design and 142 of these ideas were adopted by designers, engineers and planners before the first vehicles rolled off the assembly line.

As might be expected, the conflict between French and English Canada also leaves its mark on Canadian corporate publications. Most Canadian corporate literature is anxious to point out contributions the corporation makes to Quebec (for possible explanations, see Dion 1988: 282–317). For example, "Alcan in Quebec" argues that Alcan has raised living standards in the province. While most of the pictures in this brochure portray highly industrialized, unattractive settings, the cover itself is a panorama of a traditional Quebec village, complete with a venerable church steeple. Industry therefore need not befoul the pastoral scene. By juxtaposing the bucolic and the industrial — the machine and the garden (Marx 1964) — the brochure implies that modernity and tradition can be partners in Quebec.

The Bell "Profile" includes a section entitled "Presence in Quebec," which states proudly, if a bit defensively, "Bell was founded in Montreal in 1880 and Montreal remains the location of its head office. The province of Quebec thus benefits from the economic advantages that an international enterprise always confers on its country and province of origin" (12). This statement not only highlights Bell's economic contribution to Quebec, but also assures the Quebecois that Bell is no cultural "imperialist" exploiting the province for the benefit of Anglo-Canadians. Instead, Bell is culturally rooted in Quebec. But by suggesting the possibility of economic imperialism, the argument perhaps reproduces the very regional sensitivity it means to allay.

Tension in the Canadian corporation's collective representation appears most clearly in the Alcan material. In "Alcan, Its Purpose, Objectives and Policies," the corporation proudly describes "the Alcan group" as "a multi-racial, multi-cultural and multi-lingual enterprise" (1), and implies that, within this variegated structure, an almost utopian harmony reigns. For example, Alcan enjoys the support of "a complement of able employees who place a high value not only on the interests of the Company, but also on the interests of other individuals and entities with whom they relate both inside and outside Alcan"(3).

An important aspect of this positive image is advanced technology, to which Alcan devotes a separate brochure (*Alcan Today*). Alcan argues that it derives much of its scientific strength from its diverse employees; while in other companies ethnic diversity often causes disarray, ethnic diversity in Alcan is a source of strength. Here Alcan reproduces its own version of the Canadian ethnic mosaic.

This mosaic image recurs throughout *Alcan Today*. The brochure describes how Alcan encompasses "the activities of many people in many lands" (*Alcan Today*, 4). Shareholders also comprise "a broad spectrum of individuals from every walk of life" (3). On pages 4–5, pictures depict Alcan's unique mosaic; a veritable United Nations of employees are shown cooperating with each other at Alcan. In sum, Alcan is a productive machine of talented, varied, but competitive individuals — a machine utopia of diverse nationalities.

But, despite its best efforts, Alcan still must struggle to keep peace among its constituent parts. As we have seen, *Alcan in Quebec* attempts to reassure Alcan's Quebecois public; Alcan is also a leading depictor of blue-collar workers, especially in *Alcan Today*. Thus, the primary sources of Canadian tensions, region and class, repeatedly disturb Alcan's utopia of diversity. In response, Alcan attempts to construct a self-image which tries to transmit these potential sources of disarray into appreciation for human diversity and "identity through difference." Alcan, like Canada itself, attempts to draw strength from rather than fall prey to its many differences. But in so doing, it must depict and help reproduce the differences themselves, which are the heart of Canadian culture and politics.

Conflict as a Dominant Theme: The World of Politics

Canadian provincial governments select secondary school texts for schools. The eight texts (Hux and Jarman 1987; Grearson and King 1971; McFadden, Quinlan, and Life 1982; Mitchner et al. 1976; Evans and Martinello 1978; Lower 1970; Evans and Diachun 1976; Kirbyson et al. 1983) which I examine in this section are widely used in Saskatchewan, Ontario, Manitoba, Alberta (perhaps the most "American" of Canadian provinces), and British Columbia. Of these provinces, only Ontario contains many French Canadians. Therefore, these texts provide a conservative comparison to the American materials; if these predominantly Anglo-Canadian texts feature regional and class conflict, we may expect even more in New Brunswick and Quebec texts, for in these provinces large French-Canadian populations attend French schools manned by educators with a long memory for the French side of Canadian history.

For comparative purposes, I first examined three subjects: the portrayal of political parties; the portrayal of individual rights; and the depiction of labor unions. In the previous chapter we examined these three topics in their American guise. How do they appear in Canada?

It is fortunate for comparative purposes that the history of unionism in Canada resembles in many ways that in the United States. Like American unions, Canadian unions have not been bastions of socialism, nor a vital part of party politics. Furthermore, agrarian radicalism in the Canadian west somewhat resembles American agrarian radicalism, with carryovers into union formation and strikes (Lipset 1950). On balance, Canadian unions seem no less devoted to capitalism than are American unions. Moreover, Canadian and American unions are about equal to each other in political power. Differences in the texts' portrayal of unions, therefore, probably cannot be explained solely as reflections of fact, rather than as representations of culture.

Of course, Canadian unions did once mount a general strike, the

Winnipeg Strike of 1919, an event which remains central to Canadian political consciousness (Jordan 1975). But the United States has its own examples of severe labor conflict, such as the UAW sit-down strikes of the 1930s, the conflict over unionization in the Appalachian coalfields (Gaventa 1980), and the national steelworkers' strike of 1952, during which President Truman seized the steel mills (Donovan 1982: 387). On balance, there seems little to choose between the two countries on this subject.

Whatever the historical differences between unionism in the two societies, these can hardly explain the marked cleavage in the way the two countries' social studies texts portray unions. Where American texts portray unions as voluntary ogranizations led by charismatic leaders, the Canadian texts see unions as durable organizations expressive of the distinct, class-rooted interests of workers. In fact, McFadden, Quinlan, and Life's *Canada: The Twentieth Century* (1982) even implies that the government's intervention to break the Winnipeg Strike was unwarranted and unfair. The authors go on to suggest that government generally sides with managers against the legitimate demands of workers. No similar pro-union message ever appears in American texts.

Canadian texts also picture a decidedly noncharismatic relationship between union leaders and the rank-and-file. As we have seen, American texts typically portray unions as the creations of charismatic leaders, such as John L. Lewis or Walter Reuther. By contrast, not one of the Canadian texts mentioned a single Canadian union leader. Canadian unions thus emerge as the creations of their members, not of their leaders.

Canadian texts also treat the relationship between workers and employers as conflictive. The texts treat the two groups as inherently opposed economically; strikes or collective bargaining therefore become the normal forms of labor-management relations. Indeed, Evans and Martinello's *Canada's Century* (1978) actually portrays in some detail a hypothetical sequence of collective bargaining.

The Canadian depiction of individual rights also promotes conflictive democratic participation more than does the American version. As we have seen, although individual rights are a vital part of American political history, the Bill of Rights — the cornerstone of individual rights in America — receives surprisingly superficial attention in American texts. By contrast, perhaps it is the very *absence* of a strong rights tradition which elevates individual rights to salience in Canadian texts. After all, not until 1982 did Canadians adopt a written Bill of Rights. In 1970, the federal government suspended civil rights during the Quebec kidnapping crisis, an action which created a national outcry (Handler 1988: 15). Debate over these events and over federal and provincial protections of rights intrudes deeply into Canadian texts. Unlike Americans, Canadians perhaps do not feel they can take rights for granted.

Significantly, four of six Canadian texts picture individual rights as the product of collective struggles and debate. Examples include the Bill of Rights (Evans and Martinello, *Canada's Century*, 1978); specific court cases; Trudeau's advocacy of a Canadian Human Rights statement in the 1960s (Evans and Diachun, *Canada: Towards Tomorrow*, 1976); and the 1970 suspension of civil rights in Quebec (Mitchner et al., *Forging a Destiny: Canada Since 1945*, 1976). Indeed, after warning that the government might again abridge civil rights in Quebec, Mitchner et al. are even willing to criticize the government's actions in 1970, claiming that there was too little evidence of a conspiracy to justify so repressive an action (119).

Five of the six relevant Canadian texts also attempt to situate individual rights within a philosophical tradition. The arguments range from a discussion of natural law, Hobbes, Locke, and Mill (Mitchner et al.), to democratic theory (Evans and Diachun), to the need for equal treatment in a democratic society (Hux and Jarman 1987: 351). Evans and Martinello even describe an arrest and trial sequence as seen by the defendant (119). The text carefully points out every legal means by which citizens can resist arrest and imprisonment. In this way, Evans and Martinello emphasize the presumption of innocence in criminal proceedings.

The Canadian texts also pay attention to the problem of rights interpretation. Mitchner et al. explicitly discuss the recurrent struggle between social order and individual liberty; in fact, the authors treat rights interpretation as a *political* process, a tack no American text takes (1976: 119). Another text distinguishes specifically between public and private, characterizing the latter in terms of the right to privacy and property. In sum, as compared with American texts, Canadian texts treat individual rights within a context of continuous political debate. Given the comparative weakness of individual rights in Canadian history, this treatment stands up well.

The emphasis upon conflict continues when we consider Canadian text treatments of political parties. On this subject there is perhaps better reason to expect differences between Canadian and American texts. Canada is a parliamentary system, and Canadian parties are cohesive instruments of governance. Yet the two major parties, the Progressive Conservatives and the Liberals, are in reality no more polarized ideologically than are the American Republican and Democratic parties (Clarke et al. 1979). But despite this fact, Canadian texts accord parties greater ideological distinctiveness than do American texts.

Of the four Canadian texts which discuss political parties, two present parties as mobilizers of conflict. Only one (Evans and Diachun) sees Canadian parties as mainly pursuing a consensus; however, even Evans and Diachun depict a refined left-right party spectrum, to which they apply terminology such as "radical" and "reactionary" (7). No American text provides a comparable depiction.

Moreover, to a greater extent than American texts, Canadian texts define parties as issue-oriented, rather than as preoccupied solely with winning elections. Grearson and King, for example, define a party as "a group of people who have similar political ideas" (1971: 40). Hux and Jarman state that, "an individual joins the political party which shares that person's opinions on most issues" (1987: 366). To these authors, parties reflect the ideological views of the electorate.

Given the salience of ideology, it is not surprising that Canadian parties emerge as cohesive coalitions. For example, Grearson and King explain that parties must be united if they are to perform their parliamentary functions effectively (40). Of course, this image reflects reality. Many actual features of Canadian parties do favor party coherence. For example, to nominate candidates, Canadian parties rely on party *activists*, while American parties turn to primary elections which are open to all party voters. Indeed, until the early twentieth century, Canadian parties did not even employ a convention system to choose their nominees for leadership (Engelman and Schwartz 1975: 240). But texts which choose to depict this particular version of reality also help reproduce it.

The texts waver between seeing parties as ideologically coherent instruments of governance or broadbased electoral coalitions. Most texts characterize the parties as being broad in electoral appeal, never dominated by single cleavages along ethnic, regional, or class lines. However, Hux and Jarman do discuss the regional cleavage between Liberal support in Ontario and Quebec, and Conservative domination in Western Canada (366ff.). Aside from this brief mention, however, Canadian texts portray the heterogeneous social backgrounds of party supporters much as do American texts. The texts do not even see the CCF and the NDP as uniquely appealing to workers.

But, unlike American texts, Canadian texts are divided in their assessment of the parties' electoral role. Two treat the subject very much in the American style, that is, as more important than the party's role in governance. However, all the texts devote considerable attention to the governance role of parties. McFadden, Quinlan, and Life imaginatively combine the two functions into a single sequence. They write as follows: "Everything a party does is geared toward the next election. The election is the key. Only if elected will the party have the power to put its ideas into effect" (1982: 297). In this treatment elections become the means to a more important end, namely, governance. A similar argument appears in Grearson and King's *Canadian Democracy at Work*: "Members of a party support the same platform and organize themselves so that they may win elections and take over the responsibility of governing the nation" (1971: 40). This characterization differs from the standard American treatment, where the function of parties often seems to end on election day. More important, party governance promotes conflictive democratic participation.

The Canadian texts also view parties as more distinct from than similar to each other, despite the fact that the two major Canadian political parties are actually no more distinct from each other philosophically than are their American counterparts (Cooper, Kornberg, and Mishler 1988: 8). Nevertheless, two of the relevant texts treat the major parties as quite different from each other, while a third (McFadden, Quinlan, and Life 1982) treats the two *major* parties as largely alike, but then contrasts the two with the New Democratic Party's socialist alternative. Only Evans and Diachun (1976) treat *all* parties as compromise coalitions seeking votes. But Evans and Diachun then go on to *denounce* this practice for producing "wishy-washy" politics (7), an accusation absent from the usual American encomiums to party compromise. The Canadian approach clearly favors conflictive democratic participation.

Canadian images of conflict reach their zenith in text treatments of Quebec. The Quebec issue provides an opportunity for the texts to discuss whether mass political movements abet democratic politics. Of course, the closest American counterparts to Quebecois nationalism in this study—Jacksonian Democracy and Progressive reform—cannot equal Quebec separatism in intensity, for neither American movement seriously threatened national unity. All the more reason, therefore, why the Canadian texts might choose to minimize the Quebec conflict (for comparison, see Trudel and Jain 1970). In an effort to preserve Canadian unity, the texts could attempt to deprecate French-Canadian demands, picture Quebec separatists as unrepresentative French Canadians, or focus on corruption and charisma in the separatist movement. Moreover, since these are *Anglo*-Canadian texts, the temptation to derogate Quebecois separatism might well be high. Of course, in the interest of national unity, the textbook writers may wish to *placate* the Quebecois by portraying French nationalism sympathetically. But if so, the writers by implication legitimize Quebec separatism, and thus reproduce cultural bifurcation.

In any case, the struggle over Quebec includes at least some themes prominent in the two American movements. These themes include conflicts between rich and poor (i.e., Anglo businessmen against French-Quebec workers and "habitants"); between majority rule and minority rights (i.e., controversies over language policies); between federalism and centralization (i.e., French-Canadian separatism); and between elite and populist versions of democracy (e.g., the 1982 referendum on sovereignty association). Therefore, comparison between Quebec separatism and the two American movements, though not exact, is at least suggestive.

All the texts devote extensive attention to Quebec, running from one to several chapters. Indeed, one text (Mitchner. et al. 1976) devotes a full sixty pages to the subject. Thus, the texts make no effort to avoid this most controversial issue.

One principal question of democratic theory raised by the Quebec issue is that of majority rule versus minority rights. The Westminister model emphasizes majority rule, while the Canadian charter principle of two founding "races" possessed of equal rights elevates the position of a minority (French-Canadians) to that of a majority. Do Canadian texts raise this difficult theoretical conflict, or do they avoid it?

The texts are divided in their approach to this question. Hux and Jarman (1987) confine the discussion to "minority *language rights*" (my emphasis), thereby avoiding the connection between language and more encompassing issues of ethnicity and democracy. More bravely, Evans and Diachun (1976) extend the issue to the rights enjoyed by French minorities *outside* Quebec. Thus, Evans and Diachun move the majority-minority theme into ill-defined, dangerous terrain. Evans and Martinello (1978) pursue a third approach by focusing explicitly upon separation as a constitutional option, thereby raising the issue of majority rule and minority rights in an indirect and circuitous fashion. Finally, Mitchner et al. (1976) discuss the issue of provincial versus federal power and, unlike the other authors, use the terrorist campaign to examine the question of conflict between intense minorities and moderate majorities (189ff.).

Thus, in various ways, all these texts confront the issue of majority rule and minority rights. By contrast, American texts do not employ Progressivism or Jacksonian democracy as opportunities for raising fun-

damental issues of democratic governance. Considering the fact that—
to some disputed degree—textbooks always function as idealizations
(Patrick and Hawke 1982: 39–51), the candor in these Canadian treatments comes as a surprise.

The texts admit that the problem of Quebec threatens Canadian unity,
and they concede that reform alone will not solve the problem. For
example, Evans and Diachun consistently use the terms "races" and
"founding people," thereby emphasizing the elemental character of the
struggle over Quebec. These authors also describe various proposed
solutions to the problem, running from complete separation to cooperative federalism. Lower, in *A Nation Developing*, presents a more conservative version of the problem, but even he concedes the Quiet Revolution of the 1960s failed, thereby triggering more damaging struggles
between the "founding races" (1970: 230). Evans and Martinello dramatize the struggle by citing multiple examples of anglophone prejudice
against French Canadians. These authors directly inquire of readers
what each has done to make French Canadians feel at home in his or
her community (242–43ff.). Mitchner et al. actually print the full text
of the FLQ's 1st Manifesto advocating terrorism in Quebec. The authors' nonjudgmental tone even implies some sympathy for the terror-
ists' cause (1976: 189).

The texts insist that the problem of Quebec is essentially cultural.
For example, Mitchner et al. treat the Quiet Revolution as an effort to
insure *la survivance*—the survival of French Canadian culture. However, the texts offer no clear meanings for the concept of culture. Instead, culture appears as a primitive, undefined term, a polyglot of
religious, linguistic, and economic differences between Quebec and the
other provinces. Only McFadden, Quinlan, and Life attempt a sophisticated rendering of the culture concept. They argue that the Acadians
of New Brunswick embodied a different culture from the Quebecois,
despite the fact that both cultures are French-Canadian in origin. They
also discuss how Quebecois art contributed to French nationalism during the 1960s. Today's francophone culture, they claim, provides a new
identity for Quebec (242ff.). No other text utilizes the concept of culture so self-consciously as a means of discussing French Canada.

Most important, the texts use the issue of Quebec separatism to promote democratic education and conflictive democratic participation
(for a contrary American case, see McNeil 1986: 174). Several texts
point out that the Quebecois are not only raising issues central to democratic participation, but are also effectively manipulating the instruments of Canadian democracy. In addition, the texts use the electoral

fortunes of the Parti Quebecois in order to introduce the topic of voting in democratic societies. The Referendum on Sovereignty Association also allows the authors to discuss how referenda are connected to democratic political change. In addition, the texts highlight specific Quebecois grievances, such as customary limitations on the number of French-Canadian ministers in Ottawa. This subject naturally raises the question of elite recruitment in Canada — and in other democratic polities. Finally, all of the texts use the Quebec issue to consider the place of protest and violence in democracies. These topics appear especially in discussions of De Gaulle's 1967 visit to Quebec, which sparked many protest rallies throughout Canada. Finally, the FLQ's bombings and kidnappings provide an opportunity to discuss terrorism in democratic polities.

Though willing to discuss protest and violence, the texts never *endorse* such methods. Yet their opprobrium is surprisingly muted. For example, Mitchner et al. only imply disapproval when they observe of the FLQ kidnappings and the state of emergency, "Outright revolution seemed possible" (1976: 116). Only a single text directly attacks terrorism; it presents a cartoon of a terrorist brandishing a rifle and a grenade, and commanding, "Do what I want or I will kill somebody." The authors attribute the terrorist's actions to poor education, hostility to teachers, personal frustration, a broken home, the desire to be "something special," the need to overcome inferiority, egocentrism, the equation of power with violence, impatience, and slum living (McDevitt et al. 1979: 327)! This list not only qualifies as pop psychology overkill, but also denies any legitimate political motives to terrorism. The depiction perhaps reveals the boundaries of Canadian tolerance for political conflict; legitimate grievances may justify political separation, but can never justify political violence.

In our analysis of American texts, we observed how frequently reform movements appear to be the personal creations of charismatic leaders. Is the same thing true of Quebecois separatism in Canadian texts? Partly. All the texts pay considerable attention to galvanizing events and charismatic figures, including De Gaulle's 1967 visit (especially his allusion to "Quebec *libre*"), Duplessis's reforms, and René Levesque, whose media manipulation two texts believe crucial to crystallizing support for Quebecois nationalism (Evans and Martinello; McFadden, Quinlan, and Life). On balance, the Canadian texts treat the separatism movement very much as the American textbooks treat Progressivism and the Jacksonian Era, that is, as a mixture of personal, situational, and structural phenomena.

In summary, Anglo-Canadian texts generally tackle the Quebec issue with honesty and even some sympathy. More important, they use the issue to discuss and promote conflictive democratic participation. They do so, I think, because, unlike American writers, they work within a cultural model of politics which legitimizes group solidarity and political conflict. From this perspective, the problem of Quebec, though dangerous, remains a comprehensible and legitimate element of the dominant Canadian collective representation of politics. The texts can therefore employ Quebec to test the compatibility between rooted primordial loyalties and liberal democracy.

Conclusion: Canadian Culture and Conflictive Democratic Participation

In the configuration of Canadian popular culture, many forms of group-generating conflict play a fundamental role. Nevertheless, this culture still produces less actual conflictive democratic participation than one might have expected. Why is this so? Two possibilities spring to mind.

The first possibility focuses on the private realm in Canadian popular culture. As we have seen, American individualism and Canadian collectivism vie for dominance in Canadian images of the family. Moreover, Canadian television contains many depictions of family disarray as well as family solidarity. In addition, advertising images of the consumer are less developed in Canada than in the United States. In short, the private realm appears divided and weak in Canadian popular culture. While private division may turn Canadians toward public conflict, it may also diminish the emotional tension between public and private. Put differently, although private bifurcation is a micro model of the dualism in Canadian politics, this model perhaps does not fuel Canadian political action effectively.

A more modest argument is that Canadians *do* possess strong ties to the private world, but that this world lacks narrative and mythological force, and therefore does not stimulate political conflict. Certainly Canadian sitcoms and advertising are narratively more straightforward than their American counterparts, and therefore perhaps encourage Canadians to construe political action only in terms of *public* problems, not in terms of private needs. As a result, though perhaps better structured than American participation, Canadian political action may lack emotional intensity (for suggestive findings, see Meisel 1975: 127–83).

Yet both these observations ignore the most distinctively *Canadian* aspect of popular culture: its self-reflexive quality. For example, the topic of Canadian culture plays a prominent role in many of the social studies texts I reviewed. As the texts illustrate, Canadians incessantly ask themselves whether there is in fact a *Canadian* culture (see, for example, Kirbyson et al. 1983; chap. 12), or whether "Canadian" culture is only a *bricolage* of American television, British social class, French Catholicism, and Anglican ritual. Although most of the texts argue that there is a distinct Canadian culture, more often than not "demonstrations" of this proposition become lists of famous Canadian artists who have made their reputations in New York, Beverly Hills, or London.

Cultural self-consciousness in Canada reflects the situation of a nation caught between unstable group solidarity in the public realm and division and uncertainty in the private realm. Canadian culture may therefore be too "problematized", stylized, and self-aware to generate forceful political action. By contrast, although American popular culture almost never reflects upon what "Americans" are like or whether American culture really exists, Americans also generate little conflictive democratic participation. Why? The answer becomes clear in comparative perspective. The cultural raw materials for conflictive democratic participation exist in Canada, but Canadian culture is too insecure and mannered to produce broad political action (but see *New York Times,* 20 November 1988: 1). By comparison, in the United States, people "know" that America is unique. The irony is that *being* American means eschewing conflictive democratic participation. In neither society, therefore, does culture fully realize conflictive democratic participation.

CHAPTER FIVE

British Culture: Debating Ways Of Life

The history of British liberal high culture leads us to expect British popular culture to debate enduring ways of life. This debate should encourage conflictive democratic participation. Our examination reveals that such a debate in fact takes place between working class and middle class; hedonism and community; Left and Right. On the side of the working class, community, and the Left are television programs and social studies texts; on the side of the middle class, hedonism, and the Right are magazine advertising and corporate publications. Parliamentary democracy and tradition in the form of the monarchy symbolically mediate and moderate this struggle.

The Cultural Consequences of British Liberalism

As the progenitor of liberal political philosophy and of the Industrial Revolution, Britian generated a widely esteemed high literary culture, which during the eighteenth and nineteenth centuries attempted to comprehend these two disturbing politico-economic developments. In the early nineteenth century, Blake and the Romantic poets rejected the two. In Victorian England, Eliot, Dickens, and Trollope attempted an uneasy reconciliation between industrialization and liberal democracy. In the early twentieth century, Hardy, Conrad, and Forster reformulated literary liberalism, an enterprise that continues today in the fiction of Margaret Drabble, John Osbourne, Allan Sillitoe, and David Lodge. Thus, in Britain, the political and economic evolution of liberal democracy has had an unusually marked impact upon literary culture (Williams 1960).

The uniquely British literary consideration of liberalism has also spawned a distinguished tradition of cultural-cum-political criticism. One need only mention such names as Arnold, Ruskin, Pater, Newman, Leavis, and Snow. It should not be surprising, therefore, that the British "cultural studies" school took *popular* culture seriously before analogous theoretical schools emerged in the United States or Canada

(Fiske 1987a: 254–91). Nor should it be surprising that leading exponents of cultural studies have also contributed important *political* analyses to the British Left (e.g., Hall 1988). The craft of criticism is intrinsic to the evolution of a sophisticated, aesthetically pleasing, politically engaged, popular culture. Moreover, cultural debate—or, rather, debate about culture—stands squarely within the evolution of British politics (Williamson 1986; Leavis and Thompson 1937; for a counterview, see Miller 1988: chap 1; Hoggart 1957).

Just as liberalism in Britain helped generate a politically engaged and aesthetically powerful *high* literary culture, so also might it help today to generate a comparably distinctive *popular* culture. Indeed, a principal hypothesis of this chapter is that, comparatively, British popular culture today is an aesthetically powerful means of stimulating conflictive democratic participation. As we will see, more often than American or Canadian popular culture, British popular culture depicts struggles between public and private, and between individual and collectivity. These depictions turn into debates about alternative ways of life. In turn, these debates provide a favorable cultural context for conflictive democratic participation.

This is true in part because in Britain a socialist political party that is itself the creature of the working class continually forces class issues into popular culture. The British Labour party helps keep the language and issues of class alive in Britain. No political party acts quite this way in Canada or the United States. Indeed, in a sense, British popular culture may be seen as a battleground both between working-class and middle-class political *positions* and between working-class, middle-class, and upper-class rhetorical *styles*. For these reasons, British popular culture actually *debates* social and political issues in depth, a phenomenon absent in Canada or the United States.

This debate does not always proceed overtly. After all, popular culture is not traditional literary culture; in popular culture the class-based political debate which the Labour party fosters must become suitable for mass consumption and entertainment. Thus, while British popular culture is a real political conversation, the conversation takes place beneath a sometimes distracting surface structure.

What is the topic of this political conversation? British popular culture does not celebrate American-style institutionalized individualism, nor does it sever group conflict from its personal consequences, as in Canada; instead, it rehearses a struggle between two ways of life: a selfish, narcissistic vision of life, and a selfless, communitarian vision.

British Families in Collective Representations:
The Meaning of the "Coronation (Street)"

In "The Meaning of the Coronation," a classic of British sociology, Edward Shils and Michael Young argued that the crowning of a monarch revives British communal bonds (1953: 63–81). The coronation of young Queen Elizabeth II in 1953 brought British society together in ritual form, renewing a sense of community in a country recovering slowly from World War II and racked with class hatreds. Shils and Young claimed that the coronation helped the British temporarily to surmount these difficulties and to reconstitute themselves symbolically as a unified nation.

For the last twenty-eight years, the most-watched British television series has been *Coronation Street*, a prime-time soap opera set in a fictional working class northern town modeled on Manchester (Tinker 1985). Although the producers happened upon the title of the series accidentally (Nown 1985: 25), in a cultural sense the title could not have been more appropriate, for it connects the imaginary activities on Coronation Street to the real coronations from which the street draws its name. In this case, popular culture turns metaphor into homology, paralleling meanings in different cultural spheres. The identification of such meanings in *Coronation Street* and other popular British prime-time television series constitutes our present subject.

Before embarking on this enterprise, a word is necessary about some aspects of British television. While American television programs are seen on British television, they do not dominate the screen, as they do in Canada. Indeed, the British television industry itself thrives. Both the British Broadcasting Corporation and the Independent Television Authority consistently produce situation comedies and soap operas of high quality and sustained popularity. Therefore, in analyzing British television, we do not confront methodological complexities of the sort we encountered in considering Canadian television.

But British television is unusual in its scheduling practices. Along with other factors, the mixture of public and private networks in Britain has created quite short broadcasting cycles. Many prime-time entertainment series appear, for example, in an eight- or nine-week format, leave the air for some time, then return some months later for another short "season." Short cycles do not characterize prime-time soap operas such as *Coronation Street*, however, which not only appear in long seasons, but also occupy two evening time slots per week.

The prevalent pattern of interrupted scheduling makes it difficult to identify established, popular series, which may take longer to establish themselves in Britain than in the United States. Ratings of audience popularity are, therefore, not entirely reliable. By contrast, longer seasons in the United States make audience ratings of popularity more accurate. I have attempted to minimize this problem in my choice of programs for analysis.

I base my analysis on a random thirty-five episodes chosen from eight of the most popular British prime-time series during the 1986–1988 period. Because of their longer, more stable patterns of production, and their faithful viewing audiences, prime-time soaps such as *Coronation Street* dominate the sample. But the popularity of these soaps is not really the consequence of scheduling. The soaps endure because they dramatize in particularly evocative ways certain central, yet contested, themes of British culture. These themes are also central to the sitcom series I analyze. Though more evanescent in appearance than prime-time soaps, British sitcoms play their own variations on the themes which dominate British television culture.

As in Canada and the United States, families are central elements in British soap operas and sitcoms. However, British families are anything but cooperative, egalitarian teams along the American sitcom model. The "structure of feeling" (Ang 1985: 45) in British family depictions — both soap opera and sitcom — is not warm, loving, and cooperative. Instead, the British family is very often competitive, contentious, even anarchic. In fact, instances of outright cruelty are not uncommon. Nor does the British television family idealize inflexible traditional authority, as does the Canadian family. True, as in Canada, family roles in British television are inflexible. But *British* families often find no effective solutions to the many problems their inflexibility presents. In British television, the family is anything but a "haven in a heartless world" (Lasch 1977). On the positive side, however, these conflicts expose viewers to conflict as an *expectable* aspect of life, and thus prepare the way for conflictive democratic participation.

Two examples help illustrate the conflictive nature of British television families. In *Only Fools and Horses*, a sitcom set in the East End of London, the main characters are two brothers of contrasting temperaments. One is gentle, idealistic, artistic, and not very bright; the other is crafty, amoral, pragmatic, and — above all — anxious to make his hapless brother look foolish. In one episode, the plot revolves around a film Brother #1 is making for his film class. Brother #2 appropriates the film and turns it into a piece of pornography for his own financial benefit, much to Brother #1's horror and embarrassment. In a second episode,

Brother #2 gulls Brother #1 into believing that the latter assaulted a woman sexually and that the police will shortly arrest him. So terrified by this wholly untrue story, and so shy and inexperienced with women is Brother #1, that he flees to the roof of his apartment house, where he hides in a ventilating system in order to escape the police, who, of course, are not really on their way. Throughout this ordeal, as his brother mocks him, his elderly father stands by helplessly, showing by turns amusement and helpless sympathy at his plight.

Only Fools and Horses turns destructive sibling rivalry and paternal weakness into sources of comedy. No American or Canadian sitcom derives humor from so unpleasant a set of basic themes. Needless to say, this combination of humor, weakness, and bitter rivalry turns "home" in *Only Fools and Horses* into a vastly less comforting place than home is for, say, the Keatons of *Family Ties*, not to say the Huxtables of *The Cosby Show*. In *Family Ties*, the children poke fun at each other (especially at Alex), but they never drive each other to hysteria—or into ventilating systems. *Only Fools and Horses*, however, establishes the primacy of conflict in the British private sphere.

Indeed, even comparable earlier American sitcoms, such as *The Odd Couple*, never took rivalry to the destructive limits of *Only Fools and Horses*. When push came to shove, the ill-matched roommates of *The Odd Couple* became "buddies; but, though brothers, the protagonists of *Only Fools and Horses* are anything but buddies. The difference lies in the real malice that informs *Only Fools and Horses*; the protagonists of *The Odd Couple* were ill-starred, but never deliberately malicious to each other. The American sitcom uses conflict to get to consensus; the British sitcom uses consensus to get to conflict.

But sibling rivalry is less destructive to British families than is the struggle between generations. Of course, in American and Canadian television programs, generational combat also occurs, sometimes quite destructively. But role diffusion, role flexibility, and the growth syndrome usually help parents to "reform" or children to accept the "wisdom" of their elders, as in the sentimentalized *Anne of Green Gables*. Few such easy resolutions of generational conflict appear in British television. For example, in one episode of *Eastenders*, a prime-time soap that now contests *Coronation Street* for primacy in the ratings, a teenage girl reveals her identity to the mother who had abandoned her at birth, and whom the girl has sought for years. The girl, unstable and unhappy, desperately begs her mother to take her in. But, though moved by her daughter's plea, the mother sends her away, claiming that they have long been "strangers," and must remain so. The mother argues that she has no room for her daughter in the new life she has made. Indeed, the mother actually throws her daughter out physically, after which the girl blindly stumbles to an alleyway and vomits. Events of this sort are sufficiently common in British television as to belie any notion of the British family protecting its members against a hostile outside world. Instead, hostility in the private world turns family members outward — to society and the polity.

The most extreme example of family conflict in my sample is the last episode of *Andy Capp*, entitled ironically "The Anniversary Waltz." The series depicts the relationship between working-class Andy and his long- suffering wife, Flo. Interestingly, the series uses some of the same stylistic devices as does *Moonlighting*, such as the visual quotation marks created by characters addressing themselves to the camera about events in which they are supposedly participants. But in *Moonlighting* such self-reflexive distancing ceased once Maddie and David became lovers. By contrast, in *Andy Capp*, self-reflexive distancing is pervasive, complementing the series' main theme of estrangement between husband and wife. *Andy Capp* inverts the sentimental norms of marriage, just as visual quotation marks invert the norms of story telling.

In "The Anniversary Waltz," Andy repeatedly insults and degrades Flo. Although it is their anniversary, Andy refuses to admit the fact, nor respond to Flo when she reminds him. When Andy reluctantly recollects their actual wedding day, he remembers only how he brought Flo dead flowers, how he was arrested at the wedding, how he and Flo visited a marriage counselor even *before* they married, and how, during the marriage ceremony, he dispatched Flo to place a bet on a horse. Andy pretends to give Flo some potato chips as an anniversary "gift," but then ostentatiously gobbles them up himself. He tells Flo he loves her only because she promises *not* to kiss him. His reluctance to celebrate the anniversary finally drives Flo into the Thames. The fact that Andy actually does plan a pub celebration of the anniversary never diminishes the humiliation to which he subjects Flo (as symbolized by the river mud which covers her), nor does it dispel the grim reality of their marriage.

It seems only reasonable to expect prolonged and chronic family conflict ultimately to destroy the family unit. Yet family dissolution is not common in British television. In fact, dissension actually helps families hang *together*, if not exactly in harmony, at least in intense, painful, and enduring mutuality (for related historical examples, see Hartcup 1984: chap. 7). For example, in *Emmerdale Farm*, a prime-time soap opera set in Yorkshire, Jacob Sugden, the family patriarch, quarrels with his ambitious, talented, rebellious older son Jack, who then leaves to pursue a writing career in London. Were this situation to occur in an American sitcom, the son's leaving would probably begin a new chapter in everyone's life. After all, the principal function of the American television family is to help children leave, not to return. Not so in *Emmerdale Farm*.

Instead, the dying Jacob Sugden wills his farm to Jack, who has long despised the place. Why does Jacob make so seemingly bizarre a bequest? According to the program guide, "It was the one sure way to get Jack back to Emmerdale" (*The Story of Emmerdale Farm*, n.d.: 6). Jacob knew that Jack would be too proud to refuse his father's deathbed challenge. Thus, in death Jacob Sugden accomplishes what he cannot accomplish in life. He forces Jack to return. Once back, as Jacob no doubt hoped, Jack stays to fight for his own values. Hence, Jacob used his struggle with Jack to unite the family and save the farm.

The theme of conflict-based family unity extends also to brothers. Jack's return deprives his younger brother Joe of the farm. Although Joe worked long, faithfully, and well for his father, he receives nothing. Meanwhile, Jack who rejected his father, gets the farm. These conditions create sibling conflict; the struggle between Jack and Joe continues to hold the family together in rivalrous concert. As we can see, the British television family's embrace may not be affectionate or even forgiving, but it is real, powerful, and enduring. More important, projected outward family conflict expresses itself in conflict-based *political* unity, as we will see.

Why is family conflict more common on British than American or Canadian television? One answer to this question is the malign role of business — especially big business — in its relationship to the family. Earlier we analyzed friction between the business world and the family in American soaps, such as *Dallas* and *Dynasty*. In these two series wealthy families become divided and fragile because their members also are business rivals with divergent agendas. Nevertheless, sheer wealth cushions these struggles. By contrast, many British television families must struggle to make ends meet. They are often the "little people" of business, rather than kingpins of commerce. Therefore, when big business undermines British family stability, the family has fewer emotional or financial resources with which to strike back.

For example, in *Brookside*, a prime-time soap set in Liverpool, a middle-aged couple suffers the near-collapse of their marriage when the husband, a union steward, not only leads a time-consuming strike against a large company, but also uses family money to support some strikers (see for a relevant study, Pollard 1984). In *Emmerdale Farm*, a shepherd refuses a much-needed job at another farm during hard financial times, takes to drink, and destroys his marriage. Why, asks his distraught wife, does he not accept the job? He can't, he replies, because he would be depriving one of his mates of the job (for a relevant study of friendship networks, see Willmott and Young 1960: chap 9). Though his wife rightly accuses him of placing loyalty to his friends above family welfare, he remains adamant. The real villain, however, is a corporation which buys up farms in the area, eliminates jobs for shepherds, turns men against each other, and destroys families. In the process, however, the family/business clash creates political action.

Similar cleavages affect even affluent British families. For example, in *Emmerdale Farm*, the idealist Jack Sugden is determined to protect traditional farming practices and the bucolic village of Beckindale; by contrast, his pragmatic brother Joe—embittered by losing the farm—accepts a job with "New York Estates" (an oblique reference to crass American commercialism), the corporate conglomerate which is destroying village life. So Jack and Joe, though both distinctly middle class, are nevertheless divided by their attitudes towards corporate farming. And their division causes as much family—and political—strife as does the struggle amongst Beckindale's poor shepherds.

Even the upper middle class responds to corporations skeptically. In *Howard's Way*, the hero, a wealthy aircraft designer, loses his job at a private aerospace corporation. Furious, he denounces the corporation's heartlessness to him after twenty years of loyal service; he admits ruefully that not only members of the working class lose jobs when times get hard. Predictably, his unemployment soon destroys his family. The family thus becomes a victim of the corporation.

An overarching theme unites these examples of conflict between the family and the corporation. In each case we encounter a political struggle between tradition, in the form of the selfless family, and modernity, in the form of the selfish corporation. The struggle between New York Estates and Emmerdale Farm (and between Jack and Joe Sugden) is actually a political conflict between the rural, pastoral values of the family and the urban, industrial values of the modern corporation (for a novelistic version of the struggle, see Drabble 1977). In this light it is significant that the hero of *Howard's Way*, after losing his job in the aircraft industry, decides to build traditional wooden-hulled yachts for a living. His occupational transition depicts a dialogue between the modern, efficient, but cold corporation, and the traditional small business, with its time-consuming craftsmanship and its harmonious melding of work and play, production and reproduction. In Canadian television, we encounter this struggle between modernity and tradition, but only in truncated form. In the United States, we rarely see it at all; American television takes corporate modernity as the norm, so there is nothing to debate. Besides, American families successfully adapt to modernity. Indeed, their growth syndrome, role flexibility, and team play serve to humanize corporations. But in Britain the traditional family and the modern corporation wage war ceaselessly.

Given the many corporate attacks on the family, as well as the family's own internal struggles, how does the British family manage to survive? Certainly not through American-style teamwork or through the cultivation of nostalgia (as in the Canadian case). How then does the British family function?

The British family relies upon a community which both sustains and regulates it. Therefore, the British family does not stand alone, as does the American or Canadian family. However, the community which shelters and controls the family never eliminates hostility between the family and the forces which beset it. Instead, the community becomes a partner in the fight to save the family. In a sense, the community mobilizes the family in the service of continuing political struggle (Ginsberg 1986: chap. 3).

The protective "little community" (Redfield 1955) takes three principal forms in British television: the marginal firm, the pub, and the neighborhood. When combined, these institutions help the family both to survive physically and to strike back politically. Most important, the community forces family members to rise above their selfish personal interests, and to become, in a sense, better than they "really" are. They thus oppose the modernizing, but debasing forces which threaten the family's intimate world (see also Sennett 1970).

While big business is usually an unmitigated evil in British television depictions, the small family firm is almost always a force for good. The firm keeps the family solvent, helps family members overcome personal crises, and forces family members to remain in touch despite personal disagreements. For example, the series *Crossroads* is set in a middle-sized family-run hotel. When the hero in *Howard's Way* leaves corporate life, he becomes a partner in a small firm which makes yachts; he and his teenage son can now work together in the boatyard, alongside the boatyard's previous owner and his daughter. In *Eastenders*, three family businesses comprise main settings: a small cafe and taxicab company run by a Cypriot immigrant and his English wife, a laundromat, and a pub. In *Emmerdale Farm*, the family farm is the focus of the action. In *Coronation Street*, a small family busines takes in as a partner a faithful, long-time worker. In the *Lenny Henry Show*, most of the action occurs in a West Indian pirate radio station hidden in the rear of a small restaurant run by a Cypriot immigrant and his wife. Thus one small business cradles another, symbolically uniting Cypriot and West Indian.

Continuing business relationships force personally opposed family members to work out their difficulties with one another. For example, a middle-aged alcoholic father and his daughter who both work at the *Crossroads* hotel remain associated with each other, thus allowing the daughter to persuade her defiant father to give up drinking. Small business also promotes broader social interaction. In *Brookside*, all major characters are cultural bricoleurs who do marginal jobs which draw them together constantly in unpredictable, nonspecialized intercourse (on *bricolage*, see Goody 1977: 24). One runs a window-cleaning company; another runs a taxi service. The window cleaner spends much of his time drinking tea with his clients, and the taxicab driver makes friends with his fares. Work and social life comprise a seamless web. The job serves both as a safety valve for family tensions and a springboard for new relationships. From these relationships, it is but a short step to political action.

Most important, the small firm turns collective representations of the family into the expression of class tensions. These tensions take the form of "us" versus "them," the little guy versus the big guy (for a related distinction, see Parkin 1971). This conclusion may appear surprising, given the iconography of the "little guy" in American culture. But the American "little guy" is generally a solitary, principaled idealist struggling against a corrupt, alienating, and unheeding society (Christensen 1987). In this struggle, all notions of community or class have fled. By contrast, in Britain, the struggle between "us" and "them" is a class struggle to impose a particular political vision on an organic, identifiable community.

For example, in *Emmerdale Farm*, the family business is the setting for a struggle between selfless tradition (the rural yeomanry) and selfish modernity (New York Estates, with its glitzy appeal to trendy Londoners). In *Howard's Way*, the boatyard becomes a community which must choose between craftsmanship and mass production. A large corporation offers to purchase the boatyard and make it "efficient"; the owners resist in the name of traditional quality and family pride. Significantly, the class conflict theme in this case cuts across economic groups. The class struggle between us and them occurs within the upper middle class as well as between the yeoman and the corporate executive. Ultimately, this is a struggle about selflessness and selfishness, not about alternative patterns of ownership.

Of course, class conflict has also appeared in American sitcoms. *I Love Lucy* depicted awkward encounters between the lower-middle class Ricardos and high society. Bus driver Ralph Cramden (Jackie Gleason) and his sidekick, sewer repairman Ed Norton (Art Carney), often found themselves at odds with their employers on *The Honeymooners*. More recently *Taxi* featured many jokes about social class. However, in American sitcoms, class conflict is occasional and usually peripheral to the main plot, whereas in British sitcoms and soaps, it is pervasive and central. Moreover, in the American case, class differences dissolve through personal reconciliations between upper- and lower-class characters. Indeed, more often than not, class conflict in the American version becomes primarily a means to poke fun at the personal inadequacies of characters like Lucy or Ralph Cramden. In England, however, class conflict on television does not necessarily expose personal inadequacies *or* strengths; rather it excites individuals to political action.

Class conflict is particularly bitter in British television when class becomes linked to race (see also Vanneman and Cannon 1987: chap. 10). The pirate radio station in the *Lenny Henry Show* is the "*Brixton* (emphasis mine) Broadcasting Corporation" (BBC), a tongue-in-cheek reference to the real BBC's supposed inattention to West Indians, who become "us" against the Establishment. The us/them dichotomy thus becomes racial, helping to keep the idea of class struggle alive.

The link between family and organic community often occurs via the pub (for a discussion of gender in this context, see Hunt and Satterlee 1987: 575–602). Sometimes a family actually operates a pub, a fact which keeps the family together. For example, in *Eastenders*, an alcoholic woman and her philandering husband remain together as proprietors of a pub. In *Coronation Street*, Alec, a pub owner, meets his future wife when she works for him as a barmaid. Thus, the pub simultaneously keeps the family in a community and keeps the family a community itself.

The pub also serves as a site for the family's political debate between tradition and modernity, us and them. In *Emmerdale Farm*, the pub attracts customers from both the farm itself and New York Estates. In the pub, advocates of these two opposed ways of life debate their relationships. But the pub does not necessarily reconcile opponents. In *Eastenders*, the abandoned teenage girl takes a job in the local pub, where she encounters her mother, who is a regular habitué of the establishment. But, as we have seen, the girl's longed-for reunion with her mother fails, and so the struggle continues.

Whole families come to the pub to socialize and to gossip about other family's doings. Therefore, the pub becomes a means of social control, bringing community norms to bear on errant family members struggling against each other. The pub thus brakes the fissiparous tendencies of family conflict. For example, in *Emmerdale Farm*, young Nick Bates, consumed with love for Kathy (who works at the pub), yet sure she will reject him, blurts out his love for her in front of the astonished community at the pub. Then, embarrassed, he flees. The community now finds itself privy to the romance of Nick and Kathy. Later, like a combination Greek chorus and *deus ex machina*, the pub community assists in reuniting the lovers.

The pub is an inextricable part of the neighborhood, which also specializes in family maintenance and the selfless pursuit of community. The neighborhood especially supports the family during periods of personal transition (for a relevant study, see Young and Willmott 1957). Thus, in *Coronation Street*, mortality becomes not only a family event, but also a neighborhood sadness, as signified by the death of a regular customer in the pub. The publican admonishes the television audience that one "can't hide death," but that *Coronation Street*—as a sort of visual neighborhood—softens death. When death is shared by the *neighborhood* assembled in the pub, strain on the *family* eases.

Similarly, "leaving the family" becomes a community event in *Coronation Street*. In the American *Kate and Allie*, as we saw, a daughter negotiates the delicate psychological separation from her mother without any support from others, even schoolmates. By contrast, in *Coronation Street*, the elderly Hilda, single and alone, decides reluctantly to take a job with a rich family. Her departure from the neighborhood is marked by a surprise goodbye party for her at the pub. Gifts are given and speeches made. Hilda announces that her heart will always be in *Coronation Street*. The episode closes as the community gathers around to sing her a song, wishing her well. Ritual thus affirms the values of the community during a period of transition and loss.

The neighborhood even moderates the disruptive effects of racial prejudice and poverty. In *Eastenders*, the neighborhood helps Mary, a poverty-stricken, unstable, adolescent mother. After the health visitor from the local government authority encourages Mary's neighbors to befriend her, the neighbors respond appropriately. In *Coronation Street*, the neighborhood unites behind Shirley, a young black girl, whose desire to rent an apartment is frustrated by the racially biased neighborhood grocer, who owns the apartment building. The community brings pressure on the grocer, who ultimately confesses to his racial prejudice and then rents Shirley the apartment. In this case the neighborhood helps a flawed individual to reach beyond himself to help another; Shirley and the grocer thus become part of the *same* neighborhood, a newly expanded community stronger and better than the individuals who compose it.

Rituals also reinforce neighborhood tradition. Significantly, many community rituals allow people to display their *individual* skills, thus demonstrating that the community endorses individuality (see also Hutchison and Forrester 1987). For example, in *Crossroads*, a traditional Christmas party provides a setting for family members and co-workers to perform a skit or sing. The community thus sponsors individual creativity. Of course, people do not become "stars" American-style, and they are certainly not "discovered." But they do experience a psychological growth *within* the community, rather then having to leave in order to "find themselves"; therefore, they can *use* the neighborhood to promote their political purposes.

In the final episode of the *Andy Capp* series, "The Anniversary Waltz," the themes of family conflict, community control, and family reunification powerfully combine. The theme of family conflict we have already described: Andy spends almost the entire episode demeaning Flo, who, resolutely ignoring his piggishness, continues to avow her love for him. But then the community intervenes. From the vicar to the marriage counselor to the policeman to the local beauty whom Andy courts, a single message emerges: Andy *must* take Flo out to celebrate their anniversary. Andy finally succumbs and promises Flo a night out. Flo dresses up, thinking Andy plans something grand. But, apparently all too true to his usual colors, Andy heads Flo straight for the local pub. When Flo realizes their destination is the "local," where they always go, she finally loses her temper and runs from Andy, only to stumble into the Thames. Covered from head to foot with mud, now thoroughly debased, Flo is lured into the pub. But to her delight, she discovers that the neighborhood has gathered one and all to celebrate the Capps' anniversary, and to drink a toast "To the Capps." Even Andy smiles. The Capps' marriage is not theirs to destroy; their marriage is community property, and the community will rescue them from the slime into which they have fallen.

There is a real Beckindale in Yorkshire, where exterior scenes for *Emmerdale Farm* are shot. Coachloads of faithful *Emmerdale Farm* viewers regularly visit the village, some hoping to encounter fictional *Emmerdale Farm* characters. "Despite the fact that only the exterior of the pub is shown in the TV series, tourists still expect to find their favorite characters in residence" (*Emmerdale Farm: Celebration Edition*, n.d.). Of course, pilgrimage plays a major role in traditional religions (Turner and Turner 1978). But in modern, secular societies, pilgrimage has not died. Today secular icons—such as the homes of television stars and the physical settings of television drama—have taken on a religious quality (for a related argument, see Sennett 1976). Stars are demigods; Beckindale is a shrine. The pilgrims who flock to Beckindale follow in the footsteps of penitents to Lourdes. Should we doubt the capacity of popular culture to penetrate deeply into public consciousness, we need only consult the collective representations which television viewers imitate, thereby making fantasy the basis of reality. In Britain, the culture of television idealizes a tradition of selflessness and, in so doing, uses tradition to give the family a political role.

British Advertising: The Wedding of Tradition and Narcissism

Interpreting British magazine advertising is difficult because of the comparative paucity of material. The most popular British magazines average 2.5 times less product advertising than do their American counterparts. Although this fact is consistent with our basic argument, which would predict such a country ordering based on differing national "doses" of liberalism, it permits certain magazines, such as *British Cosmopolitan,* to dominate the material.

Because *British Cosmopolitan* carries a heavy load of advertising, it has a disproportionate impact on our conclusions. In particular, the mix of products this magazine advertises becomes influential. After all, there is a danger in confusing value appeals with the qualities of particular products advertised. As Daniel Pope puts it, "advertisements appealing to desires for intimacy are more likely to be found in ads for perfumes than for sewing machines. If perfume advertising volume has risen as sewing machine advertising has diminished, this might account for the alleged change in 'values'" (1983: 230).

Although Pope's admonition is important, it is not crippling. After all, the combination of products and appeals in any society directs consumers to particular ways of life. As Erving Goffman puts it, "the job the advertiser has of dramatizing the value of his product is not unlike the job a society has of infusing its social situations with ceremonial and with ritual signs facilitating the orientation of participants to one another" (1979: 27). Thus, the fact that societies choose to dramatize and display (Merelman 1988: 335–55) particular products is no cultural accident. Goods promote values just as values promote particular goods. Together goods and their associated values in magazine advertisements doubly inscribe a particular way of life.

In any case, as I have already argued, the cultural materials examined in this book are not meant to be seen as fixed entities. Cultural expressions in the form of magazine advertisements, television sitcoms, corporate publications, and social studies texts change their surface features over time; a cross-sectional analysis depicts only certain *tendencies*, major *themes*, and *directions* of change within a society's whole *configuration* of collective representations. As we will see, the uniqueness of British advertising in this sample suggests a rather distinct set of cultural tendencies, dynamics, and themes.

I emphasize this observation because British magazine advertising augments the dialogue in British culture between conflicting ways of life, that is, between selfishness and selflessness. Indeed, the content of magazine advertising suggests that British popular culture is less concerned with the liberal democratic division between the private and the public than it is with the division between the modern personality (for a related view, see Lasch 1984) and the traditional collectivity. Magazine advertising in Britain thus helps construct a political dialogue between the collective good and the selfish desires of the individual.

The sample of British magazines I investigated includes the five with largest mass circulation (*Readers Digest, Woman, TV Times, British Cosmopolitan,* and *Living*) and two "quality" magazines for comparison, *Punch* and *The Economist*, a total of twenty-seven individual issues in all. The first clear indication of how British magazine advertising deviates sharply from North American advertising appears in the way consumers use products. In the British sample, people use the product in private and alone three times more often than they use the product in a group. As compared to his or her American counterpart, the British consumer is extremely isolated socially, unwilling to blend effortlessly into the social world.

Even products designed to make the user attractive and erotically stimulating appear in a thoroughly solitary fashion. For example, consider the ad for Armani perfume. Juxtaposed against a beautiful woman's face, we see a small insert of the Armani perfume jar. Both the jar and the face are alone, floating in a disembodied space; the woman is not even shown applying the perfume. The caption, which reads "style goes beyond time," reinforces the sense of isolation and distance. The text implies that the fusion of style and perfume lifts the woman out of her constrained temporal existence entirely; therefore, she can neither be touched by nor participate in the world around her (*British Cosmopolitan*, May 1987: 11).

I do not mean to overstate the point, for in most ways British magazine advertising resembles North American advertising. Yet consumers are more often alone in British ads than in North American ads. The contrast with British families on television is strong. As we have already seen, the British *family* is *more* publicly visible than its North American counterpart. Thus, as individual consumers, the British use products to escape from the family. Meanwhile, the family unit attempts to lure its members into public pursuits. *Together*, the two spheres present distinct ways of life.

British ads are also more privatizing than American ads. In the United States, individual consumers use products almost as often in public as in private settings. But in the British sample, private settings are twice as frequent as public settings for individuals. Only a bare 3 percent of British magazine ads depict product use in public; indeed, only 8 percent depict clear settings of *any* kind, public or private. The world of the British consumer is an isolated, reified world dominated by the image of the product.

The isolation of the British consumer springs from the centrality of personal appearance as an advertising theme, and from the high frequency of beauty products advertised. Indeed, improved personal appearance accounts for twice the percentage of advertising appeals in Britain as in the United States. Personal appearance even outranks product quality as a selling point, in contrast to Canadian and American product appeals.

However, the care that British magazines lavish on appeals to personal appearance cannot be explained solely by the high frequency of beauty products for sale. Rather, the unusual beauty of the ads *themselves* suggests the primacy of an apparently widely shared value, namely, *style*. Not only is the reader struck by the visual sophistication of these beautiful paens to personal appearance, but also by their frequent reference to things French. Even more than in North America, in Britain France equals style (Vestergaard and Schroder 1985: 154). And style is opposed to the substantive concerns of collective life.

Significantly, appeals to personal appearance do not promise the British consumer greater spontaneity, freedom, or even better health.

Spontaneity and freedom appeals, which might pierce the consumer's cocoon of the self, are more common in North American than British magazines. For the British, however, glamour is self-contained—perhaps even the containment of the self. Glamour is presented as its own reward; the consumer becomes a narcissist, a voyeur of the reflected self, set apart from society.

Narcissism receives further support from British advertising's inattention to such staple North American appeals as quality, convenience, and progress. Explicit comparisons of product quality appear only half as often in British as American magazines; nor are appeals to progress or convenience any more prominent. British magazine ads imply that people should use products to enhance their "self-of-the-moment," not their "self-of-the-future." Perhaps *sic transit gloria mundi*; but, to the British, the *transit gloria* seems worth the *mundi*.

What makes a product desirable to the British, *aside* from its capacity to improve personal appearance? The answer lies in the product's capacity to elevate the consumer in the status order or to connect the consumer with British tradition (for a relevant study, see Bourdieu 1984). It is only through symbolic appeals to status and tradition that British advertising attempts to join the isolated, narcissistic consumer to society. In a sense, British advertising enlists tradition to bless self-absorption, whereas in the United States advertising enlists technological progress to bless an anonymous democracy of equal consumers.

Judith Williamson has observed that art symbolizes high social status in ads by deliberately obscuring connections between image and product; an "artistic" ad is subtle, and "subtlety" is classy. The "hip" reader gains membership in an "exclusive" club, that is, those clever enough to see the sales link only hinted at by high culture in the ad. Thus, the traditional reclusiveness of "high art" becomes the product's social penumbra. Ultimately, the ad fuses art, status, and commerce. As Williamson puts it, "it is the very difficulty in understanding the images, and the absence of obvious connections, which indicates the genuinely 'cultured' status of the ads, and therefore, of the product" (1986: 69).

Not surprisingly, given its particular history of class-based liberalism, British advertising contains more status appeals than does North American advertising: almost twice as many as American advertising, for example. Indeed, not only products, but also consumers are ranked in British advertising to a much greater extent than they are in North America. Consider, for example, the fusion of rank, tradition, and art in Liberty's *Cosmopolitan* ad for October 1987. Liberty fabrics—the products—are barely visible in a small space within the ad. Most of the space is given over to a lovely young woman standing alongside her horse in a traditional English park setting. The horse wears a blanket of Liberty fabric. The text consists of definitions which trace Liberty patterns to their artistic origins. For example, the pattern entitled Gilbert comes from Glaswegian art teacher and part-time painter Colin Kerr, who, with suitable artistic disdain for mere commerce, delivers his drawings to Liberty Studios rolled up in his trouser legs (1). The ad aligns Liberty with personal beauty, with English tradition, with aristocracy (the park, the horse), and with art. The purchaser of Liberty thus gains instant upward mobility into a world of traditional rank and refinement.

The Liberty advertisement summarizes everything that is distinctively British in magazine advertising. *Liberty*, of course, is the name both of a corporation and of a political concept. Indeed, the ad's text actually defines *Liberty* as "the power of choosing, thinking, or acting for oneself. Freedom to pick and choose as one wishes, with no outside interference" (1). But as we have already seen, liberty as *spontaneity* is rare in British advertising. In this ad, as in British advertising generally, tradition, rank, and hierarchy serve a self of appearance, not of action. "Liberty" turns out to be confining and status-ridden, not pragmatic or impulsive.

British advertising thus calls upon tradition to adorn a self interested primarily in its own embellishment. British magazine advertising asks tradition to legitimize a self turned inward. By contrast, British television invokes tradition in order to idealize a citizen turned outward from the family toward the community. Thus, television entertainment and magazine advertising debate contrasting ways of life, each vying with the other to control collective memory in Britain. In turn, the debate itself provides raw material for conflictive democratic participation.

British Corporate Self-Images: Consecrating the Marriage of Tradition and Narcissism

There is reason to expect British corporate publications to resemble Canadian corporate publications more than American corporate publications. After all, like a few Canadian corporations, some British industries are nationalized, and are therefore directly vulnerable to the winds of British politics. For example, the Thatcher government undertook to restructure British coal mining by bringing in a new director of the National Coal Board, Ian McGregor. When Mrs. Thatcher supported McGregor's decision to close a number of pits, the National Union of Mineworkers undertook a major strike designed not only to cripple the Board, but also to bring down the Thatcher government (for a relevant study, see Mishler, Hoskin, and Fitzgerald 1988: 54–96). The example demonstrates how in Britain the politics of the large corporation can often become the politics of the nation and class, with the Labour party representing workers, and the Conservatives representing employers.

In addition, the Thatcher government strongly—and controversially—promoted "privatization," that is, selling public enterprises to private entrepreneurs. The government argued that privatization increases the efficiency and competitiveness of British industry. Recent examples of privatization involve British Gas, British Telecom, and British Steel. As we will see, the question of privatization makes its way subtly into British corporate self-images.

Yet there exist countertendencies against these impulses to depicting conflict. All collective representations are idealizations, and therefore resist the widespread depiction of disruptive struggle. British corporations naturally desire to downplay their political role and to present themselves as harmonious contributors to the public good (a relevant British study is Fidler 1984). Moreover, so far as conflictive democratic participation is concerned, the proximity of British corporations to government is a two-edged sword. Proximity invites the British corporation to portray itself not as a self-interested entity, but rather as a quasi-public agency faithfully implementing policies devoted to the public interest. Corporations everywhere wish to make similar arguments, of course, but the direct linkage between some British corporations and government policy particularly encourages such appeals in Britain.

Moreover, British corporations faithfully served and extended the Empire. The intimate linkage between British corporations and imperialism goes back at least as far as the East India Company (Hamilton 1975); British corporations therefore enjoy a unique historical opportunity to portray themselves as crucial to the promotion of national power. Neither American nor Canadian corporations can draw on so complete a history of service to the state.

Thus, in addition to the universal appeals corporations use to promote themselves—employee consumership, job mobility, satisfying real needs, being efficient producers—British firms might attempt to enlist government itself in their campaign, just as American firms enlist images of family warmth and personal growth. While the American corporation presents itself as a benign extension of the private world, the

British corporation may present itself as a useful extension of government. If so, the image parallels that of British advertising, which uses
history and tradition to promote narcissism and self-interest. Perhaps
British corporations pursue their own version of narcissism — the narcissism of *profits* — under the pretext of serving the public good.

Which of these two possible collective representations do we encounter: the first, which portrays corporations as settings for class-based
conflict; or the second, which appeals to self-interest under the cloak
of politics and history? At first glance, we find examples of the conflict
image, examples which certainly promote conflictive democratic participation. Certainly British corporate publications acknowledge class
conflict more than do American or Canadian publications. For example,
in "The British Steel Corporation," *British Steel* notes, "The very damaging three-month steel strike of early 1980 arose from the Corporation's pressure for change and a dispute on pay. The stoppage made it
obvious to steel consumers in Britain that, with a world excess of steel-
making capacity, they could still obtain their requirements by import-
ing. BSC lost a significant share of its home market as a result . . . "
(2). BSC thus blames the strike (and, by implication, the unions) for
its declining profits. Although it attempts to subordinate class conflict
to its version of consumer priorities, the statement admits that industrial conflict exists in Britain. American corporations rarely go this far.

The National Coal Board, which has been struck several times in the
recent past, can hardly avoid the subject of conflict. The NCB grudgingly accepts the reality of conflict, but then tries to transcend the subject. In its "Your Project is Coal," a brochure directed to school students, we read:

> During the Industrial Revolution, coal-mining — like every other
> industrial activity — suddenly assumed completely new
> significance. Men became millionaires on coal. Other men
> worked their short lives out in the mines, to die young of
> silicosis or of injuries. During this century, the battle for coal
> was attended by many other battles to do with wages and
> strikes, lockouts, disasters and reforms. (1985: 14)

Following this frank description of past industrial conflict is a brief
discussion of how mining came to be nationalized in 1947. According
to the brochure, the movement from private to public ownership "suit[ed]
the needs of the nation and the dictates of common sense" (14). The
sequence of the two statements seems to imply there is no longer much
reason for class struggle in mining. Unlike the private corporation of

the nineteenth century, today's nationalized firm meets public needs and accords with common sense. Thus, the Coal Board concedes conflict in the past, yet attacks class conflict today.

Not surprisingly, therefore, in discussing the bitter 1983–1985 strike, the NCB extends sympathy to individual strikers, but none to the unions. Reflecting on the strike's collapse, the NCB observes:

> The strike had lasted nearly a year. With the 29 weeks overtime ban which preceded it, the dispute had cost the average miner who remained on strike throughout about 10,000 pounds in lost earnings. . . . Some 70 million tonnes of coal were not produced as a result of the strike and 71 coalfaces were lost or irrecoverable and some pits will never recover from the damage caused. (7)

Forced at last to admit that class conflict remains a major part of its contemporary structure, the NCB attempts to delegitimize this conflict by claiming that *workers* and the *country*—not the Board—are the main losers. The NCB thus pursues a two-pronged strategy of vindication. First, it blames the strike on the workers. Then it argues that workers suffer the adverse consequences of the strike. Significantly, the NCB's policy of pit closures is exempted from blame. The industry is powerful and innocent; the unions are weak and callous.

British corporate publications thus simultaneously incorporate and deprecate instances of conflict. Some corporations employ the tactic of "nationalistic displacement" in this endeavor. Nationalistic displacement projects the theme of conflict abroad. For example, British Petroleum's *Shield* observes that in Switzerland there is considerable political opposition to fuel-induced air pollution. "But," the *Shield* notes, "the company (BP Schwiz AG) has ammunition of its own with which to combat the continual 'strafing' through which the politicians hope to win extra votes" (1985, no. 4: 16). In this comment the *Shield* not only avoids discussion of pollution within Britain (Vogel 1986), but also implies that the pollution "issue" is only a means for unscrupulous politicians "to win extra votes." The *Shield* thus sidesteps corporate responsibility for air pollution. In sum, although British corporations depict conflict more explicitly than do their American and Canadian counterparts, they also construe conflict in a self-exculpatory fashion.

Another acknowledgement of conflict may be found in the limited self-confidence of British firms. Unlike corporate publications in Canada and the United States, those of British firms do not exude optimism. In fact, some British firms present themselves as under siege. After beginning his 1984/1985 statement to employees with an invocation of company harmony, British Gas's Sir Denis Rooke moves to a less pleasant subject. First, there is the positive side: "Nearly 100,000 people work for British Gas. It is not possible, of course, for everyone's efforts to be highlighted in these pages. So we have chosen just one employee from Headquarters and each Region to be featured on our front cover as a way of acknowledging particularly the vital contribution of gas people to the continued progress of our industry" (1985: 1)

But Sir Denis then evokes a few storm clouds: "[We] were able to maintain our undertaking to keep rises in gas prices to tariff customers generally in line with the rate of inflation" (2). Inflation pressures are bad enough, but then the storm breaks. Sir Denis must acknowledge the government's plans to privatize British Gas, a policy that implicitly disputes the rosy picture Sir Denis has attempted to paint. The best Sir Denis can muster is a reassurance to workers that, "When announcing the Government's privatization plans he [The Secretary of State for Energy] said that provision will be made for employees to acquire a stake in the industry. The Government has also accepted that the integrated structure of the gas industry should be kept intact—something which we have always insisted was vital to the interests of both the industry and our customers" (1).

After his brave opening, Sir Denis is reduced to rear-guard actions—British Gas workers can acquire stock in their newly privatized company; the company will not be broken up. But British Gas has been forced to acknowledge the political strain it has come under, and to recognize—albeit reluctantly—that policy towards industry can stimulate conflict.

British corporations also recognize the existence of public hostility towards industry, a subject absent from Canadian and American publications. Needless to say, British publications deprecate such hostility by reinterpreting history to suit their interests. For example, *Esso Magazine* (Winter 1985/1986) features as its lead story an article entitled "Industry Matters," which argues that industry actually *doesn't* seem to matter very much to many Britons. The author is a respected historian, Kenneth Adams, through whom Esso undoubtedly aims to achieve an aura of objectivity. Adams intends the article to "continue the work which I had developed towards effecting a change in the cultural attitude to industry in Britain from one of lack of interest, or even dislike, to one of concern and esteem" (4). No Canadian or American corporate publication admits to comparable cultural antipathy toward industry (but see Jones 1986).

As Adams states, his article is intended to reduce public hostility toward industry. Not surprisingly, Adams turns to history in this endeavor. He vigorously defends the impact of industry on British culture during the eighteenth and nineteenth centuries, and he argues that a renewed harmonious relationship between industry and culture is vital to Britain today. What explains the contemporary denigration of industry? Adams argues that, "some very influential figures affected . . . our view of education at the very time when the public schools were rapidly expanding and compulsory education for all children was being introduced. They saw the purpose of education as the pursuit of beauty and truth, but they narrowed their view of that pursuit so that education was seen in intellectual and not in voactional terms" (4). In short, government and the schoolmaster are made the villains, a depiction which surely promotes an image of corporate/government conflict.

A final example of the way British corporations recognize, yet denigrate, conflict is the publications' de-emphasis of employee growth, development, and self-fulfillment. There are few American-style psychological themes in most British corporate publications; to the British, a job is just a job, not a way of becoming a better human being. Consider "British Gas Apprenticeships," as glossy a recruitment brochure directed to workers as any directed to future managers. The brochure says nothing whatsoever about personal development. It observes only that "joining British Gas could prove to be the first step in a well-worthwhile career, providing you with a whole range of job opportunities. For instance, many of our supervisors and managers started their careers as apprentices" (4). This is hardly a confident prediction of mobility for the future mechanic. By publishing this brochure, British Gas at least accepts the working class ideologically (as American and Canadian corporations do not). Moreover, the hesitant tone of the brochure suggests that social class limits personal development, and, therefore, that class differences are real and potentially conflictive.

However, a closer examination of British corporate publications reveals that, despite the presence of conflict, conflict is not really a major theme. Rather, to soften the conflict perception, British corporate literature ingeniously blurs the line between public and private (for a relevant supportive study, see Wilson 1985: chap. 4). To do so, the British corporation draws upon its connections to politics, history, and tradition. In this way, it hopes to circumvent opposition from the family, the neighborhood, the community, and the political Left. However, while it does succeed in blurring the public/private boundary, it is less successful in blurring the boundary between partial and collective interest.

For example, a favorite British corporate argument is that industrial expansion and innovation increases the British public's appreciation of history. Thus, British Petroleum's *Shield* (no. 4, 1985, 37–38) describes Tony Finn, a BP chemical engineer, who has used the expertise BP provided to discover a buried treasure in Bedford, Co. Virginia. The article mentions British Petroleum only in its identification of Finn. The search for the treasure is thus presented only as an interesting historical detective story, not as a commercial for BP. Yet the reader should conclude that, with people like Finn working for British Petroleum, history and tradition — public entities — are safe, despite BP's own sometimes ecologically worrisome terrestrial explorations.

British corporate publications often string together historical appeals of this sort. For example, immediately preceding Finn's "Keying in Gold" is "Chisels Sound Again," an article which begins, "The ring of chisel on stone announces that an old quarry on the Isle of Portland has taken on a new lease on life — as a sculpture park, sponsored by BP" (34). According to the story, British Petroleum's sponsorship has renewed interest in the ancient art of quarrying. Moreover, BP has pioneered in the use of rock for sculpture rather than for building. British Petroleum thus not only preserves historical continuity (i.e., quarrying), but also promotes contemporary artistic innovation. More important, BP is just as devoted to British tradition as is the government or the family.

British corporations also produce unusually many attractive corporate histories, which argue that the corporation has always pursued public service, not private gain. General Electric's "A National Asset for a Hundred Years, 1886–1986," reprints on its cover attractive pages from earlier GE publications (e.g., catalogs, supplements, advertising) (1986). The cover thus refers to publications like itself in order to reproduce company history. More important, the text argues that, though a private corporation, GE is a "national asset." Typical is the observation that, "With the outbreak of the First World War, GEC demonstrated its ability to act in support of the nation. . . . Before the war ended in 1918, nine-tenths of GEC's production was dedicated to the British armed forces which, thanks to the foresight of the company's engineers, found themselves well-equipped with improved field wireless sets, signalling lamps, motors and wiring" (3). Also noteworthy is the way the passage overlaps religious with secular terminology; for example, the term *dedication* carries a penumbra of religious associations, such as dedications of shrines or *self*-dedications to religiously inspired good works (Weber 1963). As an ensemble, this collection of images surely is meant to defuse political hostility to the corporation and to reduce the incidence of conflictive democratic participation.

Of course, the most favorable historical political linkage British corporations can forge is with the Royal Family, for the monarchy epitomizes the long, glorious, political domination of Britain. It is, therefore, not surprising that General Electric's *Topic*, the corporation newsletter, reported in December 1986 on the meeting between several of its prize-winning technical apprentices and Princess Diana, the Princess of Wales. "At a luncheon . . . the Princess presented Keith and Paul with a plaque to mark their achievement and a cheque for 600 pounds from *The Engineer* magazine" (3). The accompanying picture of Princess Diana with Keith and Paul complements the article visually.

The several appeals in this article are intertwined. First, royalty plays the role of a *deus ex machina*, rewarding competition for excellence among General Electric workers. Second, the royal family compliments GEC for its foresight in employing such intelligent engineer apprentices. Third, awarding of the prize by the royal family connects GEC to a norm of impersonal, fair competition (the prize competition). If the "royals" are involved, British fair play must be safe; meanwhile, GEC as a powerful, occasionally *unfair* corporate entity vanishes.

The corporate uses of royalty appear most ingeniously in British Petroleum's *Shield*, no. 4, 1985. The cover features an attractive, full-color close-up of Princess Diana, which refers to a story on the Princess' visit to a North Sea oil drilling platform ("Delightful Diana," 23). Preceding this story, however, the *Shield* briefly discusses BP's workforce:

> It is no good putting in sophisticated management systems
> when the management structure is inadequate and the attitude
> of the labour force unsuitable. (3)

The question, of course, is how to remedy "unsuitability" among workers.

One possible answer is royalty. The *Shield* reports that "delightful Diana" "charmed the men of Fifties Charlie" (the oil drilling rig) (1). The article (one of the few in my sample with photographs of workers) copiously illustrates Diana's charm, particularly in pictures of the men responding animatedly to the Princess. "The royal visitor put all she met and talked with at ease with her relaxed manner and surprised some by asking questions that displayed more than a nodding acquaintance with offshore oil" (25). And later, "Planning engineer Mike Stephen runs the platform's Princess Diana fan club. . . . His verdict, 'She has a great charisma'" [*sic*] (25).

The meanings in this number of the *Shield* may be read dialectically. First, the reader learns obliquely that labor discontent is a problem in British Petroleum. Then Princess Diana charms the men with her "charisma" (or, as the article puts it, "Princess Diana became the other Charlie's darling too") (25). Thus, royalty quickly disposes of worker discontent by winning "the men" over. Soon, with luck, the united ensemble of workers, managers, and monarchy can turn BP into another "national asset," rather than a conflicted corporate enterprise.

The most powerful argument in British corporate publications is that British business effectively promotes the traditional values that all British people venerate. With corporate help, tradition not only survives, but also flourishes in the modern world. Commercial and technological innovation thus renew rather than destroy the past. From this perspective the Romantic rejection of the Industrial Revolution was unwarranted (a full treatment is Beach 1956). Instead, technology *promotes* Romanticism. No publication illustrates this theme of "technological Romanticism" better than *Esso Magazine*, especially in its Winter 1985/1986 number. This issue contains four interrelated stories which subtly develop the idea.

First, in "Industry Matters," Kenneth Adams describes industry's social and cultural—not economic—contributions.

> There is . . . the importance of what I have called shared values which band those working for a company together in their common enterprise. More importantly, they bond members of a community and citizens of a nation together. (5)

For Adams, there is no essential distinction between public life and private life. This difference dissolves once industry is doing its job properly.

But how to achieve this happy condition? Technological Romanticism is one possibility. The next story ("What Are the Wild Waves Saying?") describes how Esso technology assists a new company, Marex, to forecast dangerous tidal and meteorological conditions in desolate coastal areas. The article carefully points out that Marex is merely perfecting the ancient art of weather forecasting. Modern technology extends tradition and the pastoral virtues; it does not destroy these things.

The magazine next offers a copiously illustrated story about the River Clyde, which, although "flowing through Scotland's busiest industrial areas . . . still manages to maintain a character of its own albeit in a variety of disguises" (10). The muted, watercolor riverscapes provide an appropriately traditional artistic complement to the story's message that industrial development has improved the river's environs. Wise use of contemporary technology has transformed ugly industrial sites along the river into objects of tourism. The author writes, "I would recommend anyone paying a visit to this area to spend some time absorbing the historical beauty of New Lanark" (10), which has been both a center of industry (through the invention of the waterframe), and a center of political progress through Robert Owen's "humane treatment of workers and children at the time of the Industrial Revolution" (10–11). Technology, social reform, and even utopian socialism flow harmoniously together along the River Clyde, at least as seen by *Esso Magazine.*

The final story in this sequence reports on Westminister, the ancient seat of British government and of the monarchy. According to the writer, "Fresh life is being brought into Westminster by a revitalization project linking local government with the business community" (17). Technological Romanticism thus not only brings government, industry, and the monarchy together to preserve British tradition, but also incorporates the entire business community into that tradition. In neither the United States nor Canada do corporate publications so deftly describe business as a bridge between tradition and modernity, the public and the private.

The companies whose publications I have so far surveyed are old-fashioned, heavy-industry corporations: gas, steel, coal, petroleum. An exception to this pattern, however, is Grand Metropolitan, which is a conglomerate of companies in the "leisure industry" ("Finance Graduate Scheme, The Berni and Host Group Ltd." 1). These companies include hotels, alcoholic beverage producers, child-care providers, and so on. Grand Met provides an opportunity for us to compare the appeals of a "modern" British corporation against comparable American or Canadian firms. Significantly, Grand Metropolitan elaborates upon the wedding of tradition and consumer narcissim that is the distinctively British version of private-sector collective representations; indeed, in both style and quality, Grand Met's publications surpass those of any corporation in this study.

We begin with one Grant Met subsidiary, Children's World, a child-care provider. Children's World's brochure joins familial and corporate imagery together in a seamless web. Consider the following statement:

> High ideals, attractive facilities and strategic marketing plans do not make a child care company excel. People do. That's why we spend considerable time and money to attract, train, and promote the best available talent in the industry. Their dedication, skill and unbounded enthusiasm transform the principles of the Children's World Concept into caring reality. (1985: 5)

The phrases "a child care company," and "caring reality" introduce familial images of nurturance and protection into the corporate presentation. The third sentence joins these themes to the growth syndrome. The "growth" of employees thus parallels the "caring reality" provided children. Of course, financially, Children's World is like any other company; but it makes money by nurturing people rather than by producing goods. Therefore, it naturally employs familial themes.

The merger of corporate with familial imagery runs throughout the *Children's World* presentation. For example, after Children's World announces that the company "has developed an intensive training program for all members of the Children's World family," it devotes two paragraphs to the "childcare marketplace" (6). Children's World thus becomes a business family, if not a family business. Children's World's business, childcare, apparently encourages the company to see no possibility of conflict between personal growth and business competition.

The primary appeal of the Grant Metropolitan group, however, is its claimed enhancement of public tradition, not its merger with the private world of the family. In fact, Grand Met offers a distinctive theory of tradition. The company argues that tradition is a means toward the end of consumer — and employee — satisfaction. Instead of people sacrificing themselves to preserve tradition (for a related perspective, see Janowitz 1983), tradition should serve the narcissistic impulses of individual consumers. For example, in its *1986 Annual Review*, Grand Met discusses its Berni and Host Group, which consists of over 1700 pubs and restaurants in Britain. The *Review* states that, "Clifton Inns specializes in managing high quality pubs in the traditional style" (11). Apparently, one can "manage" tradition, for tradition is "style," not substance. The *Review* also depicts employees who are camouflaged to be indistinguishable in demeanor, uniform, and mood from their customers. The waitress who smilingly serves the young woman in the "Old Orleans" restaurant in Richmond looks very much like her customer — and certainly appears to be having as much fun (10). In a sophisticated, consumer-oriented company such as Grand Metropolitan, work as such disappears, to be replaced by the new theater of tradition and hedonism.

Tradition is also the subject of another Grand Met theatrical presentation, in the form of a company called Tuxford and Tebbutt, whose promotional brochure features an aerial photograph of a British pastoral scene, with a small insert picturing the cheeses Tuxford and Tebbutt has produced "since 1780." The brochure reads, "In the small market town of Melton Mowbray, deep in the heart of traditional Stilton country, lies the creamery of Tuxford and Tebbutt. Built in 1780, the frontage is unchanged and its atmosphere and appearance still retain their period charm. . . . The Tuxford and Tebbutt cheeses of today are made using the time-honoured methods and traditional craft skills which ensure the same high standards as have been achieved over the last 200 years" (1). There are no references at all to the technological changes Grand Metropolitan must surely have introduced to mass produce and market Tuxford and Tebutt's cheeses.

Grand Metropolitan returns to its traditional nurturing-parent persona throughout its publications. Express Food Group's "milkman of the year" has fully incorporated into his own identity this feature of Grand Met's image. He observes of his relationship to his customers:

> I just give them good service. There's lots of things I do for them. I feed their dogs and cats, chop the wood up. I've even changed nappies. She's 30 years old now and won't let me change her nappies any more. I suppose good manners is what makes a good milkman. (*Express News*, Autumn 1986, 9)

Here the blurring of familial and corporate functions is complete.

The zenith of Grand Met's power as collective representation is embodied in "employee reification," where the Grand Met employee uses his spare time to construct imaginary models of the company. The company thereby becomes not only a livelihood, but also an object of intrinsic pleasure, imitation, and identity formation. Arthur Law, of Appleby, "express driver of the year," is himself a model for his co-workers. In his spare time Arthur Law constructs models of the trucks he drives for Grand Met. In fact, his basement overflows with miniature versions of these trucks. For Law personal identity and corporate identity merge.

Ultimately, the distinctive cultural feature of Grand Met remains its ingenious melding of traditional themes with consumer narcissism. In this respect, it resembles other British companies and also British magazine advertising. Not surprisingly, Grand Met celebrates its 25th anniversary by returning to—or, better, by manufacturing—its own particular tradition in the form of a company hallmark. As its chairman explains:

> A hallmark on a piece of gold or silver communicates the intrinsic value of an object over and above the design and character of the piece itself. Thus, analogously, the use of a corporate symbol based on the traditional English system of hall-marking allows Grand Metropolitan to communicate the added value that membership of the group confers on its component companies and brands. ("Grand Metropolitan, 1962–1987," 1)

Grand Metropolitan celebrates its identification with the British political tradition by depicting the traditional British lion in its hallmark. Grand Met's *respect* for tradition thus becomes simultaneously an attempt to *appropriate* the public sphere for its pursuit of profits. In a sense, it is Grant Met itself which is really a hallmark, for the corporation epitomizes British firms which marry tradition and politics to narcissim and the pursuit of private pleasures.

Contesting the Marriage: British Social Studies Texts

British schooling is a combination of centralization and decentralization. Unlike American students, secondary-school graduates in Britain must pass standardized examinations to enter higher education. These passports are distributed to only a small percentage of British students. Admission to higher education is thus not only more centralized than in North America, but also more competitive, and, inevitably, socially stratified (Halsey, Heath, and Ridge 1980). Moreover, government inspectors from Whitehall regularly visit and advise in British schools.

At the same time, in Britain, in contrast to Canada or the United States, there is no central, regional, or local government determination of textbook choice. In British schools headmasters and headmistresses reign supreme in the selection of texts; therefore, it is difficult to identify "the most popular" or widely read British history and government texts. Not even British publishers could supply us with a useful list. We therefore chose our texts from verbal reports by social studies department heads in a small but regionally and socially diverse set of British secondary schools. Fortunately, there was considerable overlap in the texts named, so that we know these particular books are widely used. The five British history and seven British politics texts we chose are directed to students preparing for 0-Level and GCSE exams in British Government and British history. These students average fifteen or sixteen years of age (for recent developments, see Lister 1988).

The struggle between two ways of life — one based upon self-interest, the other based upon collective interests — is the leitmotif of this chapter. We would expect British history and government texts to favor the second of these visions. Schools, after all, are entities which help define collective interests. Moreover, since the 1960s, educational policy has become a central issue for conflictive democratic participation in Britain (Lodge and Blackstone 1982). Labour has pressed for the cessation of governmental support for selective grammar schools, while Conservatives have resisted these reforms. The ensuing party debate has contributed to conflictive democratic participation. By contast, in neither the United States nor Canada have the political parties divided so markedly along lines of educational policy. Therefore, it seems reasonable to expect British texts to contain images of group struggle, of cohesive, ideologically distinct political parties, of class tensions, and even of conflictive democratic participation itself.

Yet we must remember that schools in Britain share the same fear of controversy and dissent that other school systems exhibit (Tapper and Salter 1978). Moreover, the long history of liberal democracy and Parliamentary governance in Britain provides an image of continuity that text writers and school heads may find irresistible in their effort to control controversy. Indeed, as a distinct subject, politics did not even occupy a place in British classrooms until the 1970s (Brennan 1981). One could hardly expect a fledgling, insecure subject to risk introducing too much conflictive democratic participation as a topic in the curriculum (but see Swann 1985). At least one expert on British political education would agree with this guarded assessment; Tom Brennan writes, "What has been stressed in British society and its schools are the virtues of a 'representative' model of democracy . . . , while the possibilities inherent in the 'participatory" model . . . have been ignored" (1985: 6).

Our examination of the texts, however, does not fully support Brennan. The texts neither endorse the marriage of tradition and narcissism, nor do they make a strong case for conflictive democratic participation. Instead, they resemble the proverbial rejected suitor at the wedding—wounded, critical, yet somewhat withdrawn.

Several topics the history texts discuss invite the imagery of conflictive democratic participation. I examined three: labor-union formation in the late nineteenth century; the Parliamentary Reform Act of 1867; and the selective nationalization of British industries after the Second World War. These three topics somewhat parallel comparable American and Canadian espisodes whose textual treatments we have already examined. The question is whether the texts represent conflict in these episodes so as to stimulate conflictive democratic participation.

Contrary to the American and most of the Canadian texts, several of the British texts argue that unions represent durable class interests, not transient worker grievances. For example, Peter Lane writes, "In 1870 most politicians believed in the idea of self-help. But by 1900 there were a growing number, even of the ruling class, who no longer believed that self-help was enough" (1987: 162). The term *ruling class* never appears in North American texts; however, Lane avoids such terms as *working class* or bourgeoisie. His ruling class is thus a political, not an economic class. But his treatment of unionization certainly implies the class origins of the union movement.

By contrast, two of the five history texts develop a more particularistic analysis. Christopher Culpin, for example, fragments the modern history of unionization, dividing the topic by individual climactic events (e.g., the Match-Girls' strike of 1888, the London dock strike, the Taff Vale Judgment). Culpin does not employ the concept of class to connect these events to each other; he also claims that socialism and syndicalism were "not common in the union movement as a whole" (1987: 204). To Culpin, early British unions concerned themselves only with "bread-and-butter" issues and local problems.

The texts generally agree, however, that industrial relations were basically conflictive during the modern period of unionization. Indeed, R. J. Cootes emphasizes this point when he contrasts the unionization of the unskilled worker during the late nineteenth century with the unionization of craft industries a generation earlier. He writes:

> These new unions differed from the older "model unions" in several ways . . . above all, they were less prepared to cooperate with employers. They wanted higher wages and better working conditions right away and would not listen to excuses. (Cootes 1982: 195)

On other aspects of unionism, the texts take a less clearly conflictive stance. For example, most state that unions are essentially voluntary associations, not interest-based conflict groups. Despite socialist and Marxist influences on British unions (Flanders 1970), the texts argue that British unionism is essentially instrumental, rather than philosophical or ideological. Only Peter Lane argues that skilled workers formed a new political party because of "the writing of the socialists and the fear of unemployment" (1987: 167).

The treatment of unionism supports conflictive democratic participation most strongly in two additional respects. First, the texts portray unions as the creations of ordinary workers, rather than as the creatures of charismatic leaders. Although a few leaders, such as Annie Besant, Ben Tillett, and Keir Hardie, receive attention, they are subordinated to the workers they represent. Typical is R. J. Coote's observation on the dock strike of 1889: "It was a remarkable achievement of discipline and organization when . . . Ben Tillett . . . brought 10,000 poverty-stricken

dockers out on strike in the hot summer of 1889" (1982: 193). Although
the statement applauds Tillett's leadership, the real achievements of
discipline and organization appear to be those of the workers themselves.

Finally, three of the four relevant texts portray the unions as socialist
rather than capitalist. A particularly good example is Peter Lane's description of the Labour party's foundation: "The socialist societies
argued that only when there was a socialist government would the poor
get cheap housing, old age pensions, unemployment benefit, free medical care, and so on" (1987: 166). Here socialist societies push the unions
toward a socialist political party in order to attain otherwise unattain-
able economic goals.

Does class struggle reappear in the texts' characterization of the 1867
Parliamentary reform? Although the texts pay surprisingly little attention to the 1867 Reform Act, the little they do say attributes Parliamentary reform largely to working-class agitation. Richards and Hunt (1983)
offer the most sophisticated analysis, portraying the Reform Act as a
product of party strategy within Parliament and working-class pressure
outside Parliament. Other authors reverse the ordering. Cootes, for example, attributes the Act to new model unions which pushed for electoral reform; to Cootes the political parties played only a minor role
(1982: 196–97). Culpin agrees, noting that while working men initiated
the drive for reform, the Conservatives under Disraeli positioned themselves effectively to *benefit* from electoral change (1987: 212). Significantly, all the writers agree that the Act had nothing to do with charismatic leaders; there are no British Andrew Jacksons.

The texts say surprisingly little about the electoral consequences of
the 1867 Reform Act. In the comparable American case, the texts treated
electoral expansion during the Jacksonian period as stimulating mass
political-party organization. Not so the British. Only two of the five
British texts view parties as being in any major way affected by the Reform Act. Yet the Act significantly influenced the organizational structures and electoral styles of both the Liberal and Conservative parties
(for a relevant Parliamentary history, see Kinzer 1982: esp. 90–93). The
fact that the texts eschew such connections reveals a weakness in their
treatment of conflictive democratic participation.

On another point, however, the British diverge positively from the
American treatment of electoral reform. The British texts never asso-
ciate electoral expansion with political corruption. All treat the Reform
Act as a pure expression of democratic progress untainted by anything
like the spoils system or political machines. To some degree, of course,
this judgment simply reflects historical reality; British electoral expan-

sion *was* less corrupt than electoral expansion in the United States. But reality is less the issue than perception and image. Emphasizing corruption in the American case, while ignoring it entirely in the British case, surely promotes conflictive democratic participation in the latter country and retards it in the former. After all, if people believe electoral expansion inevitably to be corrupting, they are likely not to desire it. But if they view expansion as a means of redistributing power *fairly*, they will not be deterred from acting to effect reform.

The texts' treatment of the post–World War II nationalization program contrasts interestingly with the way American texts treat the Progressive period. Both Progressivism and nationalization were programs of government intervention designed to restructure and regulate industry. American texts characterize Progressivism as piecemeal social engineering guided by charismatic political leaders, such as Teddy Roosevelt; Progressivism therefore lacks qualities of enduring group conflict or conflictive democratic participation. Do British texts treat nationalization in the same way, or do they view nationalization as a working-class attack on capitalism through the medium of the Labour party? Is nationalization merely a reform of capitalism, or a substantial step towards socialism?

The texts compromise between capitalist reform and socialist control. On the one hand, nationalization is portrayed as a fundamental reconsideration of free enterprise; on the other hand, the texts do not characterize nationalization as socialist control over the economy. Rather, the texts emphasize that nationalization was simply a pragmatic response of the Labour party to its experience during the Second World War, when the nationalized industries first came under government regulation. As we shall see, portraying class and economic issues as party struggles within Parliament is one way text writers render conflictive democratic participation legitimate in Britain.

The texts certainly do not view nationalization as an expression of socialist philosophy. Rather, they follow the American practice of treating industrial reform as a purely piecemeal reaction to recurrent economic weaknesses. The to-be-nationalized industries were simply inefficient and uncompetitive in world markets. A typical characterization is Robottom's: "[The] main reason for nationalizing industries was to modernize them so that they could offer a better service . . . Nationalization of coal gave a chance to end the bitter disputes between miners and owners. It was possible to mechanize small pits and make overdue improvements, such as providing pithead baths" (1987: 258). Pragmatism, not idealism, drove nationalization.

Not surprisingly, therefore, nationalization appears as a genuinely collective political effort, not a triumph of and for workers as a class. Even Peter Lane's text, the furthest left in the sample, stresses collective rather than working-class action. Lane reprints a picture of a sign displayed at a colliery. The sign's caption reads, "This colliery is now managed by the National Coal Board on behalf of the people." In the foreground a miner is shown reading the sign, symbolizing working-class deference to "the people" and the National Coal Board (1985: 262).

On explicitly political subjects, such as individual rights and political parties, the theme of conflictive democratic participation emerges more explicitly in British textbooks. For example, where most American and even a few Canadian texts treat individual rights as permanent and secure, British government texts often treat individual rights as insecure and in need of constant protection. Robins, Brennan, and Sutton (1985) observe that the British government has abused individual rights in Northern Ireland, and that even within Great Britain, welfare recipients have suffered harassment. David Roberts (1986) argues that newspapers sometimes destroy a person's rights through unfair publicity. Only two of the six government texts demur from this cautionary view. For example, J. Harvey argues that Parliament protects individual rights through the institution of question time; he never explains, however, exactly how Parliamentary questions provide effective protection for the rights of citizens (1983: 94–95). On balance, of course, recognizing that rights are always a matter of debate favors conflictive democratic participation.

British texts, however, are but marginally more attentive to the philosophical underpinnings of individual rights than are American or Canadian texts. Only three texts mention any philosophical justification at all; these three are cursory, referring the reader either to American sources—such as the Declaration of Independence—or to the "need" to protect individual rights in a democracy (Roberts 1986). Why democracies must protect rights remains unclear, however. Moreover, only one of the six texts mentions the public/private divide as basic to individual rights (Robins, Brennan, and Sutton, 1985).

Still, British texts are unusually sensitive to varieties of struggle over individual rights, a major topic in much conflictive democratic participation. For example, Gabriel and Maslen (1986: 7–8) allude to constant friction between the government's legitimate power to make laws and the citizen's right to be free. The authors mention Parliament, the courts, and social customs as sites where this conflict occurs. Scott and Kobrin begin their chapter on "The Rights and Liberties of Citizens" by stating, "The freedom currently enjoyed in this country has been attained only after a slow process of constitutional development over the centuries, but it will not inevitably last forever. It must be guarded constantly . . . " (1979, 1983: 204). After this brave beginning, however, Scott and Kobrin confine their discussion to only *legalistic* conflict. David Roberts (1986) provides a fuller discussion. He focuses particularly on the struggle between free speech and racial slurs.

British government texts truly excel in the treatment of political parties. This superiority is understandable given the British history of party government. But the texts so nicely render this history as to help extend it in the form of recurrent conflictive democratic participation. For example, five of the six politics texts characterize parties as basically conflictive, rather than consensual in the American or Canadian sense. J. Harvey is typical in listing as the first of his eight party functions the necessity to organize public opinion into opposed policy options (1983: 55). Only one British writer, Philip Gabriel, demurs from the positive vision of party conflict when he writes, "Some party conflict is very trivial. . . . Occasionally it has harmful effects, as when rival politicians give misleading accounts of each others' policies . . . " (1986: 23).

British texts also devote more attention to party structure than do American or Canadian texts. The parties are not pictured as loose aggregates, but as stable institutions with durable memberships and effective organizations. However, the texts usually distinguish between Labour and Conservative in this regard. Some writers characterize Labour as divided and decentralized, and Conservatives as unified and hierarchical; others see Labour as more disciplined than Conservatives, at least at election time. All writers agree, however, that leadership choice is not as divisive for Conservatives. Most important, the texts all attribute greater organizational autonomy and cohesion to British parties than American or Canadian texts attribute to their own country's parties.

British parties also emerge as comparatively ideological and issue-oriented, not as catch-all organizations devoted mainly to electioneering. One reason for this distinctively British emphasis is that the authors use socialism as a way of polarizing Labour against Conservatives. By implication, therefore, they characterize debate over capitalism as normal. For example, after first observing that "socialism has had a considerable influence on Labour Party thinking," Gabriel and Maslin (1986: 33) use the issue of party conflict to demonstrate the importance of socialism's effect on Labour. In this way, ideology contributes positively to conflictive democratic participation.

The texts emphasize that class cleavage divides the parties from each other. Neither Harvey nor Roberts pays attention to recent declines in British class voting, a significant omission, for it helps to reinforce the strong image of class cleavage in British collective representations. Most of the other writers briefly mention class dealignment, but then stress that class remains the dominant party cleavage. The contrast with American and Canadian texts, which generally ignore class entirely, is quite palpable.

The texts also emphasize that, in Britain, winning parties become the Government: therefore, parties are not solely representational devices, as they are in the United States and Canada. In Britain, the parties transport conflictive democratic participation from representation to governance itself. Statements such as the following typify the dominant view: "[By] means of the party system the elector votes not only for a candidate, he votes for a Government" (Scott and Kobrin 1979: 69); "Through parties, . . . effective government is possible" (Harvey 1983: 59); "Political parties dominate British politics" (Robins, Brennan, and Sutton 1985: 56); and "in practice most people are voting for a party which they hope will form the next government" (Roberts 1986: 91). These statements not only *reflect* the reality of a Parliamentary system, but also help *reproduce* this reality. In so doing, they elevate conflictive democratic participation to a greater role in British texts than it occupies in Canadian or American texts.

Conclusion: Cultural Visions and Political Debate in Britain

No two aspects of contemporary British politics are more conspicuous than the simultaneous rise of Margaret Thatcher and the decline of class voting. Not surprisingly, writers link the two phenomena causally. Crewe (1986: 620–38), for example, explains the former by reference to the latter, while Elliott and McCrone consider both phenomena as the "new right's" attempt "to reconstruct the terrain of what is taken for granted in social and political thought—and so form a new common sense" (1987: 485–515, 487). If Elliott and McCrone are correct, contemporary British political parties are engaged in a fundamental struggle over culture as embodying distinct ways of life.

This conflict differs profoundly from that which presently simmers in North America. In the United States, neoconservatism remains encased within a dominant liberal ideology that lacks a socialist antagonist; therefore, neoconservatism's possibilities of polarizing the electorate

culturally are few (Conover and Gray 1983). In Canada, neoconservatism is subordinated to more divisive political cleavages involving language and region. The New Democratic Party's socialist alternative is
still too new and too weak to trigger a proportional neoconservative
response. Only in Britain is there true struggle between philosophically
and sociologically distinct cultural alternatives.

In this cultural fight, Labourite England finds allies on television and
in social studies texts, each of which promotes class consciousness,
party solidarity, selflessness, and community values. By contrast, Conservative England finds allies in British advertising and corporate publications, each of which weds tradition to narcissistic, selfish pleasure.
Ultimately, the struggle in British political culture is not between public
and private, but between collective endeavor and personal indulgence.
Because this struggle suffuses British popular culture, its embodiment
in *party* struggle emerges sharply and evocatively. Culture thus stimulates greater conflictive democratic participation in Britain than in Canada or the United States.

Two factors moderate these cultural tensions in Britain: the party
system and "tradition" itself. Although the parties sharpen visions of
culture in Britain, they also reshape these visions into instruments of
legitimate governance. British parties, therefore, illustrate how political
institutions can occasionally function both as cultural symbols and as
political instruments (see also Sahlins 1981). As cultural symbols, the
parties stimulate conflict, but as political instruments, the parties moderate conflict. The parties thus empower a democratic majority to rule
legitimately without encountering forceful resistance.

In addition, the two cultural antagonists both defer to and venerate
tradition. Corporations and advertisers appeal to tradition in order to
promote narcissism; television entertainment and social studies texts appeal to tradition in order to build community. As a symbol, tradition
plays the role of mythological unifier, simultaneously available to all
comers, yet sufficiently aloof as to remain above the ideological fray
(Edelman 1964). When royalty makes itself available left and right, it
legitimizes both Left and Right. More important, it mediates in the
name of tradition between these two bitter opponents.

CHAPTER SIX

The Political Embodiment of Liberal Democratic Culture

Public opinion and the language of political elites in Britain, Canada, and the United States embody and transmit the collective representations described in previous chapters. Analysis of the literature on opinions regarding class, race, partisanship, and protest generally supports this proposition. An original analysis of political language regarding bilingual education and party reform also generally supports this proposition. Public opinion and political language present distinctive analytic problems as surface manifestations of liberal deep-cultural structures. The chapter addresses these problems and finds that they do not vitiate the cultural approach.

Introduction: Reasonable Misgivings

I have argued that liberal democracy has combined with particular historical circumstances in Canada, Britain, and the United States to produce three national variants of popular culture. In the United States, there exists a cultural configuration I have termed *institutionalized individualism;* in Canada, there exists a cultural configuration of *restrained conflict;* and in Britain there exists a cultural debate between opposing visions of life. Each of these cultures differentially supports conflictive democratic participation.

But do these three cultures really themselves shape and limit conflictive democratic participation, or are they only reflections of other forces? After all, there are other, more traditional explanations for the incompleteness of liberal democracy. For example, if many people do not vote frequently or stably, then the properties of political parties and electoral systems provide an explanation, not television sitcoms (Jackman 1987: 405–24). If only a few people participate actively in politics, the explanation lies in Downsian theories of rational choice (see also Barry 1970). Why should a rational person make the considerable effort to advance a political alternative that is only incrementally different from other alternatives? And if group solidarity and polarization

174

are limited, the reason lies in the strategic vagueness of leaders' political appeals (Page 1979), or in the growth of an affluent complacent, middle class (Bell 1976), or in the decline of class conflict (Ingelhart 1990). These conditions have little to do with culture.

My response to these misgivings is threefold. First, by having defined the "political" only as the workings of governmental institutions and public policies, political science arbitrarily excludes culture and thus prejudices the argument from the outset. But once we recognize that politics is as much a struggle for minds and hearts as for stomachs and pocketbooks, the shaping of culture returns as a central political issue.

Second, no single approach should be expected to explain everything political. Popular culture cannot explain marginal allocations in, say, agriculture programs, any more than political economy can explain why Americans are institutionally individualistic, Canadians drawn to solidary groups, and the British torn between narcissism and selflessness. But both agricultural policy and institutional individualism are clearly political topics of importance.

Third, I maintain in this chapter that cultural configurations do in fact influence certain aspects of politics directly enough to satisfy even the most skeptical political scientist. A cultural configuration is a model of values and cognition which individual citizens imitate and reproduce in their political enterprises. In this chapter we investigate two political expressions of culture: first, patterns of public opinion in Canada, Britain, and the United States; and second, the language political elites use to grapple with salient political issues. As we will see, the cultural configurations we have described infuse both mass opinion and elite discourse.

The fit between cultural configurations, on the one hand, and public opinion and political language, on the other, is not direct and unmediated. Cultural configurations are deep structures whose surface embodiments in the forms of public opinion and political language will vary, yet remain true to the underlying structure (for example, see Fowler 1977). After all, different people construct different sentences from the same language, even the same words. And, as David Laitin puts it, "within a culture there are diverse strands of opinion and conflicting values" (1988: 589), yet the culture itself endures.

Moreover, as collective representations, culture embodies ideals which each citizen and group adapts to particular circumstances. The circumstances themselves—whether they be the tedium of an assembly line, the despair of a ghetto, the red tape of a bureaucracy, or the pragmatism of a political deal—always escape somewhat the idealizations of culture.

Yet adapting cultural ideals to reality does not render the ideals power-less. Instead, cultural ideals become internalized, refined, enriched, and changed through application (Berger 1981; Varenne 1977). For ex-ample, to apply the ideal of individual freedom to the practice of child-rearing requires that we raise children in conformity to the ideal as fully as possible. But we also encounter the limits of freedom as a guide to raising children, and therefore reconstitute the ideal itself. Though our practice may not fit the ideal completely, neither will it be intelligible in the absence of the ideal.

Put differently, a culture does not provide rigidly enforced values, but rather "points of concern" (Laitin 1988: 589) which define political issues and the acceptable range of policy solutions. Politics turns cul-ture's heady ideals into sometimes grubby realities, yet simultaneously *valorizes* culture, by glorifying pragmatic bargains as "political wisdom." It is this paradox—political action as both cultural negation and cultural affirmation—which we will observe as we examine public opinion and political debate in Canada, Britain, and the United States.

Cultural Configurations and Public Opinion

Conflictive democratic participation is built upon cultural cleavage, which gives the citizen the conviction that political action is both necessary and worthwhile. In the United States, institutionalized in-dividualism reduces tension between collective representations of the public and of the private, and between selfishness and selflessness. I hypothesize that this cultural configuration also minimizes cleavages in public opinion, and thereby retards conflictive democratic participation. In Canada, the raw materials of conflictive democratic participation are more abundant than they are in the United States. However, weakness in the collective representation of private life removes passion from pub-lic action. Therefore, Canadian culture does not fully realize conflictive democratic participation. Still our analysis so far leads us to expect cleavages in Canadian public opinion to be sharper than in American public opinion. Finally, British culture fuses private passion to public debates about divergent ways of life. Therefore, we should find deeper and more enduring cleavages in public opinion in Britain than in Canada or the United States.

Comparing public opinion cross-nationally is always risky. The wording of survey questions is rarely exactly comparable across countries; measures and sample characteristics differ from study to study; and even definitions of salient concepts, such as social class or partisan identification, often vary. Moreover, survey results are often subject to country-specific situational, demographic, period, or institutional effects (Powell 1982). For example, the Viet Nam War and the Watergate scandal shaped American public opinion in the early 1970s at the same time that industrial struggle influenced British public opinion. We may expect Viet Nam and Watergate to have had effects on American public opinion different from the effects of industrial turmoil on British public opinion. These endogenous effects render comparative conclusions always quite tentative.

These problems emerge immediately when we scan studies of political participation in the three countries. If we confine ourselves to the simple act of voting, our hypothesis holds up well; assuming that rates of voting in part respond to cultural configurations, then for the most part, the recent history of voting turnout reveals the predicted ordering: Great Britain highest; Canada second; and the United States lowest (Conway 1985: 6; Rose 1985: 272; Crewe, Fox, and Alt 1977: 45; Clarke et al. 1979: 358).

A similar order emerges in Ingelhart's analysis of political discussion rates in advanced industrial societies. Ingelhart discovered that the percentage of the public which frequently or occasionally discussed politics was 72 percent in Great Britain, 68 percent in Canada, and 65 percent in the United States as of 1984. Nevertheless, these differences, though in the predicted direction, are small (Ingelhart 1990: 343).

But things quickly become murky when we venture beyond these indices. Contrary to the hypothesis, Barnes, Kaase et al. classified 28 percent of their British sample as uninvolved in conventional politics in the mid 1970s, as opposed to only 16 percent of their American sample (1979: 169). Worse yet, Kornberg and Stewart (1983: 92) found that 21 percent of their Canadian sample in 1979 reported attending political meetings, as compared to only 9 percent of Barnes and Kaase's British sample and 18 percent of their American sample (Barnes, Kaase et al. 1979: 541). The point seems clear: the effect of cultural configurations on conventional political activity is inconclusive so far as country orderings are concerned.

More telling, perhaps, is research on unconventional political participation, such as illegal protests, violent actions, boycotts, and rent strikes. Our argument leads us to expect higher levels of unconventional political participation in the United States than in the other two countries. Institutionalized individualism draws citizens away from traditional political organizations, such as political parties. The culture thus makes way for citizens who choose to be active to venture beyond conventional political boundaries. It is therefore significant that American public-interest groups have skyrocketed in both number and membership since the 1970s (Shienbaum 1984: 67; Berry 1989: 19).

Scholarly research generally suggests that unconventional political participation is both more approved and more common in the United States than in Britain. Barnes, Kaase et al. (1979: 80) classify only 9 percent of their American sample as outright opponents of unconventional protest. By contrast, 23 percent of their British sample rejected unconventional protest. And Ingelhart found that 22 percent of his American sample had actually *participated* in unconventional political behavior as of 1980, five times as many as in West Germany, and more than twice as many as in the Netherlands (1990: 313). These findings make sense when connected to the fact that unconventional participation often bypasses intermediate groups representing social class, party, or region, which are more powerful culturally in Britain than in the United States.

The data are more striking for Canada. Lipset (1989: 66) reports that there were only 13 protest demonstrations in Canada between 1978 and 1982, as compared to 1,166 in the United States during the same period. Thus, Canadians are far more likely than Americans to pursue conflictive democratic participation through the medium of political parties, the more promising route.

Alan Marsh has challenged the claim that the British public resists unconventional political participation. After reanalyzing the Barnes and Kaase data, Marsh argues that the 1960s destroyed the last remnants of traditional British "deference" to authority. As Marsh puts it, "Especially among the young, protest potential was found to be the common property of people of all social characteristics and political persuasions and not merely of 'extremists' or 'militants' or any other fashionable *bete noir* of professional politicians and communicators" (1977: 227). Indeed, the 22 percent of Marsh's sample which endorsed "the legitimacy of non-legal protest" compares favorably with studies of Americans (Marsh 1977: 51).

Perhaps it is the *form* protest takes, rather than its sheer incidence, which speaks more directly to our hypothesis. We would expect approval of protest to be more related to *individual* psychological characteristics, such as ideological conceptualization, in the United States, and more related to *group* membership in Britain. It turns out, in fact, that approval of unconventional action *is* more of a personal choice in the United States than in Britain. For example, Barnes and Kaase report that individual attitudes towards protest are sharply polarized in the United States. They find a correlation of -.51 between protest potential (a liberal attitude) and repression potential (a conservative attitude) in the United States, as opposed to the comparable British correlation of .35 (Barnes, Kaase et al. 1979: 93). In short, in the United States, personal feelings about protest are sharply demarcated and bifurcated. In Britain, they are not.

By contrast, most *group* factors structure the potential for protest slightly more in Britain than in the United States. Union membership, for example, is linked to support for protest in Britain but not in the United States (.14–.05). Family income is also more important in Britain (.23–.17) (Barnes, Kaase et al. 1979: 100). Because the two societies are predominantly liberal, individual commitment is more important than group membership in both countries. But groups play a stronger role in Britain than in the United States.

In the United States the trend towards unconventional, individualistically based participation remains strong. In his study of the age cohort which entered the electorate in the 1960s, Delli Carpini reports an unusually strong attraction to unconventional participation (1986: 192ff.). While life-cycle effects may reduce this tendency somewhat, the sixties generation may push the American electorate to higher levels of unconventional participation than those observed in the Barnes and Kaase study.

A motivation favorable to political participation in these three countries is the belief that government ought to provide important services to the public. Promoting government services provides incentives for political action, while resistance to government programs removes an incentive for sustained public involvement. Therefore, let us consider attitudes toward the welfare state. Our approach leads us to expect the recent decline of support for the welfare state to be steeper in the United States than in Canada, and greater in Canada than in Britain. Historically, welfare-state policies have emerged from episodes of conflictive democratic participation. Where the culture somewhat supports such participation (as in Britain) we would expect support for the welfare state to remain comparatively strong; by contrast, institutionalized individualism in the United States provides less cultural support for welfare-state programs. Meanwhile, in Canada, we would expect the sharp cultural conflict between government and the corporation (but see Fox and Ornstein 1986: 481–506) to sustain considerable support for the welfare state; however, the weakness in cultural images of private life might well deny such support the depth and breadth it enjoys in Britain.

Available studies through the 1970s support these expectations. Before the current "revolt" against the welfare state, the expected country-ordering apparently held. Speaking of the 1945–75 period, Coughlin states, "on items virtually identical to those on American surveys, Canadians appear a bit more receptive towards goverment guarantees" (1980: 19). The expected ordering also emerges in popular explanations for poverty. On average, through the 1960s and 1970s, the conservative explanation of poverty (i.e., that poverty is the consequence of individual laziness) received the support of 30 percent of the Canadians and 40 percent of the Americans sampled. Finally, 58 percent of Americans condemned high levels of government spending, as opposed to 43 percent of Canadians and only 20 percent of the British (Coughlin 1980: 19).

Recent studies support these observations. In 1978–79, for example, 51 percent of Americans sampled argued that government should "let each person get ahead on his own." This view was echoed by only 38 percent of the Canadians sampled. Thus, in Canada, support for a strong welfare state appears to have remained strong (Lipset 1989: 142).

In Britain, favorable attitudes towards the welfare state persisted to the very dawn of the Thatcher era. Mack and Lansley report that in 1979, 55.3 percent of British Election Survey respondents stated that "redistribution was a very or fairly important government activity" (1985: 222), the same proportion as in 1974. Although the authors do admit a gradual weakening in British support for the welfare state, they believe that the "hardening" of opposition in the late 1970s was directed mainly at a few "spongers," rather than at most beneficiaries. Mack and Lansley characterize this modest shift as a temporary rearrangement of attitudes, attributable mainly to the 1979 "winter of discontent," which followed a period of economic stagnation (1985: 250).

It is difficult to locate comparable American or Canadian data. It may be significant, however, that American public opinion has consistently and unequivocally opposed the idea of a minimum income, a chief form of income redistribution. For example, in the late sixties, roughly two-thirds of the American public opposed income-maintenance programs which lacked a work requirement. To be fair, support rose considerably when a work requirement was included (McClosky and Zaller 1984: 275–76). On balance, however, through the seventies, the British seem to have been more supportive of the welfare state than the American public.

What then of Mrs. Thatcher's attack upon the welfare state? Did the British public support it? The most thorough investigation of British welfare attitudes during the Thatcher regime concludes that

> [t]he electorate shows little evidence of having adopted a That-cherite position on these issues. For example, between 1974 and 1979 the electorate did move to the right on the issues of whether benefits "nowadays have gone too far"; by 1983 it had reversed direction and was to the left of its original position in 1974. Nor have Thatcherites converted the electorate to the goal of a low-tax minimal welfare economy. Asked to choose be-tween tax and social service cuts or tax and social service in-creases, the public was evenly divided—37% apiece—when the Conservatives came to office in May 1979. By 1983 service in-creasers outnumbered tax cutters by 52% to 24%, and by May 1987 by the even greater margin of 64% to 13%. (Crewe and Searing 1988: 377; McAllister and Mughan 1987, 47–71; Golding and Middleton 1983; Taylor-Gooby 1985; Clemens 1983)

Similar, but weaker arguments hold for the United States. John Schwarz reports that, "as late as 1976 . . . the public was in no mood to turn the corner and reverse the [government] programs . . . the proportions of the nation that favored maintaining or increasing spending were: rebuilding the inner cities, 70 percent; programs to help the elderly, 95%; welfare programs to help low-income families, 61 percent; food stamps for low income families, 60 percent; and programs to help the unemployed, 79 percent" (1983: 163). Even during the Reagan years, there occurred no precipitous decline in public support for most welfare state programs. In fact, "an NBC News poll found that those agreeing with the statement that Reagan was 'going too far in attempting to cut back or eliminate government social programs' rose from 37 to 52 per-cent over 1981–83. Comparing the results of a 1982 survey with one commissioned in 1978, the Chicago Council on Foreign Relations found a remarkable 26 percentage point jump in those wishing to 'expand' rather than 'cut back' welfare and relief programs . . . " (Ferguson and Rogers 1986: 15).

However, in all three countries the public makes a sharp distinction between "deserving" and "undeserving" poor. Again, however, the British do so less than do Americans. For example, in 1981 Taylor-Gooby found that only 31 percent of a smallish British local sample (n = 240) wanted to make benefits available to *all* unemployed; many respondents argued

182   The Political Embodiment of Liberal Democratic Culture

that the unemployed were "scroungers" (1985: 31 ff.). But as early as 1961—
a year of economic affluence before the public turned against certain welfare-state programs—71 percent of an American sample already opposed
increased government spending for the unemployed (Coughlin 1980: 104).
By the mid-1970s, only about 25 percent of most national samples argued
that the poor deserved special government help in order to better their circumstances (McClosky and Zaller 1984: 271; see also Mead 1986).

In summary, though sorely incomplete, the available evidence suggests
that the welfare state has weathered attacks better in Britain than in the
United States. On balance, therefore, attitudes toward the welfare state
support this chapter's primary hypothesis.

A further important comparison involves cross-national group cleavages in attitudes toward the welfare state. We would expect to discover
sharper group cleavages in Britain than in Canada, and in Canada than
the United States. Certainly class differences on welfare issues have
generally been stronger in Britain than in the United States. For example,
Coughlin reports only a 10 percent class difference in American beliefs
that government should let each person get ahead on his own. In 1968
a slight majority of American workers favored the proposition, as opposed to a solid majority of managers. By contrast, in 1961 there was
a yawning gap between British manual and professional classes on the
same question; only 16 percent of the manual workers sampled stated
that each person should get along on his own, as opposed to 53 percent
of the professionals (Coughlin 1980: 34, 40).

Studies disagree about Canadian class cleavages on welfare-related
issues. In an early investigation, Mildred Schwartz reported moderate
social-class effects on welfare attitudes, once partisan identification was
controlled (1967: 131). Recently, Johnston and Ornstein utilized position in the production process, rather than the usual white collar/blue
collar distinction, to demarcate their Canadian sample into *three* classes.
They report substantially greater working-class than middle-class support across a broad spectrum of welfare issues. However, welfare state
support is no more closely related to income, education, or occupation
today in Canada than it was at the time of Schwartz's study (Johnson
and Ornstein 1985: 369–94).

Contemporary research suggests that class differences on welfare issues
are sharper in Britain than in the other two countries. Mack and Lansley report that in the early 1980s opinion differences on welfare issues
averaged about 20–30 percent from the highest to the lowest social
class in the standard British five-tiered census scheme (1985: 214, 223,
266–67).

One group which plays a key role in promoting conflictive democratic participation is the labor union. Unions can provide strong group support to party competition, a chief component of conflictive democratic participation. Therefore, attitudes and behavior involving unions are important to our argument. So far as membership rates are concerned, the hypothesized country ordering holds. Vanneman and Cannon report that in 1980 union membership among adults equaled 25 percent in the United States, 35 percent in Canada, and 49 percent in Britain (1987: 6). Of course, unions have suffered political setbacks over the last several years in all three countries; but unions in the United States have suffered most, at least judging by membership levels. Only 18 percent of employed Americans belonged to unions in 1985, while in Britain membership remains around 50 percent (Vanneman and Cannon 1987: 5–6). Meanwhile, in Canada, "as of 1989 . . . union density was more than twice that of the American" (Lipset 1989: 169).

Union membership is also more strongly connected to left voting in Britain than in the United States. When Margaret Thatcher first came to power in 1979, union members strongly resisted her appeal. In 1979, 48 percent of working-class union members voted Labour, as opposed to only 30 percent of the unaffiliated working class. Significantly, 64 percent of union members with kin also in unions voted Labour (Robertson 1984: 63). This latter finding is consistent with our contention that British culture effectively mediates between public and private via kinship, neighborhood, pub, and—in this case—unions.

Even in 1983, four years into the Thatcher regime, union membership continued to be associated with support for Labour within the working class. According to Dunleavy and Husbands, 46 percent of union members among manual workers voted for Labour, as opposed to 34 percent of the manual workers who were unaffiliated with a union (1985: 132). This gap managed to resist the overwhelmingly positive effect of the Falklands victory in encouraging support for Mrs. Thatcher.

Of course, the union-Labour link in Britain may not be entirely a product of union influences. Labour partisans may simply choose to join unions. However, this choice itself reflects the culturally-based expectation that unions will be supportive of Labour. In this case, British culture produces a self-fulfilling prophecy, for unions can hardly reject their members' expectations, and must clearly reinforce these propensities through their own actions.

By contrast, American unions did little to stem the tide of Reagan victories. Indeed, in 1984, when the AFL-CIO formerly endorsed Walter Mondale, thereby abandoning its traditional nonpartisan stance, union workers still voted only 14 percent less heavily for Reagan than did their nonunion peers. This was true despite the fact that the election itself presented an unusually clear-cut class choice, and that nothing equivalent to the Falklands triumph favored the incumbent.

I do not wish to emphasize unions in this argument, however, for public attitudes toward unions are quite negative in all three countries. Typical is the Gallup report that in 1979 only 23 percent of a Canadian sample had either a "great deal" or a "lot" of confidence in labor unions, a lower ranking than that given to any other institution ranked, including large corporations (Kielty, Hatton, and Munsche [1980]: 72). Similar findings regularly appear in American and British studies (Clemens 1983: 58–61). Even union members themselves are quite critical of labor organizations, and most participate little in union affairs. Recent ethnographic studies (Halle 1984; Nichols and Beynon 1977) describe in detail the nature of these discontents. All we can say is that British unions apparently suffer less from these problems than American unions.

A key question for our analysis is the connection between class position and "appropriate" party voting. We would expect this connection to be closer in Britain than in Canada, and closer in Canada than in the United States, but we are only partially correct in this prediction. In an important early study, Alford (1963) found sharper class/party polarization in British voting than in the United States or Canada. The same ordering appears to hold today. A discriminate function analysis of the British elections of 1964 and 1966 reveals that Conservative supporters differed from Labour voters by seventy-five points in class voting (Vanneman and Cannon 1987: 165). The comparable class difference between Nixon/Humphrey (1968) and Nixon/McGovern (1972) voters was a comparatively trivial eight points. Studies of class self-placements in relation to party choice are equally supportive. For example, in the midsixties, subjective class identification explained 46 percent of the British party placements, as opposed to only 20 percent of the American placements (Vanneman and Cannon 1987: 178).

The problem, however, is that class in the United States is a stronger voting influence than class in Canada. In the latter country, Clarke et al. report only miniscule relations between subjective class placement and vote choice in 1965, 1968, and 1974, with measures of association never rising above .10 (1979: 116).

Curiously, however, class consciousness itself is stronger in Canada than in the United States, a finding which is consistent with our hypothesis. Lipset reports that in the early 1980s, "Forty-eight percent of Canadians, but 42% of Americans, said that they think of themselves as 'belonging to a particular social class,'" and of these, more Canadians than Americans thought of themselves as working class (1989: 154). These data suggest that Canadians are less likely than Americans to translate their more prevalent class awareness into voting, perhaps a sign of the weaker role of the private sphere in Canadian culture than in American culture.

A number of political factors also help account for this weakness. Although the New Democratic Party in Canada originated in the union movement, it appeals to a quite heterogeneous class base. Moreover, the Liberal party—the dominant Canadian party in terms of identification—attracts many middle- and upper-middle-class voters, despite the mild "progressiveness" of its policies; and the Progressive Conservatives appeal strongly to lower-middle-class people.

These apparent anomalies owe much to the regional and ethnic loyalties in Canadian culture. The two main parties have quite different regional bases. Until recently, the Progressive Conservatives have lacked a strong presence in Quebec, as have Liberals in the West. Regional loyalties cross-cut social class lines; the Liberals, for example, are a strong favorite among all classes in Quebec federal elections. The New Democratic Party appeals both to affluent English speakers and to "New" (i.e., non-Anglo, non-French) Canadians in the prairie provinces. The result of this checkerboard pattern is considerable regional variation in class/party relationships. For example, in the Clarke study, class identification is *positively* associated with Liberal support in the prairie provinces, but *negatively* associated with Liberal support in the Atlantic provinces (Clarke et al. 1979: 113).

Of course, parties themselves are the chief agents of conflictive democratic participation. We must therefore consider parties in greater detail. In so doing, however, we enter contested research terrain. Not only do researchers employ different definitions of "partisanship" from study to study, but they also disagree about the acquisition and stability of partisanship in Western societies. Today a prominent group of investigators on both sides of the Atlantic argues that parties have become "dealigned" in Britain and the United States (e.g., Franklin 1985; Wattenberg 1984; a balanced treatment is Epstein 1986: 266–67). These researchers claim that the major parties no longer hold their partisans over time, no longer attract youthful cohorts entering the electorate, and have lost the social class roots the Depression of the 1930s formerly bequeathed them. If so, our task is quite complex.

Significantly, however, Le Duc (1985) argues that the trend toward dealignment is strongest and fastest in the United States, as evidenced by the upsurge of young Americans calling themselves "independents." While young voters in the United States contribute disproportionately to independence (Flanigan and Zingale 1987: 89–91), in Canada no such trend existed, at least in 1979. According to Clarke et al., "Unlike the American pattern, there is no significant increase in the number of voters without partisan attachments, nor is partisan instability higher in the younger cohorts" (1979: 385). Thus, as our hypothesis would predict, there may be less dealignment in Canada than in the United States. Nevertheless, partisanship is no stronger or more polarizing in Canada than in the United States. Indeed, in a 1978 Canadian Gallup poll, a full 55 percent of the sample claimed they did not feel close to *any* party (Kielty, Hatton, and Munsche [1980]: 26). Perhaps dealignment is less evident in Canada in part because partisanship has *always* been shallow in that country.

Our basic conceptualization of culture in Canada and the United States is perhaps more useful for understanding the *timing* than the *extent* of dealignment. A culture of institutionalized individualism promotes *rapid* dealignment; institutionalized individualism distances people psychologically from solidary, intermediate organizations, including political parties. Therefore, when traumatic political events occur—such as the Watergate affair and the Viet Nam War—people can abandon their party allegiances rapidly. By contrast, in Canada, although regionalism, ethnicity, and a culturally weak private realm have never bound voters closely to parties, the truncated group solidarity which *does* exist reduces the speed of dealignment.

There is particularly sharp debate about dealignment in Britain. Independence from partisanship is less commonly used to assess dealignment in Britain than is instability in party voting or weakened associations between social class and party support. On the latter subject, major research has been undertaken by Crewe, Franklin, Robertson, and Heath, *inter alia*. Crewe and Franklin agree that since the 1960s, social class has become considerably less powerful as a determinant of partisanship and partisan voting in Britain. Crewe notes that between 1945 and 1983 the proportion of manual workers voting Labour fell from 62 percent to 42 percent (Crewe 1986: 620–48; see also Dunleavy and Husbands 1985: 123). This observation clearly disputes our hypothesis, as does Mughan's finding that the British middle class's voting cohesion is greater than that of the working class, a differential consistent with the weakening of the class/party nexus for working-class voters (1986: 66). However, M. Franklin also notes that although *individual* class consciousness plays a less powerful role in structuring the vote, class as embodied in *communities* and organizations continues to play a major role (1984: 483–508). This finding is quite consistent with our characterization of British culture as being hospitable to images of community.

At the outset of his study, Robertson appears to concur with the dealignment position. He reports an 11 percent decline from 1955 to 1979 in the proportion of working-class voters choosing Labour (62 percent–51 percent) (1984: 26). However, he also notes that only 5 percent more working-class voters chose the Tories in 1979 than in 1964; nor has there been any tendency at all for more middle-class voters to choose Labour. Importantly, the bulk of Labour's defections are not to their "class enemies" (as in the case of the American Democratic party defections to the Republicans), but to the Alliance or to nationalist splinter parties or, indeed, to nonvoting.

Robertson's analysis of the dealignment thesis is complex and ambivalent. He proposes a novel three-class model of British social stratification, rather than the traditional two-class or five-class model; his intermediate class is composed of white-collar workers who do not supervise people and manual workers (e.g., foremen) who do supervise people. Using this scheme, Robertson describes nine class/party "families" in British political culture. As one proceeds downward in class and leftward from Conservative to Labour party identification, the propensity for the individual to vote Labour and to support the left grows powerfully. Interestingly, the relationship between class and party is nonlinear; there is an unexpectedly great affinity for left voting and left ideology among upper-class Labourites (Robertson 1984: chap. 5).

Robertson's conceptualization takes on significance for our argument when we compare it to American data gathered by Verba and Orren. In their sample of American leaders drawn from several walks of life, Verba and Orren report 5.3 times greater support for government redistribution of income among Democrats than among Republicans. By contrast, in Robertson's study, upper-class Labourites (whose social position resembles the American leaders Verba and Orren studied) are a startlingly *thirteen* times more likely to favor government redistribution of wealth than are their upper-class Tory opponents (Verba and Orren 1985: 79; Robertson 1984: 173). Partisan cleavages apparently continue to structure issue opinions more strongly *within* social class in Britain than in the United States or Canada. This pattern supports our main hypothesis.

Moreover, just as class *alone* polarizes British politics more than it does American politics, so also does partisanship remain more closely associated with class in Britain. The ratio of upper-class Conservatives to upper-class Labour supporters in Britain was roughly 3–1 (63 percent–20 percent) in the 1979 election (Robertson 1984: 120). In 1983 five times as many professionals, employers, and managers voted Conservative as Labour (Dunleavy and Husbands 1985: 123). By contrast, in the Verba and Orren study of American leaders—a group normally *more* polarized ideologically than the general public—61 percent of the sample actually identified with the *Democratic* party (calculated from Verba and Orren 1985: 65). Put differently, from a class standpoint, 61 percent of American leaders were misidentifiers. Although the Verba/Orren sample may be eccentric, the sharp difference from both the Robertson and the Dunleavy/Husbands findings is still suggestive. Perhaps a fairer comparison emerges from Flanigan and Zingale's 1984 American data. These authors report that among college educated Protestants in the North, Republicans enjoyed approximately a 2–1 advantage over Democrats (1987: 51). This figure can again be compared to the substantially greater 3–1 Conservative advantage in the British upper class.

So far, Canada has been the odd man out in our review of public opinion research. Canada simply does not display enough partisan or social class cleavage to place it significantly ahead of the United States in stimulants to conflictive democratic participation. However, it is significant that regionalism in Canada plays a greater cleavage role than regionalism does in the United States. There is certainly nothing akin to the regional salience of Quebec today in the United States. As John Meisel put it some years ago, "Whether it be the simultaneously lyrical and angry songs of the Quebec *chansonniers*; the particular intellectual universe and flavour of *Le Devoir*; the staging, by several companies, of works by the prolific Quebec playwrights; or the massive output of the poets, novelists, pamphleteers and other polemicists, who created a veritable sea of little magazines and books—these phenomena all attest to the existence of a French Canadian identity which constantly finds expression in a vigorous cultural life and an articulate national consciousness, missing in English Canada" (1975: 187). Recent interview and ethnographic studies support the contemporary relevance of Meisel's conclusions (Maxwell 1976; Menzies 1978; Handler 1988).

How do Canadian regional cleavages express themselves politically? Partly through language. Meisel found that if he assigned Canadians to five language groups ranging from pure English to pure French users, he could effectively predict attitudes towards parties and issues. French users saw the Liberals as closer to them on all issues, with percentage differences of around 20–25 percent between themselves and English users (1975: 170). The linguistic underpinnings of regionalism in Canada thus held firm politically through the early 1970s.

But regionalism is not just a matter of language. Using an imaginative "index of regional consciousness," Clarke et al. demonstrated that the highest regional consciousness lies in the prairie provinces and the lowest in Newfoundland, though both regions are mainly anglophonic (1979: chap. 2). Prairie regionalism bespeaks a belief that the federal government has exploited and ignored the West, has taken its abundant natural resources for granted, and has given the West little real assistance in integrating its many "New Canadians."

By contrast, consider the formerly distinctive American South. Recent American studies demonstrate that the South is no longer a distinctive bastion of conservatism and one-partyism, thanks to immigration of Northerners south, to regional industrial development, and to the emergence of blacks as a significant force in southern state Democratic parties (Black and Black 1987). However, as of 1979, Clarke reported "no support whatsoever for any argument that deregionalization, or declining regional consciousness, is taking place in Canada. The data is [sic] far more consistent with an argument that regional feeling is increasing" (Clarke et al. 1979: 44). Clarke shows that younger and better-educated Canadians are especially drawn to regionalism. Interestingly, speakers of languages other than French or English are less sensitive to regional differences than are speakers of the two "charter" languages, a fact which suggests that if "New Canadians" should drop their native tongue as a first language, they may well enter into and reproduce a regionally polarized polity.

To summarize, recent studies indicate that Britain, Canada, and the United States generally display in descending national order social welfare, regional, class, and party cleavages — the cultural faultlines along which conflictive democratic participation emerges. These findings are consistent with the cultural arguments advanced in earlier chapters.

There appears to be one major exception to the argument I have made: race in the United States. Racial polarization in the United States clearly contributes to the mounting of conflictive democratic participation. As Carmines and Stimson argue, in the 1950s "racial issues were not aligned with the party system; they cut across it. Now they are clearly aligned" (1989: 138). In the mid-1950s there was no significant difference between Democratic and Republican party identifiers in attitudes towards desegregation. By 1980, there was a 14 percent difference, with Democratic identifiers the more liberal (ibid., 150). Moreover, by 1972, black voters were almost unanimously aligned with the Democratic party throughout the country (ibid., 46).

In addition, the institutionalized individualism that dominates American culture has until recently omitted blacks. But instead of accepting their exclusion, blacks have protested successfully against it. Particularly has this been true regarding the collective representations we have examined — textbooks, advertisements, sitcoms, and corporate publications — which blacks have denounced for their insensitivity to race. Thus, blacks have *not* been absorbed by or accepting of institutionalized individualism.

Still, if Sears and his associates are correct (e.g., Sears, Hensler, and Speer, 1979: 369–84), Americans at least now apply a common value language to whites and blacks. Moreover, Sniderman and Tetlock argue (1986b: 129–150) that this language is not a cover for racism, but an actual application of color-blind political values. Recent electoral successes by moderate black Democrats, such as David Dinkins and Douglas Wilder, suggest that many white Americans will disregard race if other considerations dominate an election. Finally, former Republican Party National Chairman Lee Atwater embarked upon a serious effort to attract black voters back to the Republican party. These phenomena are consistent with what we would expect in a culture dominated by the institutionalization of individualism.

Race constitutes the most strenuous test of institutionalized individualism in the United States. If black political distinctiveness does erode, the argument in this book will receive important support. Institutionalized individualism will have once again limited conflictive democratic participation (for a different view, see Wilson 1978). But if racial polarization continues to structure American politics — especially party politics — our argument must be seriously qualified.

Cultural Configurations and Political Language

The study of political language presents formidable problems. Paradoxically, language is both too close to us and too far from us to permit easy analysis. As to closeness, language is to culture as oxygen is to breathing — the "taken for granted" which sustains and surrounds us. How then can we extract ourselves from speech so as to consider it afresh, to see it as an embodiment of culture?

Moreover, analysts of language, unless they employ the jargon of semiotics or linguistics, must use the very language they are attempting to analyze. The language which we study leaves its footprints — its *traces,* as deconstructionists put it (Balkin 1987: 743–86)—in the language *of* our study. No wonder some theorists see the analyst of language as actually language's puppet.

But how can language simultaneously be distant from us? Recent efforts to analyze language testify to the complexity of linguistic meaning. Consider literary language, the recipient of so much recent attention. Literary language is both representational and self-reflexive; reading literature comprehends "style" (the point of view of the author) and content (what the story "represents"). The problem is that different forms of analysis apply to style and content (Ruthrof 1981: chaps. 1–2).

And what exactly *is* content? Since Wittgenstein, we have recognized that even apparently pellucid language is neither purely referential nor isomorphic to some underlying reality (Pitkin 1972). A word reaches beyond itself to an unarticulated family of meanings which shadows its every usage. Moreover, words take on meaning through their opposing, though unverbalized, terms (see also Leitch 1983). This is true of literary themes as well. Thus, Hemingway's "manly" heroes become comprehensible to us because we can imagine their opposites—the "effeminate" cowards who *might* have peopled the story, but whom Hemingway left out. Thus, the boundaries of language are unclear, and certainly not coterminous with the written text.

It is not surprising that attempts to capture literary language often frustrate even the most comprehensive analysis. Roger Fowler, for example, devotes six full pages to an admittedly inadequate account of thirty-four sentences from Hemingway's short story, "The Killers" (1977: 48–54). Though informative, these six pages capture only a few elements at play in the passage. Moreover Fowler writes in a far more complex language than Hemingway himself. Six densely written pages for thirty-four typical Hemingway sentences, such as "It's twenty minutes fast," or, "It isn't ready yet." The reader can be excused for declining to venture into a comparable analysis of, say, thirty-four sentences from Joyce's *Ulysses* or Faulkner's *Absalom, Absalom*.

Why then does so astute an observer as James Boyd White enjoin us to

> seek a cultural criticism that is literary rather than theoretical in character. It should take place in the space between abstract theoretical argument on the one hand and particularized judgments of individual texts or actions on the other . . . it should be tentative and poetic, recognizing the limits of its own terms and open to possible shifts in perception and in the very language in which it is constituted. (White 1985: 125)

Put bluntly, doesn't White realize the trouble he is pushing us toward? More important, can we avoid this trouble while still doing an adequate piece of language analysis?

One step forward is to realize that much political language is a form of persuasion. Legal rules attempt to persuade citizens that a particular course of action is prudent and correct (White 1985: chap. 2). Political compromises are exhanges of mutually beneficial, persuasive promises, in a word, deals. Power threats are efforts to persuade people to comply with demands or else face dire consequences. The campaign speech is an attempt to persuade voters. The public opinion poll is a factually based persuasive argument about the state of the public's political attitudes (Marsh 1982), and so on.

Because political language is often a form of persuasion, our analysis can draw on the ancient study of rhetoric. Rhetoric, after all, is the study of persuasion; therefore, rhetoric should help us identify some of the unique persuasive devices which appear in political language.

But rhetoric points us mainly towards specific persuasive devices, such as arguments from design, synedoches, arguments from contraries, and so on (for other devices, see Hairston 1982: chap. 9; see also McCloskey 1985). There is no reason to predict any particular connection between these literary contrivances and the three cultural configurations we have been analyzing. Moreover, even if such a connection were to exist, persuasion is more than an accumulation of specific rhetorical devices. Thus, to focus solely on rhetoric is to miss the forest for the trees.

Political persuasion is more than rhetoric because politics is always about conflict in some form. For this reason the study of fiction, which also centers on conflict, is instructive (see Rabinowitz 1987). Imaginative literature uses rhetoric to create *narratives* about conflict. The same thing is true of political language, which combines narrative and rhetoric to represent power in persuasive and enlightening tales: cautionary tales, tales of vindication, morality tales, even tales of the picaresque.

Consider, for example, the campaign speech. The speaker narrates a stylized and perhaps fanciful version of his opponent's policy views. Meanwhile, he tells a heroic story about himself. He refers to certain climactic events—perhaps the intervention in Viet Nam, the bomb at Hiroshima, the March on Selma. He pictures a glowing future which can be ours if we vote for him. The speaker also narrates his version of how things work politically. A rise in the consumer price index "means" "hard times." The "inevitable" Democratic increase in taxes "means" trouble for middle-income families. The "spiraling" tax deficits "mean ruin for our children." He uses metonymy and synecdoche; he claims that the AIDS victim or the homeless child are parts of a larger problem, such as "malaise," "moral decay," a lack of "caring." He employs peripetiea—the rhetorical device of reversal—to argue that when his opponent became president things were fine, but now they're not. He divides the world into villains and heroes—perhaps it is the Sandinistas who are the villains, or perhaps, as Rogin (1987) argues, the Communists, the Indians, the Blacks, or the immigrants are our perpetual demons. He constructs a chain of cause and effect which "explains" what has happened. Perhaps American exploitation of the Third World called forth the Sandinistas, or a callous Republican administration created the homeless (Edelman 1988).

Culture rejoins us at this point. I hypothesize that a culture's configuration predisposes political narratives toward certain forms of language, or collective figures of speech. Although politicians may disagree about "the issues," as communicants in the same culture, they share the same issue language. Moreover, because they share the same culturally coded language, they can never dispute the culture itself, even though culture often *creates* the issues. For this reason, a culture may be compared to a neurosis, whose painful symptoms—in the form of issue conflicts—recur time after time, never to be fully resolved. Therefore, political issues in the United States will be fought out in a language of institutionalized individualism; political issues in Britain will be fought out in a language of conflict about ways of life; and political issues in Canada will be fought out in a language of bifurcation and truncated group solidarity.

Paul DiMaggio argues that, increasingly in modern life, symbols rather than property create power (DiMaggio 1987: 440–53). All the more important, therefore, that we understand how cultural configurations appear through political language. The Bible states, "In the Beginning there was the Word, and the word was made Flesh." But prior to the Word there was God, who turned word to flesh. Today fewer of us trace words back to God. One of the few propositions on which positivists and deconstructionists agree is that words lack a transcendental reality. But, curiously, words have not become unimportant because they lack the transcendental; they have instead become the vehicles of culture, which plays the role of God's poor substitute.

The Language of Party Reform in Britain and the United States

Our earlier discussion identified different cultural stances towards political parties in Britain and the United States. In Britain parties are represented as solidary, conflictive, class-based, and dedicated to governing. In the United States parties are represented as fluid, consensual, heterogeneous, and dedicated to representation. The question to which we now turn is whether these cultural configurations frame the language of party reform in Britain and the United States. Specifically, does debate about party reform in America embody institutionalized individualism? Does debate about party reform in Britain constitute a discussion of conflicting ways of life?

In my investigation of these questions I follow White's (1985) suggestions (see p. 191). First, I apply Roderick Hart's (1984, 1987) method of content analysis, in which theoretically relevant words in two equivalent political texts become quantitative units of investigation. The texts, of course, deal with party reform in Britain and the United States. I then return to the two texts, and after comparing some of their distinctive rhetorical devices, tease out the narrative themes which hold each together culturally. I will argue that each text is consistent with and largely shaped by the national culture from which it emerges.

The two texts I analyze are debates about party reform at two political party conventions. The first is the floor debate over seating the California and Illinois delegations to the 1972 Democratic national convention (Hixon and Rose 1972). The second is the two-day Labour party debate which adopted candidate reselection but postponed adopting a new electoral college method for choosing the Labour party leader. The latter debate took place on the floor of the Labour Party national conference in October, 1980 (Labour Party Conference 1982: 138–42, 148–52, 185–94).

These two debates decided issues of great significance. In the United States, the 1972 convention debate climaxed a period of Democratic party reform that had begun in 1964, when a largely black party delegation from Mississippi challenged the right of the regular, white-controlled Mississippi delegation to be seated at the presidential nominating convention. This event triggered a struggle over rules for seating state delegations, for choosing state delegates, and for controlling state delegations. The reform movement gained momentum at the tumultuous 1968 Democratic Convention in Chicago, where, amidst the struggle between Hubert Humphrey and Eugene McCarthy, party regulars and party insurgents, the Chicago police and anti–Viet Nam War demonstrators, there emerged further calls for party democracy.

Between 1968 and 1972 the movement for Democratic party reform spawned the so-called McGovern-Fraser Commission, which proposed major changes in the rules governing delegate selection to Democratic party conventions (Commission on Party Structure and Delegate Selection to the Democratic National Committee 1970). State Democratic parties largely implemented these proposed changes during the Democratic primary season of 1972. The challenges to the Illinois and California delegations at the 1972 convention were crucial tests of Democratic resolve to reform the party. Indeed, on the outcome of the debate hinged the fate of the entire reform effort.

In fact, however, more was at stake in this debate than the interpretation and application of reform rules, or even the attainment of greater party democracy. The presidential nomination itself hung in the balance. Both in California and in Illinois, the seated state delegations supported different candidates from their challengers. Ironically, if the convention decided to seat a California delegation pledged entirely to McGovern, it would violate one guideline the McGovern-Fraser Commission itself had proposed: namely, that a state's delegates should be distributed in proportion to the votes each candidate received in the state's primary. Applying this guideline to California would have significantly reduced McGovern's chance for the nomination, for he had won but a narrow plurality of the California vote. However, ignoring the guideline meant seating an entirely pro-McGovern California delegation, and thereby bringing McGovern's nomination within reach. McGovern therefore had to choose between his own commission's reform principle and his personal interest in winning the nomination. Ultimately, the convention seated the Illinois and California pro-McGovern delegations, in the case of California overruling its own convention officers (for a treatment, see Ranney 1975: 82–91).

Like the Democratic convention debate, the Labour party conference debate also culminated a period of intense party self-examination. Following the first Thatcher victory, Labour found itself in a wrenching struggle over internal reform (for an account, see Shaw 1988: chaps. 9 and 10). In the debate we examine, the party conference adopted two important policy changes. First, the conference required all Labour candidates for Parliament to submit to mandatory reselection, in which local party activists could play a crucial role. Second, the conference removed the choice of party leader from the hands of the Parliamentary Labour party, envisioning instead an electoral college composed of labor unions, constituency parties, affiliated organizations, and the PLP. Moreover, like the Democratic debate of 1972, this debate also was complicated by uncertainty about party leadership—in this case James Callaghan, whom Mrs. Thatcher had soundly defeated in the 1979 general election.

What did these two debates ultimately decide? The Democrats decided to seat an entirely pro-McGovern California delegation, overruling the Convention Credentials Committee. In so doing, the Democrats exempted California from the McGovern-Fraser rules. In addition, the convention accepted the Credential Committee's seating of contested Illinois delegates, on the grounds that the Illinois Democratic party had discriminated against minority groups in its delegation, and had engaged in the newly prohibited practice of "slate-making," that is, predetermining the contestants for convention delegate.

As indicated above, the British debates established mandatory candidate reselection in all constituencies. A management committee of the local constituency party must decide whether it wishes to renominate its sitting Labour MP as a constituency candidate in the general election. Other potential candidates have the right to challenge the sitting MP for the management committee's endorsement. In addition, the party accepted the principle of an electoral college for selecting the party leader.

These decisions represented efforts towards greater party democracy. As Byron Shafer has pointed out, party reform can reflect either of two perspectives, both of which are related to culture and conflictive democratic participation. The first perspective sees parties as instruments of democratic governance only if they remain strong, disciplined organizations. The second perspective "emphasizes the *obstacles* to democratic governance presented by party organizations as traditionally constituted" (Shafer 1983: 99). This perspective de-emphasizes parties as unified organizations in favor of lowering barriers to membership participation. Reformers drawn to this second perspective strive above all to escape Michels' "iron law of oligarchy," which states that any mass political party must become internally undemocratic (for a sympathetic treatment, see Crotty 1978).

These two versions of party reform contradict each other. Indeed, according to Robert McKenzie, in making the party leader formally responsible to the whole Labour party rather than to the Parliamentary Labour party alone, the reforms substitute private for public control over policy. As McKenzie puts it,

> If a political party is successful in an election and its leaders form a government then, *whatever the party's internal arrangements . . . , the party leaders . . . become the chief*

decision-makers within the political system. And almost every political system has rules which provide that the government and ruling party in the legislature cannot be subject to the direction of any body of political decision-makers outside the legislature. (1982: 195, emphasis mine)

If McKenzie is correct, the Labour party's efforts to lodge control over its leader outside Parliament prevents the party from acting as a legitimate instrument of democratic governance. A Labour Prime Minister cannot be responsible both to Parliament and to the Labour party.

In point of fact, *four* conceptions of party reform appear in the two texts we examine: increased participation; preferential representation; demographic representation; and constituency control of party policy. Party democracy as *increased participation* requires that more candidates run for party office, that more partisans become active in the party, that more citizens join the party, and that more citizens vote. Party democracy as *preferential representation* attempts to incorporate a wider range of views in the party, by connecting such views to their numerical support within the party. Party democracy as *demographic representation* argues that party leaders should reflect accurately the size of important subgroups within the party. Finally, party democracy as *constituency control of leaders* assumes that leadership actions must reflect the views of party activists.

These forms of party democracy often conflict with each other. Consider, for example, preferential representation and demographic representation. "[T]he 1972 [Democratic] convention was a hodgepodge of representative inconsistencies. It closely approached full representation-by-quotas for blacks, women, and youth . . . but 57% of its first-ballot vote and the nomination went to a candidate who had won only 27% of the popular votes cast in the primaries . . ." (Ranney 1975: 196). Thus, although the delegations were demographically representative of important subgroups in the party, these delegations did not accurately express the candidate preferences of voters. In essence, this conflict was the issue in the California debate we will shortly discuss.

Or consider increased participation and constituency control of leaders. Increased participation may permit small groups of radicals, such as the Labour party's Militant Tendency (a Trotskyist group), to exercise power disproportionate to their numbers over candidate reselection. The constituency activists may then select candidates who are to the left (or right) of most party members. The majority of party members may thus be denied full control over their leaders. The fear that expanded participation would render the Labour party *less* open to constituency control haunted the debate over candidate reselection in the 1980 Labour party conference.

How were these issues debated in the 1972 Democratic national convention and in the 1980 Labour party conference? Did the two debates differ in ways our analysis of cultural configurations would predict?

Our initial investigation of these questions involves an adaptation of Hart's technique for studying verbal styles (Hart 1984, 1987). I created a few "dictionaries" of frequently used words in the two debates. Appropriately classified, these words become examples of the two societies' cultural configurations. I then simply counted these words as they appeared in the debates. But to make sense of these word counts, we must relate them to British and American culture.

Earlier we observed that American culture places emphasis upon individuals rather than groups. Therefore, references both to individuals and to personality characteristics (such as feelings, beliefs, and opinions) should appear more frequently in the American than in the British convention debates. By contrast, British culture encourages references to aggregates, such as the party itself, social class, "unions" and the "movement." Our first hypothesis is that references to such aggregates will dominate the British text, and references to individuals will dominate the American discourse.

Of course, the British debates considered a proposal to give unions as such power in leadership selection; no such proposal was discussed in the Democratic Party. Yet this distinction is less important than it at first seems. The substance of the Democratic party debates revolved around demands that the party include specific subgroups more completely. Therefore, if anything, the Democratic party debates actually *encouraged* references to aggregates, albeit within a culture of institutionalized individualism that is normally ill-disposed to such considerations.

We also argued that debating ways of life in British culture creates sharper conflicts than does institutionalized individualism in the United States. Therefore, we hypothesize that specific references to conflict and to related terms, such as *struggle, attack,* and so forth will be more frequent in the British debate than in the American debate. By contrast, American culture blurs the public/private cleavage and the collectivity/ self-interest boundary. Parties more often appear as producers of consensus than as instruments of polarization. Therefore, we expect terms such as *compromise, consensus, consent,* and their relatives (e.g., *harmony, peace,* etc.) to appear more often in the American text than in the British text.

Third, institutionalized individualism in the United States promotes sensitivity to individual opportunity, access, participation, and representation, rather than to public control over leaders or policy. A culture of institutionalized individualism favors process as much as outcome; the individual must take part; leaders must respond; access must exist; the party must be open; communication must occur. By contrast, in a cultural configuration more hospitable to group solidarity, popular control over elites is paramount. The term *democracy* itself will be used mainly to describe actual control rather than just access. And, since British culture promotes conflictive democratic participation, we would expect less use of the term *democracy* at all in the American debate.

Fourth, a culture of group — especially party — solidarity naturally should emphasize unity. After all, without unity, neither the party nor any other group can struggle effectively against its enemies. Hence, we would expect the term *unity* to appear more often in the British debate than in the American debate.

Finally, we need to consider abstract political symbols, which include such terms as *country, fairness, equality, freedom, law, rights, socialism,* and *capitalism.* Symbolic anthropology suggests that, being comparatively conflictive, British culture will produce highly polarized political debate. In turn, polarization encourages symbolic mediation. Hence, we would expect to discover more use of symbolic terms in the British debate than in the American debate. At the same time, however, the *institutional* nature of American individualism also promotes resort to symbols. Lacking strong group representations, American culture adopts institutional formulations of political events. But institutions often disseminate symbols in an attempt to achieve legitimacy. Symbolism may, therefore, permeate the American debate; indeed, symbols and symbolic usages may actually be more frequent in the American than in the British texts.

Table 6.1 below sets out the data, based on a total of 11,200 words in the British debate and 6,860 in the California and Illinois credentials fights. The British debate makes up 62 percent of the data; word usage must be compared to this base figure in order to discover the relative frequency of particular word classes in each text.

Examination of Table 6.1 supports several of our hypotheses, but also reveals a number of surprises. To begin with, as hypothesized, *party, class, unions, movement,* and *group* appear disproportionately in the British debate. Seventy-three percent of the party and class references are British, as are an overwhelming 96 percent of the *union, movement,* and *group* references. Reference to specific minorities appears

Table 6.1 Word Frequencies in Credentials Committee Challenges, Illinois and California Debates, 1972 Democratic National Convention; and in British Labour Party Conference Debates on Candidate Reselection and Electoral College, 1980.

References (by subject)	British Labour Party	California		Illinois	Total
Personality					
individual	3	0		1	4
self	1	1		1	3
ourselves	3	8		0	11
personality	10	0		0	10
growth	4	0		0	4
development	2	0		0	2
esteem	0	0		0	0
feel	12	1		1	14
believe/belief	19	1		13	33
opinion	0	0		1	1
confidence	1	1		0	2
attitude	0	0		0	0
Totals	55 (68%)	12	+	17 = 29 (32%)	84
Group					
party	211	24		54	289
class	13	3		0	16
Totals	224 (73%)	27	+	54 = 81 (27%)	305
union	54	0		0	54
movement	24	1		0	25
group	7	1		0	8
Totals	85 (96%)	2	+	0 = 2 (4%)	87
Specific Groups					
young	5	8		15	28
blacks	0	5		15	20
women	1	6		43	50
old	1	1		3	5
whites	1	0		2	3
males	2	0		2	3
Chicano	0	8		0	8
Latin America	0	0		6	6
Mexican-American	0	2		0	2
Jewish	0	0		1	1
grassroot Democrats	0	2		0	2
Totals	10 (8%)	32	+	89 =121 (92%)	131

Table 6.1 (*continued*)

References (by subject)	British Labour Party	California	Illinois	Total
Conflict				
conflict	0	0	0	0
struggle	1	0	2	3
attack	4	1	0	5
compete	0	0	0	0
fight	22	3	1	26
argue	19	0	2	21
dominate	0	0	0	0
enemy	5	0	0	5
defend	3	2	1	6
opposition	8	0	4	12
conspiracy	2	0	0	2
elite	4	0	0	4
Totals	68 (76%)	6	+ 15 = 21 (24%)	89
Democracy				
democracy	59	3	7	69
participate	6	7	8	21
elect	97	0	58	155
select	55	5	18	78
vote	60	28	53	141
Totals	277 (60%)	43	+ 144 = 187 (40%)	464
Representation				
represent	13	10	12	35
respond/responsible	9	0	5	14
openness	1	2	23	26
opportunity	13	7	2	22
access	0	0	2	2
Totals	36 (38%)	19	+ 44 = 63 (62%)	99
Symbols				
country/nation	22	5	6	33
fairness	5	2	11	18
equality	4	0	1	5
freedom	0	1	10	11
law	0	15	13	28
right/rights	12	1	2	15
socialism	15	0	0	15
Totals	58 (46%)	24	+ 43 = 67 (54%)	125

(*continued on following page*)

Table 6.1 (*continued*)

References (by subject)	British Labour Party	California	Illinois			Total
Consensus						
agree	12	0	3			15
compromise	1	0	2			3
harmony	1	0	0			1
peace	0	0	0			0
solution	3	2	0			7
(resolve)	2	0	0			
friends	8	0	0			8
comrades	33	0	0			33
share	1	0	0			1
accept	15	1	0			16
consent	0	0	0			0
Totals	74 (87%)	3	+	8 (13%)	= 11	85
Unity						
Purpose: to struggle against outside forces	6	0	0			6
Purpose: to create harmony within party	24	0	2			26
Totals	30 (95%)	0	+	2 (5%)	= 2	32

mainly in the American text, as might be expected from the Democrats' emphasis upon demographic representation in the Illinois and California delegations; but on balance, of all group references, 68 percent appeared in the British text, slightly more than the base rate of 62 percent.

Our first surprise, however, occurs when we compare group references with references to personality. Surprisingly, the British also refer to personality slightly more than the base rate would predict. There apparently is no necessary tension between a group frame of reference and an individual frame of reference. Notice, however, that within the Labour party debates, references to party and class are four times more frequent than references to personality (224–55), while within the Democratic debate, the comparable ratio is but 3–1 (81–29). In summary, our first hypotheses gains substantial support: the British are more given to group references.

We also hypothesized that the British debates would contain disproportionately many conflict references. The data support this hypothesis. Of the 89 conflict references in the two texts, 68 (or 76 percent) are British.

But again we encounter a surprise, for references to consensus are also more frequent, relatively speaking, in the British text. A full 87 percent of consensus references (74) occur in the Labour party debates. However, if one eliminates the largely honorific term *comrade,* the British use less consensual language than do the Americans (41–44), as we hypothesized.

Our third hypothesis receives unequivocal confirmation. As expected, terms referring to representation (*represent, respond, openness, opportunity,* and *access*) appear considerably more frequently in the American debates than in the British debate. Although the American debates comprise only 38 percent of the word total, a full 62 percent of the 99 references to representation occur in the Democratic convention. Moreover, of the 21 uses of *participation,* 15 are American. And, as expected, the British use the term *democracy* far more often than do the Americans (59–10). To the Americans, party reform means representation, openness, and participation, as would be expected in a culture of institutionalized individualism.

As our fourth hypothesis suggested, the British also pay more attention to party unity than do the Americans. For the British, intraparty unity is meant mainly to perform internal functions, but it also augments the struggle against the Conservatives. Of the 32 references to party unity, an overwhelming 30 are British.

Finally, contrary to symbolic anthropology, the Labour party debate does not resort heavily to symbols as conflict-mediation devices. Instead, 54 percent (67) of the symbolic references occur in the American text. Particularly revealing are the three most widely used symbols in the American text: *freedom, law,* and *fairness.* Together these three symbols portray party reform as a rule-governed, impartial competition among unconstrained delegates, an image of reform which fully reconciles institutionalization with individualism. Not surprisingly, the British are the only disputants to mention *socialism;* more surprising, however, is the frequent British reference to *rights.* This finding seems anomalous, for *rights* appears to fit more comfortably in the American culture of institutionalized individualism. Apparently, a culture of group conflict need not exclude individualism.

It could be argued that these differences in language merely reflect the different political conditions that each convention confronted. After all, the Democratic party had already adopted the McGovern-Fraser reforms before the convention, while the Labour party was actually debating *new* rules. Therefore, the more conflictive character of the Labour debate is wholly predictable; adopting new rules is inherently more difficult than applying established rules.

This argument is unconvincing. The McGovern-Fraser rules were new and controversial, and their interpretation open to debate. Moreover, reluctance to apply the rules (as charged by some in the debates) raised bitter charges of betrayal and hypocrisy, charges that could not have existed at all had the rules not been previously adopted. Therefore, the impetus to fundamental conflict was as strong in the American as in the British case, but the outcome—for cultural reasons—was different.

Our next task is to pursue a qualitative analysis of the debates as self-contained narratives. As Lucaites and Condit argue, "narratives need to do more than simply plot conflicts between and among characters. They must also offer some formal resolution or solution to the crises they portray" (1985: 99). Our first step, therefore, is to discover how the two debates construct and resolve their basic conflicts. As we will see, the narratives portray both conflict *and* resolution quite differently; significantly, *within* each debate, opponents and allies share the same conflict framework and strive toward culturally equivalent resolutions. Though opposed on the substantive issues at stake, they share a culture. Therefore, cultural differences appear *between* the two countries' debates, not between participants within a debate.

Both debates employ a governing metaphor to frame the conflict. For the Americans the governing metaphor is that of a *game*. Appropriately, the game metaphor appears at the very outset of the debate, when the first participant, Gaylord Nelson of Wisconsin, argues the case for overturning the Credentials Committee Report on California. Nelson states:

> We set up a commission [the McGovern-Fraser Commission]; it examined our procedures; it drew up rules and we all adopted them. Everyone knew exactly what they meant; everyone played by those rules; nobody questioned their validity until somebody won and somebody lost. (Hixon and Rose 1972: 175–76)

This short excerpt reveals much about the way rhetorical devices shape political controversy. Note particularly how Nelson slips from an initially neutral recounting of recent history (i.e., the first sentence) into terms which evoke the game metaphor (e.g., *rules, played, won, lost*).

In fact, however, Nelson is not actually the first speaker to frame the debate as a game. Instead, appropriately enough, a "neutral" umpire introduces the game metaphor. The temporary chairman of the convention, Mrs. Patricia Harris, introduces the debate in the following way:

The task is here in this great hall and the time is now. Shall we change the rules by which the game was played? That is the question. (176)

The significance of the game metaphor lies in the fact that, for the game to proceed, the players must cooperate with each other. Thus, whatever their other differences, opponents are likely to remain in league with each other, even after one side eventually wins. Whether opponents *will* remain together, however, depends upon the "fairness" of the game's rules, as well as the fairness of rule application. Understandably, then, the game metaphor encourages the debaters to pursue the goal of fairness and impartiality.

One way to insure fairness for one's own position (and to advantage this position substantively) is to employ the time-honored rhetorical argument for balance and symmetry (McClosky 1985: 109). A common political version of this argument is a demand for compensation. Here is one version of the argument in Willie Brown's appeal that the entirely pro-McGovern California delegation be seated:

> Seat my delegation. I did it for you in Mississippi in 1964, in Georgia in 1968, and it is now California in 1972. I deserve no less. Give me back my delegation. (177)

Of course, both sides can employ this device. Thus, Doris Davis argues against Brown and in favor of the Credentials Committee position, claiming that as follows:

> The problem here is the same things that we fought for in 1968 and I thought we resolved it with Mississippi but the same liberals are trying to put it down on us again. They are not going to run this same game in 1972 that we changed the unit rule to let them know that 100 percent cannot be represented by 44% of the delegates. (180)

Only one participant in the debate attempted to challenge the game metaphor. However, this lone challenger eventually succumbs to the metaphor himself, recasting only the *players*. In supporting the Credentials Committee position, Robert Begam of Arizona observes:

> Now we hear that the rules of the game should not be changed after the game is played. Let's analyze that. *Is this a game or are we about the serious business of selecting a Presidential candidate* [emphasis mine]? Who are the players in the game — the candidates? I submit no. I submit to you that the players in the

> game are the voters, the voters. [applause]. And we should not
> reduce 1.9 million voters to spectators, which is what a yes vote
> would do here. (178)

But if the voters too are players, the game embraces everyone. Who then
is left to make the nomination a more "serious business" than a game?

Another method of achieving the fair application of the game's rules
is through *openness*, which insures that everyone who wants to play
can do so. The argument for openness employs the McGovern-Fraser
Commission's goal of a more accessible process of nomination. Here,
for example, is George Shipley, arguing in support of the challenge to
the seated Illinois delegation:

> All that is required to be a candidate in Illinois is for someone
> to get 600 signatures and they are on the ticket . . . They [the
> Credentials Committee] said that we had private meetings,
> which is untrue . . . I know that our laws in Illinois are open
> and free for anyone to be a candidate and our so-called or-
> ganization has no control over who is going to run and who is
> going to be elected. (197)

Shipley's opponent, Jean Wallein, also employs openness as a measure
of fairness. Speaking in favor of the seated Illinois delegation, she argues:

> The issue in this majority report is abundantly clear. Just
> because the final phase of the delegate selection process is fair
> and open, does that mean that the whole process is fair and
> open? In this case, the answer is no. Just as when you start with
> bad yeast you wind up with bad bread, therefore, when you
> start with a bad, discriminatory, and closed slate-making pro-
> cess, you wind up with bad delegate selection. The delegate
> selection process must be open and free at all levels. (198)

Ultimately, the participants' search for a fair, balanced, open game
demands that impartial institutions adjudicate the struggle. As Frank
Kermode notes in the case of more deeply felt oppositions—the Old
Testament struggle between the pure and the polluted—"Between the
opposites clean and unclean there are inserted—intercalated—figures of
sexual or magical force" (Kermode 1979: 133). The Democratic party
is not the Old Testament; therefore, no "sexual or magical force" finds
its way into Democratic party debates. Instead of magic, Democrats
settle for mundane institutions to insure fair, balanced, open competition. Two such institutions emerge in the debate: law (see Arnold 1935),
and the party itself.

Law can mediate the California challenge because, prior to the convention, the courts had considered a legal challenge to the winner-take-all primary which the McGovern-Fraser Commission permitted only in California. Robert Begam relies upon the U.S. Supreme Court's decision in the case to support the Credentials Committee position:

> That action was dismissed for the same reason that last week
> the Federal Courts right up to the United States Supreme Court
> said no, the Democratic Party makes its own rules. (178)

In Begam's view, the lawsuit permitted one legitimate institution (the Court) to confer on another legitimate institution (the Democratic party) the power to regulate party affairs. Thanks to the legal system, the party in convention has the right to seat any delegation it chooses. Law thus legitimizes party decisions.

For her part, Marilyn Clancy observes during the Illinois debate that the game metaphor requires the *party* to play the role of umpire:

> My experience over the last few months has been that of a new-
> comer who is a woman playing in a serious game with male
> party officials who have been playing in the game for a long time
> unchallenged, because they made up the rules as they went along
> and had all the necessary equipment, the playing field and the
> scoring devices. I am delighted that the umpires remain free and I
> am hopeful that they will always remain faithful to the Call to
> the 1972 Democratic Nominating Convention, in spite of threats
> of some of the players to take their ball and go home . . . (202)

It is worth wondering whether a party which portrays itself as a neutral umpire can also be a fighting force—an army in the struggle of opposing ideologies. Can the cool objectivity of the referee fuel the passion of the ideologue? Perhaps the answer to this question lies in the fact that ideological rhetoric—disfavored in a culture of institutionalized individualism—never emerges at all in the credentials debate. Ideology vanishes once the game metaphor triumphs.

If by chance the courts and the party cannot fairly arbitrate the struggle, American culture offers a last resort: youth. Young people are not an organized, partisan force; rather, they are spontaneous, free, and impartial. They are therefore culturally appropriate for the convention. Indeed, just as the children on *Family Ties* or *The Cosby Show* keep their parents in line, so also can "American youth" keep the Democratic party in line. No wonder Doris Davis closes the debate on the California challenge by proclaiming:

> Our youth are looking at us tonight. They are saying that all of these politicians are hypocrites and if you don't vote no, you are going to show them what they are saying is right. (180)

If law and party serve as the *institutional* terms of the Democrats' cultural equation, then children serve as the *individualistic* term of the equation. Thus, the debate both *displays* institutionalized individualism rhetorically to the delegates in the hall, and *reproduces* institutionalized individualism for the television audience at home.

The British Labour party debate is quite different in style and substance from the Democratic party debates. The opposing Labour factions see the struggle not as a game played by individual competitors, but as a war fought by groups. Near the beginning of the debate, a passionate supporter of candidate reselection, Ivor Crees, clearly enunciates the war metaphor:

> Party workers and Party members have become aware that they are not, nor have they ever been, a meaningful part of our movement. They have been used by the PLP (the Parliamentary Labour Party) and Party Leaders, past and present, as election campaign fodder — just as working people have been used as factory fodder by industrialists and the flower of our youth used as gun fodder by the generals. (Labour 1982: 149)

Just as Gaylord Nelson in the Democratic convention slid effortlessly into the game metaphor, so does Crees effortlessly glide from a comparatively moderate observation about party members into increasingly warlike images of conflict. He first compares political campaigns to a war in which campaign workers serve as infantry ("election . . . fodder"). Next he compares this "war" to industrial exploitation, the ideological nerve center of Labour party history. He concludes by comparing party leaders to imperialist generals sacrificing their troops in foreign wars. Like a deconstructionist, Crees metaphorically turns the Labour party on its head, portraying the party's usual heroes as actually its villains (Balkin 1987: 743–87).

The sheer power of the war metaphor stimulates a resort both to historical arguments and to multiple rhetorical devices. Whereas in the American text references to history functioned mainly as appeals for compensation and balanced *processes*, in the British case historical references serve to advance *substantive* policy positions. Here are two examples:

[Gavin Strang] Let us also dismiss the argument that because there is a difference of view about the composition of the college, we should not have one. Let us settle that later. It is a bit like saying that we should not have nationalized the steel industry because there were different views about the representation of the workers on the board. No! (150)

[Mike Rogers] I have heard a lot of shouting this afternoon. I was also reminded yesterday that we are celebrating the 600th anniversary of the Peasants' Revolt. I felt yesterday like an agricultural worker who in the 19th century was shown the possibility of a vote, only to have it removed by the barons and by the princes of this country. I felt cross last night. Am I not an adult that I can help select the next Prime Minister of the United Kingdom? (188)

Rogers and Strang are especially skillful rhetoricians. Rogers uses history to evoke the specter of illegitimate class conflict *within* the party. Strang rests his appeal on an historical symbol of Labour success, that is, nationalization. Both arguments are powerful within a culture which, as we saw earlier, esteems tradition.

The war metaphor also stimulates analogies to nature. The most elemental of all cultural conflicts is that between nature and civilization. Therefore, the more bitter the political conflict—and the "war" over reform in the Labour Party *is* bitter—the more tempted opponents are to use elemental imagery. Here are two images of nature:

the issue of democracy is not something dreamed up by tiny conspiracies or something which floated down from space. It is rooted in the experience of working people within and without our movement. . . . The question of why we say this Party is so unique is that this Party is the only mass social democratic party which is actually rooted in the trade union movement. (Pat Wall, arguing in favor of the electoral college, 154–55)

I represent the true Labour Party in Smethwick, not the Workers' Revolutionary Party, nor the militant Trots (applause). They have infiltrated so many constituency parties, as you know [applause]. Madam chairman, the baying of the beast betrays its presence; you can hear them. (Andrew Faulds, arguing against the electoral college, 186)

Wall embeds his support for the electoral college in a narrative about the naturally benign roots of the Labour party. To Faulds, however, the nature of the party is not at all benign; instead, nature has unleashed the "beasts" of baying Trotskyism, who have "infiltrated" the civilized Labour movement. Indeed, so bitter is the Labour debate that participants not only disparage opposing *arguments*, a quite acceptable rhetorical device (McCloskey 1985: 127; see also Bennett and Feldman 1981: chap. 6), but also disparage opponents as *persons*. For example, later in his statement, Faulds attacks by name Tony Benn, a major left-Labour spokesman: "We know where most of the leadership contenders stand. . . . None of them has welshed on the Labour Government they have served in. But what of the Rt. Honorable Anthony Wedgwood Benn?" [cheers] (186) At this point, the Chair prevents Faulds from continuing, on grounds that he is attacking an individual, rather than debating an issue.

Another indication of the debate's virulence is the tendency of the British to question their opponents' grasp of "reality." After all, people who are out of touch with reality can hardly be parties to an American-style compromise. Crees employs this tactic by arguing that Parliamentary party leaders cannot dismiss candidate reselection on the grounds that the policy lacks "realism." To the contrary, "If they think the hallowed halls of Westminster are the real world they should come out and work in a geriatric or psychiatric ward for a few months. Have they tried working on the corporation dust cart lately? When did they last muck out the cows?" (149) By suggesting that MP's rather than ordinary party workers are out of touch with reality, Crees effectively discredits the "brains" of the party. Once again he proves himself a skillful deconstructionist in a debate whose bitterness encourages deconstruction.

The war metaphor also encourages participants to employ images of religion and ritual. War, after all, is a life-or-death matter; religion and ritual are therefore appropriate (for a literary study, see Fussell 1975). Here are two interesting examples of the sacred in play:

> [Denis Howell arguing against mandatory reselection] They [his opponents] are not in practical politics at all. They are the high priests of the theology that we have in the movement now. If it was possible for them to frame constitutional changes about MP's they would provide for the whole gamut of the ritual. We should be having confessionals and penitence and absolution. (138)

[Michael English on choosing a new Labour leader in the
case of the leader's death during a Parliamentary sitting]
There is a tradition that upon one occasion a great decision
was taken by each one of 30 individuals separately contributing a single piece of silver, not by a majority. I hope
that on this occasion this Party Conference will stick to what
it decided . . . (187–88).

Finally, the British debate is redolent with suspicions of schism, dis-
sidence, heresy, and disloyalty. Because a war metaphor is inherently
more conflictive than a game metaphor, opponents will naturally view
each other as potential traitors, secretly abetting the party's enemies
(Edelman 1988). In 1980 such fears were understandable. As a consequence, in part, of these reforms, four right-wing Labour party leaders
(Shirley Williams, David Owen, Roy Jenkins, and Bill Rogers) did in
fact defect, and shortly formed the moderate Social Democratic Party.

From a literary standpoint, a schism is an extreme political version
of the necessary narrative distinction between insiders and outsiders
(Scholes 1985: 53). In the case of the Democratic party debates, this
distinction is weak. In fact, the goal of party *openness*, which characterized the McGovern-Fraser reforms, renders the distinction itself problematic. This is because "the McGovern-Fraser commission . . . had little
to say about its underlying conception of party membership" (Ranney
1975: 150). The reforms, in an effort to facilitate openness and participation, intended to make the boundary between insiders and outsiders maximally flexible. Under these conditions, "schism" becomes
a narratively unlikely device.

By contrast, in the more solidary context of British culture, party reform focuses attention on the issue of party membership and party
loyalty. Therefore, to prove themselves loyal party members becomes
a chief goal for delegates; correspondingly, the motive to rid the party
of those who are disloyal is equally strong. Indeed, from an anthropological standpoint, purging the party cleanses it and reinfuses it with
power. No wonder Sam McCluskle imputes disloyalty and schismatic
tendencies to a previous speaker, Joe Ashton: "you get Joe Ashton com-
ing on that rostrum and telling us that Roy Jenkins, if he starts a middle
party, would have 25 MP's who are already members of the Labour
Party. Why don't you join them?" (142) No wonder other delegates strive
to escape the label of *outsider* or *infiltrator*. One is Andrew Allenby,
who offers a mini-autobiography: "I joined the Labour Party at the age
of 15. I joined the Labour Party to fight for socialism because it is what

the working people of this country need. . . . I have not infiltrated this Party. I have joined this Party to fight for socialism and I will fight for it anywhere" (187).

Every narrative must resolve the conflicts it embodies. In the Democratic convention debates, a combination of symbols—law, party, and youth—helped provide a resolution. Because Labour's conflict is more severe—and a war metaphor more inflammatory than a game metaphor—the debate might destroy the party utterly. The situation is precarious. How does Labour attempt to resolve the bitter conflicts of an internecine war?

As our quantitative analysis demonstrated, references to party unity are common in the Labour party debate. Unity in fact serves as a symbol of conflict resolution. Rhetorically, the Labour combatants continually work to confine *within* the party the struggle they so vigorously promote. A principal argument along this line maintains that party reform actually promotes unity. For example, Larry Brooks claims that, "The traditional methods of selection of parliamentary candidates— the subject of the debate at this point in time . . . has [caused] and continues to cause deep resentment and bitterness—that eats into the very heart of our party. . . . Unity can only be created by ensuring that progress is made on each of the key constitutional issues before us this week" (141). Thus, to Brooks, party reform *creates* unity out of preexistent struggle.

But the main argument for party unity is the necessity for Labour to join forces against a well-defined and ideologically polar opposition: the Conservatives. Consequently, there are more references to party unity against electoral opponents in the Labour debates than in the Democratic party debates. For example, to oppose mandatory reselection, Joe Ashton welds together the inside/outside metaphor, party unity, and hostility to the Tories. Ashton argues:

> you are letting a Trojan horse into this Party you will live to regret for many a long year. What this Party needs is unity. It needs unity to fight the next election, and mandatory reselection is not a recipe for unity. (141)

As symbolic anthropology would suggest, one solution to bitter internal conflict is the creation of a powerful external enemy whom both parties to the conflict fear (for a similar pattern, see Rosaldo 1984: 150). The process of psychological projection—in this case, projecting the Conservatives as imminent foe—helps restore internal unity.

A second promoter of party unity during the debate turns out to be the press. Various speakers charge that the press has deliberately exaggerated Labour party divisions, portrayed the party as hopelessly sundered, and intentionally assisted the Conservatives. Indeed, some speakers claim that the press is simply an *extension* of the Conservative party, which uses its journalistic privileges to "infiltrate" the party conference and advance Tory interests. The conference must unite in order to thwart the press's nefarious scheme. Here are three versions of this argument:

> [Eric Heffer] You would imagine, reading some of the articles, that we were trying to change things in such a way that we were not trying to improve democracy but bring about some Eastern European state. (190)

> [Joe Ashton] Have you seen the Tory press attacking the idea of mandatory re-selection? . . . The media cannot wait for mandatory re-selection because they will have Prentice sagas [a reference to Reg Prentice's defection from Labour] right through the country, right up to the next election. (140)

> [Andrew Allenby] People tell us, "We don't want the gutter press to put this out for the next 12 months telling us our Party is useless, disunited, and all the rest of it. We don't want the gutter press to do that." (187)

The Labour party must unite rhetorically to fight its many powerful enemies. By contrast, the Democratic party need not unite rhetorically, for it seeks mainly to represent its voters fairly and to encourage increased participation. Labour's emphasis upon external conflict helps it to manage its bitter internal struggle; in doing so, it portrays itself as *generally* prone to ideological debate. The Democrats' emphasis upon openness avoids internal sectarianism, but makes the party ideologically incoherent and incapable of effective external conflict. As we can see, each party embraces the distinctive fate which suits its national culture.

The Language of Bilingual Education in Canada and the United States

James Boyd White argues that in court cases and poetry, "the text can make its own language of meaning, its own internal discourse, out of the larger materials the writer has inherited. One function of a text in both fields is in fact to give special and related meanings to sets of words that carry with them in ordinary usage a wide and uncertain range of possible significance and to make these new meanings available to others" (1985: 112). White's argument can also be applied to the written reports of government commissions. The principal purpose of such reports is to reconstruct the language of particular political conflicts so as to gather support for the commission's policy recommendations (Lipsky and Olson 1977).

The subject of the two government reports to which we now turn is bilingual education. Each report is both a policy recommendation and what I have elsewhere called a cultural *display* (Merelman 1988: 335–55). As a policy recommendation, each report advocates particular educational and political ends. As a cultural display, each report trims its policy recommendations into a "fitting" cultural pattern, and in so doing, "displays" its country's culture, much as a peacock displays its plumage. The challenge of the commission report in each case is to mesh the cultural and the political, and thereby to persuade its audience.

Both as policy issue and as cultural artifact, bilingual education commands our attention. A generous immigration policy has attracted to Canada many "new Canadians" who speak neither French nor English (Harney 1988: 51–99). These immigrants must become part of Canada linguistically, a task complicated by the fact that "Canada" is itself a contested linguistic concept. From Quebec's Quiet Revolution of the 1960s to the Referendum on Sovereignty Association in 1982, the relationship between French and English in Canadian schools was an object of heated debate. Language remains an important issue, as reflected in contemporary debate about the form of association between Canadian regions. Ultimately, the resolution of the struggle between Francophones and Anglophones will decisively shape language education for "new Canadians"–and old.

Meanwhile, since 1965, American immigration has shifted dramatically from Europe to the Orient and Latin America (Morris 1985). With increasing numbers of Latinos entering the United States, bilingual education became a prominent issue, particularly in the Southwest. Unlike previous immigrant groups, Mexican Americans remain physically proximate to their native land. They could easily maintain their native language, especially given their continued kinship ties to Mexico. In short, they present a unique linguistic situation in the history of American immigration.

This alteration in immigration occurred during a period of heightened civil rights consciousness in the United States. The period created sensitivity to the relationship between language usage, social status, and minority rights. Many civil rights groups argued that retaining one's native language is a right every immigrant should enjoy. Others observed that school prohibitions on native language usage consigned minorities who did not command "respectable" English to the bottom of the academic heap (Stein 1986). The result was an unjust perpetuation of inequality.

The core of language issues, of course, is the question of national identity and national allegiance. For many people, the ability and willingness of minority groups to speak the national language symbolizes the group's commitment to its adopted country. Small wonder, then, that bilingual education should attract the student of culture and politics.

One of the documents we examine in this analysis is book 2 ("Education") of the Canadian Royal Commission Report on *Bilingualism and Biculturalism* (abridged), which originally appeared in 1969 (Innis 1973). We will compare this document with the second chapter ("Language Minority Students and Equal Educational Opportunity") of the 1975 United States Commission on Civil Rights Report entitled *A Better Chance to Learn: Bilingual-Bicultural Education* (United States Commission on Civil Rights 1975).

Of the two reports, the Canadian was the more influential. The Royal Commission's study not only helped reform Canadian educational policy, but also reshaped the entire range of Anglo-French relations. Hugh R. Innis, one of the Canadian Commissioners, observed that "the Commission's work has produced changes. . . . The Official Language Act of 1969 gave French and English equal status as official languages of the Parliament and Government of Canada. The ground work was laid for the bilingual districts which we had recommended in the first volume of the Report" (Innis 1973, "Foreword"). Most Canadian scholars agree that the "Bi and Bi" report was a watershed in relations between Anglo-Canadians and French Canadians.

By contrast, the U.S. Commission on Civil Rights report was only one among several Commission influences on the 1978 Congressional reauthorization of the Bilingual Education Act (Amendment to Title VII of the Elementary and Secondary Education Act of 1965). As Colman Stein, Jr., described the Commission's influence, "the U.S. Commission on Civil Rights declared itself in favor of bilingual education in the mid-1970s and uncovered important information on program operations in its hearings and research efforts" (1986: 56). The Commission's 1978 report was an important first statement of the federal government's intent to implement the U.S. Supreme Court's Lau decision

(1974), which outlawed the forcing of non-English-speaking students to confront only English in school, on the grounds that such a practice denied students a "meaningful opportunity to participate in the public education program" (as quoted in Stein 1986: 37). The Commission's report recommended bilingual education as an appropriate response to the Lau decision, and Congress incorporated many of the Commission's arguments into its 1978 reauthorization of the Bilingual Education Act.

Though both Commission reports recommend bilingual education, they define the concept in different cultural terms. In an important 1971 endorsement of the Bilingual, BiCultural Commission's Report, Prime Minister Trudeau stated, "Although there are two official languages, there is no official culture, nor does any ethnic group take precedence over any other. . . . A policy of multiculturalism within a bilingual framework recommends itself to the government . . . " (Burke 1984: 4–5). "Multiculturalism within a bilingual framework" seeks to maintain the cultural integrity of all significant ethnic groups, but only within a French/English linguistic matrix. To maintain cultural integrity, the policy countenances some degree of group separation on terms of equality, a formula for association which is closely connected to the Canadian image of a cultural mosaic.

This Canadian policy is clearly different from the American policy that "separate-but-equal" education is an impossibility, a view enunciated in the U.S. Supreme Court's decision, Brown vs. Board of Education of Topeka, in 1954. Not surprisingly, therefore, the U.S. Commission on Civil Rights develops a quite different conception of bilingual education. Bilingual education is meant to secure "equal protection of the laws" for non-English-speaking children. The report claims that, "A public school system discriminates against non-English speaking children in violation of their right to equal protection of laws under the 14th amendment of the U.S. Constitution when it fails to educate them in a language they can understand" (U.S. Commission 1975: 142). Unlike Prime Minister Trudeau, the commission does not mention "ethnic groups" or "culture." In so doing, it envisages a potentially assimilationist or melting-pot conception of bilingualism. The commission wishes only to educate all students fairly; it leaves moot any stated role for particular ethnic groups. Bilingual education in the United States, therefore, strives to achieve equal educational opportunity for individuals; bilingual education in Canada strives to achieve equality among quasi-autonomous ethnic groups.

Viewed narratively, the reports also follow quite different paths. The Canadian report follows symbolic anthropology in construing culture as a set of binary oppositions mediated by myth, in this case a myth of "Canada." By contrast, American bilingual education departs from symbolic anthropology. It envisages the subordination of antagonistic ethnic groups to fair individual competition within an impartial educational system. It encourages each student to seek his or her own niche in a never-defined, but always taken-for-granted "American Way of Life." By educating children in their cultures of origin, Canadians attempt to shore up group identities. By contrast, American bilingual education de-emphasizes group oppositions in order to *free* children as individuals from their cultures of origin. Not surprisingly, given these different cultural theories, the language of bilingual education policy recommendations differs profoundly between the two countries.

Each country's cultural model of bilingual education generates its own particular political dangers. The Canadian model of bifurcation implies that bilingualism can contribute to Canadian unity so long as the two main linguistic groups remain the major political players. The dialectical tension between these two groups can generate a powerful myth of national identity. But interminable fragmentation and even schism also become possible within the model. If linguistic *bi*furcation is legitimate, why not "polyfurcation?" Why not separate but equal status for Ukranians, Italians, Chinese, and so on *ad infinitum*? The Canadian model of unity through difference yields no defensible grounds for saying "enough difference." Indeed, as Burke points out, "A little-known proviso in the Official Languages Act was recently cited by the Official Languages Commissioner, stressing the fact that official bilingualism in federal government services was not intended to preclude or detract from promotion of nonofficial languages" (1984: 9). In short, the Canadian model of cultural bifurcation is always vulnerable to charges that it fosters a national Tower of Babel.

A quite different danger plagues the American model. The Americans must demonstrate that bilingual education will in fact provide equal educational opportunity to individual students. In practice, bilingual education must allow non-English-speaking students to *transition* (the commission's term) to English-speaking American culture more effectively than did the traditional (now unconstitutional) practice of forcing students to use English in the classroom. Put differently, because learning is ultimately assessed only in English, the model must demonstrate that the child's early use of his native language will augment his or her later English-language performance. To conservative critics, the argument seems illogical, and, in fairness, the commission never provides convincing evidence to defind its position (U.S. Commission 1975: 69–78).

If conservatives can attack bilingual education, so can radicals. To some Canadian leftists, bilingual education amidst multiculturalism is an "attempt to obscure the French-Canadian challenge to political power and deflect it into linguistic and cultural directions . . . " (Peter 1981: 60). While conservatives charge that bilingual education threatens to cause political fragmentation, radicals charge that it actually delivers false consciousness. Multiculturalism and bilingual education obscure the real economic inequalities that plague Canadian society. Somewhat similarly, American leftists argue that bilingual education turns the student's native language into an instrument for learning English, which is the voice of the "dominant class." Rather than "respecting" the culture of origin, the culture of origin collapses, and the cultural stimulus to oppositional politics disappears. What is left is a deceptive and spurious form of political assimilation, not true equality of opportunity.

We are thus entering analytically rich terrain. I will proceed as I did in the previous case study. First, I will provide a quantitative analysis of theoretically significant words in the two texts. Then I will undertake a qualitative analysis.

Initially, I hypothesize that the Canadian approach to bilingualism will emphasize group terminology, while the American approach will emphasize the language of individualism, including individual psychology. The Canadian "separate-but-equal" model of bilingualism endorses group solidarity, not individual achievement; by contrast, the American equal-opportunity model requires the individual student to pass from one culture to another, or at the very least to balance psychologically the demands of two contrasting cultures. Hence, the Canadian text should include frequent group references, and the American text should dwell upon individuals and their subjective states.

Second, the Canadian text should emphasize conflict, and the American should emphasize consensus. The Anglo-French cleavage in Canadian culture imposes group tension upon the separate but equal model. By contrast, the American equal-opportunity model assumes that education in the native language is only a necessary first step toward English, which is the consensually "all-American" language. Non-English speakers in the United States thus move from a diverse linguistic universe to a single shared language; Canadians preserve diversity through two co-equal languages. Conflict is therefore more likely in the Canadian model than in the American model, for two co-equal language groups may well struggle against each other.

Third, the Canadian text should contain more abstract symbols than the American text. Symbolic anthropology argues that the dialectical group tensions in the separate-but-equal Canadian model should encourage symbolic reconciliations. By contrast, the American equal-opportunity model contains too little group tension to generate mediating symbolism.

Fourth, and finally, the Canadian text should refer more to the term *culture* itself than the American text. The separate-but-equal model of bilingual education presumes that a group's language is the key to a group's culture. Retaining language retains culture. By contrast, the American equal-opportunity model elevates the individual above the group. Individuals cannot "make" a culture themselves; therefore, the American text should elide the term *culture*.

Again I compiled a dictionary of words which operationalize these four hypotheses. Table 6.2 provides the relevant data. Because the two excerpts are virtually identical in length, we do not need to translate the word totals into percentages in order to make sense of the data. Table 6.2 not only supports all four hypotheses, but also adds a few unexpected wrinkles. Let us examine each hypothesis in turn.

The evidence in Table 6.2 supports our first hypothesis unequivocally. The Canadian text does emphasize the concept of group. Not only does it name *particular* groups (e.g., Francophone, Anglophone, etc., versus, in the U.S., Navajo) more often than the American text, but it also uses the term *group* itself 48 times to the American 35. By contrast, as expected, the American excerpt concentrates on individualism and individual psychology. The term *development,* for example, appears more than twice as often in the American than in the Canadian text; indeed, it is not surprising that the American context in which *development* appears is the familiar *growth syndrome,* which traverses so many realms of American culture. *Individual* development is actually more dominant in the American excerpt than the quantitative data alone indicate; the Canadian text often uses *development* to refer to *group* identity. The following two examples are typical:

> Without teachers, instruction, instructional materials, and parents to which language minority children can relate, it is virtually impossible to provide an environment conducive to learning and the *development* of positive self concept. (U.S. Commission, 1975: 36; emphasis mine)

> In Canada, the principle of equal partnership leads logically to the provision of minority-language schools, whether French or English. These schools are essential for the *development* of both official languages and cultures . . . (Innis 1973: 38; emphasis mine)

Table 6.2 Word Frequencies in *Bilingualism and BiCulturalism: An Abridged Version of the Royal Commission Report, Book 2* (1973), and *A Better Chance to Learn: Bilingual-Bicultural Education, Chap. 2* (1975).

References (by subject)	Book 2 (Canada)	Chapter 2 (United States)	Total
Psychology			
individual	10	15	25
self	0	32	32
personality	0	1	1
growth	1	9	10
development	30	70	100
esteem	0	0	0
feel	6	20	26
believe	10	5	15
opinion	3	0	3
confidence	0	4	4
attitude	14	16	30
feeling states	6	7	13
Totals	80	179	259
Group			
party	0	0	0
class	0	3	3
upper		2	
middle		1	
Ethnic Minority			
Francophone	23	0	23
French/ French-speaking	21	0	21
French Canadian	2	0	2
French Catholic	3	0	3
Roman Catholic	6	0	6
Anglophone	18	0	18
Anglo (2nd)	0	9	9
English/ English-speaking	21	2	23
English Protestant	1	0	1
Anglophone	1	0	1
Spanish-speaking	1	3	4
Puerto Rican	0	8	8
Mexican American	0	7	7
Navajo	0	16	16
Indian/Native American	0	2	2
Mexican Indian	0	1	1
Chinese	0	1	1
Totals	97	49	146

Table 6.2 (*continued*)

References (by subject)	Book 2 (Canada)	Chapter 2 (United States)	Total
union	0	0	0
movement	0	0	0
group	48	35	83
Totals	48	35	83
Conflict			
conflict	1	3	4
struggle	1	0	1
attack	0	0	0
compete	2	0	2
fight	0	0	0
argue	4	1	5
dominate/dominant	8	8	16
enemies	0	0	0
defend	1	1	2
opposition	1	0	1
conspiracy	0	0	0
elite	0	0	0
separate	14	2	16
duality	11	1	12
stereotypes	2	0	2
divide/division	4	1	5
Totals	49	17	66
Consensus			
agree	2	0	2
compromise	0	0	0
harmony	0	0	0
peace	0	0	0
solution	3	0	3
friends	0	1	1
comrades	0	0	0
share	4	1	5
accept	9	4	13
consent	0	0	0
unity	2	0	2
Totals	20	6	26
culture	22	23	45
cultural	59	33	92
Totals	81	56	137
Symbols			
country	11	9	20
fairness	0	0	0
equality	31	3	34

(*continued on following page*)

Table 6.2 (*continued*).

References (by subject)	Book 2 (Canada)	Chapter 2 (United States)	Total
freedom	1	1	2
law	3	0	3
right(s)	17	0	17
socialism	0	0	0
Totals	63	13	76
Total words in text:	9,650	9,200	

Psychological terminology also differs between the two cultures. Aside from its emphasis upon *individual* and especially *self*, the American excerpt also uses the term *feel* frequently. By contrast, Canadians make heavy use of the term *believe*. *Belief* denotes greater psychological commitment than *feel*, and is therefore consistent with Canadian culture's strong emphasis upon group identity. After all, group allegiance provides a secure foundation for the development of beliefs. By contrast, institutionalized individualism grounds American opinions not in organic groups, but in impersonal institutions. Psychologically, therefore, the American is somewhat adrift. Small wonder that Americans *feel* things, while Canadians *believe* things.

Although our second hypothesis also receives support, examination of the data reveals an unexpected finding. As was true in our comparison of British and American political language, so also in this comparison: *conflict* and *consensus* do not preclude each other linguistically. The Canadian text does emphasize conflict more than the American text (49 references to the American 17), but it also refers more to consensus than does the American excerpt (20 references to 6). If, as Leitch (among others) argues, difference lies at the heart of a language's meaning (1983: 8; Saussure 1983), then the same thing may well be true for texts. The Canadian text certainly conveys different *meanings* than does the American text, for the Canadian text focuses upon difference itself, including the difference between *conflict* and *consensus*, while the American text says little about either concept.

Our third hypothesis also gains support. In accord with the predictions of symbolic anthropology, more abstract symbols appear in the Canadian text than in the American text, almost five times as many in fact (63 to 13). Noteworthy is the heavy Canadian usage of *equality* and especially *rights*. One possible explanation of this latter finding is that the American text applies the concept of rights to individuals, while the Canadian text applies the concept both to individuals and to *groups*.

Finally, the data also support our fourth hypothesis. The master concept, *culture,* appears considerably more frequently in the Canadian than the American text (81 to 56 references). Moreover, as our qualitative analysis will suggest, *culture* refers to wholly different things in the two narratives.

Qualitatively, the texts construe bilingual education very differently. The Royal Commission report sums up its vision of bilingual education in the following way: "The principle of equal partnership [between the two main cultures] implies [that] not only should children be guaranteed access to public schools, but English and French should have equal status as languages of instruction" (Innis 1973: 30). The goal of equal status leads the report to recommend special bilingual education districts in areas of substantial minority-language population. As the report puts it, "Our first recommendation is that public education be provided in each of the official minority languages at both the elementary and secondary levels in the bilingual districts" (Innis 1973: 50). The report also proposes wholly separate minority-language schools, federal goverment subsidies for such schools, and the encouragement of bilingualism for *all* students. Finally, the Canadian report recommends English and French be designated official Canadian languages with "equal status as languages of instruction" (Innis 1973: 38).

By contrast, the U.S. Civil Rights Commission omits any discussion of an official language for the United States. But it does state that "language-minority children in this country ultimately must learn English" (U.S. Commission, 1975: 56). It makes no comparable statement concerning native English speakers learning, say, Spanish or Navajo. Bilingual education, therefore, is principally a device for assisting language minorities to learn English. Naturally enough, therefore, the commission does not propose bilingual "districts," nor does it advocate separate schools for language minorities. Instead it envisages full minority-group transition to English at some unstated point during the educational cycle: "Instruction through English in cognitive areas begins when the child can function in that language and experiences no academic handicap due to insufficient knowledge of the language. Some instruction in the native language may continue even after the child is competent in English" (U.S. Commission 1975: 29). Thus, continuing use of the native language is mainly a necessary evil; by contrast, in Canada, continuing use of the native language is the ultimate good.

These differing conceptions of bilingual education are rooted in political realities. In Canada, an alienated, secession-minded, French-speaking province traces its legitimacy to a period before the English conquest. No wonder there is a separate place for French. In the United States, Spanish-speakers have never possessed their own state; therefore, within the United States, English reigns supreme.

Yet such political realities become powerful only because they are captured and refashioned by the collective representations which make up a culture. In this case, the collective representations are commission reports, which propose new public policies and disseminate novel forms of discourse, such as bilingual "districts" or "academic handicap." In so doing, culture reformulates the past to accommodate present political exigencies, and thus helps shape the future.

Indeed, differing objectives for bilingual education reflect different conceptions of culture itself. Canadians conceive of culture as the objective of personal development. Therefore, it is perfectly proper that governmental authorities impose culture, regardless of the child's own preferences. As the Royal Commission puts it, "An awareness of . . . cultural duality is essential to an understanding of Canada. Our aim has been to ensure that all students will become more conscious of this aspect of our national identity" (Innis 1973: 36). Nor does the commission hesitate to characterize education as the inculcation of collective values, rather than the development of the individual. "The aims of education are as diverse as the aims of society itself, for in the final analysis they are determined by the values accepted by the society. . . . Any proposal for change in our educational systems must . . . be ultimately based on our view of what Canada is or should be" (Innis 1973: 36). In short, Canadian culture comes first; the child, second.

By contrast, in the United States, the function of culture is only to facilitate or inhibit individual learning. At its best, culture serves personal development; however, it is never itself the *aim* of development. As the U.S. Civil Rights Commission puts it, "Since culture forms the base of all school curricula, the cultural relevance of curricula is as crucial to learning as understanding the language of instruction" (U.S. Commission 1975: 47). Further, "In a bilingual bicultural program the points of departure of learning are the cultural values, cultural heritage, and societal experiences of the language minority child" (U.S. Commission 1975: 48). Both these American statements portray culture only as a place to begin, not as a place to arrive. The child comes first; culture of any kind, second.

It is hardly surprising, therefore, that the American report emphasizes individualism. Particularly revealing is the ten pages the report devotes to the "self-concept," a subject absent from the Royal Commission text. The U.S. report claims that "current developers of curricula have given as much importance to building self-concept in school as to transmitting knowledge" (U.S. Commission 1975: 30). Is there any connection between culture and the self-concept? Yes, but again the relationship is only instrumental. "Numerous persons have testified at Commission hearings on the negative effects of the English curriculum on minority children's attitudes towards themselves" (U.S. Commission 1975: 33–34). Thus, bilingual education as a cultural alternative is useful only because it can create a strong self-concept. Otherwise, it has no value at all.

Individualism also enters the text through the report's pervasive psychologizing. The following statement is typical:

> Children who view themselves as being loved, accepted, and respected develop positive self-concepts. They are motivated to learn because they approach learning with optimism and confidence in their abilities. They approach life with openness and, thus, are able to make the fullest possible use of new experiences. Since such children feel adequate, demanding or difficult tasks do not frighten them. (U.S. Commission 1975: 31–32)

The truth of these assertions, of course, is not the issue; the point is that comparable statements simply do not appear in the Royal Commission report. Institutionalized individualism in the United States encourages resort to psychology; by contrast, truncated group solidarity in Canada culture makes the psychology of individual learning less salient or problematic.

Other features of the American text also emphasize individualism. One such feature is the frequent citing of personal experience. The American text includes six extended quotations from young Navajo, Puerto Rican, and Mexican children, all of whom attest to the difficulties they experienced in English-language classrooms. There are no such personal testimonies in the final report of the Canadian Royal Commission. How can we explain the difference? One possibility is that the Canadian group-based model of bilingual education need not resort to the rhetorical technique of personification, which rhetorically exemplifies individualism (for a literary comparison, see Scholes 1985: 146). By contrast, the American equal-opportunity model favors personification.

The American text also emphasizes the necessity for good personal relations between teachers and students (Cusick 1983), another subject that is absent from the Canadian text. Why the difference? Possibly because the American student is offered no clearly articulated collective goal, and also because the culture of origin serves only as a motivator. Under such conditions, each student is very much alone in the classroom, and therefore in need of help from skilled and caring teachers. No wonder there are such sentences as, "The lack of positive teacher-student interaction in monolingual schools was underscored by the Commission's study of Mexican-American education which documented Southwestern teachers' failure to 'involve Mexican-American children as active participants in the classroom to the same extent as Anglo children'" (U.S. Commission 1975: 40). Whether "positive interaction" improves learning is not the issue; rather, from a cultural standpoint, the relationships symbolize the unforced formation of social bonds, a chief goal of institutionalized individualism.

The Canadian separate-but-equal model of bilingual education creates its own culturally shaped peculiarities of logic—and politics. Understandably, the Royal Commission report devotes most of its attention to maintaining and strengthening separate cultures; however, almost as an afterthought, the report adds: "Cultural duality in Canada depends upon the coexistence of the two major cultures and *on cooperation between them*" (Innis 1973: 62; emphasis mine). The report recommends mandatory second-language teaching as a means of fostering cooperation between the two cultures. The report acknowledges, however, that "one does not need to be an expert in semantics to realize that words can be misunderstood if they are torn from their cultural context. . . . Indeed, the difficulty of communication becomes itself a confirmation of the existence not merely of two linguistic groups but of two cultural groups" (Innis 1973: 62).

The problem is that the more successful the Canadians are in creating separate-but-equal education, the more they risk the very "misunderstandings" they fear. After all, for people from separate cultures to cooperate, they must leave their *separate* languages temporarily behind, and settle on a *common* language, which, used in a new context, cannot be wholly faithful to separateness. At least the Canadian self-consciousness about culture creates awareness of this problem; by contrast, the American denial of separate cultures prevents even the recognition of tensions in bilingual education.

We saw in our quantitative analysis that the cultural model embodied in the Canadian text generates symbolic mediations of group struggles. By contrast, the American text yields many forms of individualism, but so far little else. Yet the envisaged "fair" competition between individual minority and majority students in American schools is also a form of struggle. Is there any narrative mediation of individual struggle in the American text?

The answer, as we should by now expect, is that impartial institutions mediate the competition. Three such institutions are prominent in the American text: science, educational measurement, and law.

Of these three, science is the most important. Indeed, the report as a whole is less a political document than it is a graduate research paper on bilingual education, complete with the requisite paraphernalia of "educational" science. The text contains 141 scholarly references to the literature on bilingual education, much of which is, ironically, Canadian. By contrast, the abridged Royal Commission text contains not a single footnote. Moreover, the American text resorts to frequent use of social science jargon. Here is one example:

> Native language arts programs, like English language arts programs, are designed to "refine and extend" children's use of language. By providing the opportunity for verbal interaction and by providing culturally relevant situations on which to base language usage, they ensure the development of expression skills commensurate with their level of intellectual and emotional development. (U.S. Commission 1975: 46)

Educational jargon (e.g., *language arts, verbal interaction, expression skills*) conveys the imprimatur of social science to what might otherwise be understood solely as a politically controversial proposal. So also does the chart on page 8 of the text, which portrays social science guidelines for implementing bilingual education. By contrast, no such charts find their way into the Canadian text.

Related to science as a mediating device is educational measurement. Equal educational opportunity promises to improve learning, but only testing can determine if the promise has been met. Thus, testing and grading are not *constraints* on children, as critics often contend, but *liberators of children*. Moreover, the report argues that

> the decision to promote children from one grade to the next is based on whether they are able to communicate that they have learned the information and concepts required . . . the fact that verbal ability is one of the two basic measures used on college entrance examinations reflects the importance of language skills for further educational opportunity. (U.S. Commission 1975: 45)

228 The Political Embodiment of Liberal Democratic Culture

The logic of the argument is that command of language permits the individual to score well on tests, so that he or she can pass from grade to grade, enter college, and ultimately enjoy the fruits of equal educational opportunity. Testing thus facilitates success.

This scenario demands that testing be fair. According to the report, because language-minority children have usually been tested against majority children, they have been at a disadvantage. So, "as a basic maxim, before children's abilities are tested in any language, their language proficiency in that language must be determined. . . . Since IQ tests purport to measure cognitive ability, an IQ test administered through a language that the child has not fully developed is not an accurate assessment of intelligence" (U.S. Commission 1975: 66). In short, IQ tests will be fair only if a previous set of tests confirms the ability of the child to *take* IQ tests. Thus, more tests, more fairness.

Finally, legal institutions mediate the strains of bilingual education. In a twenty-eight-page appendix the Commission argues that bilingual education fulfills the 14th Amendment to the U.S. Constitution. The appendix concludes simply, "Students who begin school with limited or no English skills and who as a result are unable to benefit from an exclusively English educational curriculum are . . . denied equal educational opportunity" (U.S. Commission 1975: 170). Therefore, bilingual education is the only available legal solution. Together, the trio of law, social science, and educational measurement help to construct institutionalized individualism in American bilingual education, just as symbolism and group struggle help to construct cultural bifurcation in Canadian bilingual education. Canadian and American models of bilingualism thus embody and reproduce all the contradictions, complexities, and concordances of their respective cultures.

CHAPTER SEVEN

"Partial Visions" as Partial Argument

Just as the partial visions this enterprise describes are incomplete cultures of democracy, so also is my account of these cultures incomplete. I have said comparatively little about three issues: (1) the intelligibility of culture; (2) the relations between collective representations and social institutions; and (3) the contributions, if any, of culture to political change. A proper conclusion to this "partial" effort demands that I address each of these issues briefly.

The Intelligibility of Culture

It may seem odd that only at the very end of this enterprise do I discuss the question of whether culture is intelligible. After all, the entire effort presumes that culture *is* intelligible. Yet these "partial visions" are essentially constructions. Perhaps investigators using other methods and relying upon other theories might have constructed different cultures. If so, why then assume that cultures are ever truly intelligible as anything *but* constructions? If there can be many different accounts of the "same" culture, than perhaps no fully intelligible or accurate account of culture is possible at all.

Much recent discussion of culture and politics addresses this question. Some authors, such as Marcus and Fischer, confine the problem to the capacity of ethnography to characterize cultures correctly. Others, such as Baudrillard, focus on the alleged disappearance of the object of study—the public itself. Still others, such as Edelman, target the complex interplay of political interest and linguistic ambiguity, an interplay which, he alleges, produces multiple and irreconcilable realities. Let us briefly describe each of these positions.

To Marcus and Fischer, contemporary anthropology is marked by a "suspicion of all totalizing styles of knowledge" (1986: x–xi). As they put it:

> The key feature of the moment . . . is the loosening of the
> hold. . . . of either specific totalizing visions or a general
> paradigmatic style of organizing research. The authority of

"grand theory" styles seems suspended for the moment in favor
of a close consideration of such issues as contextuality, the
meaning of social life to those who enact it, and the explanation of exceptions and indeterminants rather than regularities in
phenomena observed–all issues that make problematic what
were taken for granted as factors or certainties on which the
validity of paridigms had rested. (1986: 8).

Marcus and Fischer dub this situation a "crisis of representation" (1986:
8). Although Marcus and Fischer explore the multiplicity of recent
ethnographic strategies, from interpretive approaches like that of Clifford Geertz to autobiographical ethnography, they refrain from drawing the most radical possible conclusion, namely, that this profusion
of ethnographic approaches signals the absence of any single, comprehensible cultural "thing" to represent. Instead, they visualize a healthy
development of ethnography towards "an approximation, variably achieved through dialogue, that is, a mutual correction of understanding by
each party in conversation to a level of agreement adequate for any particular interaction" (1986: 29). Ultimately, they praise "the
practice of ethnography . . . where the vitality of anthropology remains" (1986: 165).

Considerably less optimistic is Baudrillard, whose concern is not
with ethnographic accounts of exotic cultures, but with the fate of
cultural meaning in liberal democracies. To Baudrillard (1983) such
democracies exist "in the shadow of the silent majorities." It is not that
the silent majorities are at variance with a biased, left-wing media, as
Richard Nixon thought; rather, the silent majorities can no longer be
heard at all. As Baudrillard puts it:

That the silent majority (or the masses) is an imaginary referent
does not mean they don't exist. It means that *their representation is no longer possible.* The masses are no longer a referent
because they no longer belong to the order of representation.
They don't express themselves, they are surveyed. They don't
reflect upon themselves, they are tested. (1983: 20)

The culprit in this debacle is mainly the mass media. According to
Baudrillard, "the mass media, with its [sic] pressure of information,
carries out an irresistible destruction of the social" (1983: 100). "The
social" is a prerequisite to the existence of a democratic public; but the
media's "information dissolves meaning and the social into a sort of
nebulous state leading not at all to a surfeit of innovation but to the

very contrary, to total entropy" (Baudrillard 1983: 100). Therefore, the "public" has become a kind of "black hole" into which all meaning systems disappear, leaving only an ever-expanding social vacuum where once there was democracy.

Finally, to Edelman, the unintelligibility of culture can be traced equally to the political uses which those in power impose upon the realm of ideas and to the instability of language itself. "Accounts of political issues, problems, crises, threats, and leaders . . . become devices for creating disparate assumptions and beliefs about the social and political world rather than factual statements. The very concept of 'fact' becomes irrelevant because every meaningful political object and person is an interpretation that reflects and perpetuates an ideology" (Edelman 1988: 10). But the problem is actually deeper than ideology. Language in even its most pristine form always escapes any single, trans-situational meaning. "The subject cannot be regarded as the origin of coherent action, writing, or other forms of expression; . . . actions and interpretations hinge upon the social situation in which they begin, including the language that depicts a social situation. The language that interprets objects and actions also constitutes the subject. . ." (Edelman 1988: 9). Although Edelman directs his characterization mainly toward political leaders, his argument applies to any social actor. If political leaders—specialists in political "expression"—cannot achieve coherence, why should we expect more from the mass public?

There are various ways to maintain the intelligibility of culture in the face of these assaults. For example, we could attempt to reinvigorate a positivist model of the relationship between cultural visions and political objects. From a positivist standpoint, a meaningful cultural analysis employs the traditional tests positivism recommends: tests of reliability, replicability, prediction, and "postdiction." Though the present effort applies few such tests, other researchers can easily assess the reliability of our cultural characterizations. Any competent researcher could apply the same content analysis formats we applied to the magazine ads, situation comedies, corporate publications, and social studies texts we have examined. Multiple coders could then calculate measures of reliability. To the degree that coders agree on the content of these media, and to the degree that these media continue to display the cultural themes we have described, then the visions themselves become both real and intelligible.

Moreover, we can ask, in standard positivist fashion, whether the visions this research describes predict theoretically relevant political phenomena. Indeed, the previous chapter asked precisely this question; we discovered that the three cultural visions did in fact predict aspects of culturally relevant political discourse and political attitudes in Britain, Canada, and the United States.

Yet positivism does not really answer the charge of unintelligibility, for such arguments name positivism itself as only one "multiple reality" among many. Moreover, consider Baudrillard's argument that survey research—perhaps the ultimate positivist research tool—has helped reduce the public to "a mass . . . dumb like beasts, and its silence . . . equal to the silence of beasts" (1983: 28). To Baudrillard, positivism is not a scientific method, but a political truncheon. Finally, and most important, our own interpretative approach to cultural visions is not really positivistic, for positivism would eliminate the shades of meaning from the partial visions we have described.

Of course, we could always turn these arguments upon their authors. Neither the supposed unintelligibility of culture nor the problem of "multiple realities" prevented Marcus and Fischer, Baudrillard, and Edelman from presenting their own analyses as truth. Therefore, their writings are hardly exempt from the general critique they offer of others. A form of the Mannheimian paradox thus emerges. Either the claim of cultural unintelligibility may be correct but unverifiable, or it may be verifiable and, for that very reason, incorrect.

Unfortunately, this line of argument attempts to solve a serious problem through cheap philosophical gimmickry. The important claims of Marcus and Fischer, Baudrillard, and Edelman deserve better. Let us therefore suppose the most damaging case to be true. Suppose culture is unintelligible. What then follows? Not really very much. The absence of a stable, knowable cultural referent does not relieve the individual of the need to act. Regardless of whether culture does or does not "make sense," we live in a world which forces us to make decisions. Should be take this job or that? Should we obey the law? Should we vote? Should we support the war our leaders have just declared? Decisions impose themselves upon us no matter what our philosophical stance may be on the question of culture.

At the point of unavoidable decision, people must attempt to make sense of their worlds. To do so, they turn to the cultural tools at hand, including collective representations. Therefore, at the point of irrevocable choice, culture reappears in a form intelligible to social actors, if not to academic observers. Of course, "multiple cultural realities" may compete against each other to control decisions, but this fact does not make the decisions nonsensical to their makers nor culturally incoherent to the observer. Multiple realities simply render personal decision and cultural analysis problematic.

I have characterized my approach in this study as interpretative rather than positivistic. Interpretation does not allow the author to impose selectively his or her own undisciplined preconceptions on the cultural materials. Instead, the materials constrain the interpretation. I combined the content analyses in chapters 3 through 5 with qualitative illustrations to develop broad cultural themes in each of the three countries. The method of interpretation is best represented in chapter 6, where the initial quantitative analyses of political debates and reports pointed the way towards qualitative thematic analyses of the same texts.

The method of interpretation often produces surprising conclusions. For example, at the outset of the study, I did not expect to find American culture so heavily institutionalized; nor did I foresee finding the Canadian private realm so weak; nor did I anticipate the narcissistic withdrawal that dominated some of the British materials. Interpretation yielded new formulations which modified and sometimes contraverted my preconceptions.

Institutions and Culture

The partial visions this study describes emerge from mass media representations of society. But what about the institutions which produce these visions? How textbooks get written and marketed; how corporate public relations firms work; how advertising agencies operate; and how sitcom creators go about their business—all these institutional processes the present discussion ignores. For this reason, a critic so disposed could well characterize "partial visions" as reifications floating in a social void absent of all human habitation.

Appropriately enough, the initial objection to this "dematerialized" account of culture emerges from cultural materialism. As Marcus and Fischer put it, "a weakness of the culture theorists is that they failed to come to terms with issues of political economy. . . . Because of the compelling hold on Western thought of the importance of politics, economics, and self-interest as the fundamental explanatory frames for what happens in social life, any effort to argue for the power of symbols, no matter how persuasively, is bound to be taken lightly if it does not seriously address or rephrase materialist explanations" (1986: 141). Of course, it is precisely this task the present effort avoids.

Indeed, the problem extends even beyond materialism. A more broadly gauged attack emerges from the perspective of institutional interest and social control. From this Weberian standpoint, institutions are structures of power which manipulate symbolic and material resources in struggles against other institutions. Therefore, "partial visions" *are* partial because they say so little about the role culture plays in institutional conflict and domination.

The chief contemporary theorist of institutions is Michel Foucault. Foucault's *Discipline and Punish* begins with a horrific account of standard operating procedures in the seventeenth century for regicides: a public execution by burning, skinning, and drawing and quartering. The purpose of this punishment was to impress a simple message of deterrence upon the assembled populace: the state offered no pretense of rectification; no opportunity for sinners to atone; no chance to expiate guilt; no forgiveness; and, above all, no possibility of reform.

Today things are even worse: "Whereas in the eighteenth century criminals were punished bodily . . . punishment, primarily, has become psychological . . . we move from 'punishment of the body to that of the soul'" (Wuthnow et al. 1984: 163). "Punishing the soul" is both more intrusive and more effective than punishing the body, for psychological punishment removes the very impulse to reject authority. Punishing the soul offers "therapy" and "cure" under the pretense of encouraging the criminal's "better nature." No longer does the institution stand as the implacable Other; now the state and the prisoner are bonded intimately together. Everywhere coercive institutions use codes of legislation to mask their abuse of power, turning all theaters of human endeavor into increasingly uneven struggles between the powerful state and the helpless, vulnerable subject.

Even if we choose to reject Foucault's grim view of institutional development, we must still confront other theories of institutional domination of culture. In fact, Mary Douglas invokes Durkheim in this regard; she writes, "Durkheim and Mauss [in *Primitive Classification*] proposed to analyze the extent to which the mundane classifications we use are projections of the social structure partaking in the aura of sacredness" (1986: 97). For Douglas's "mundane classifications" we need only substitute "culture," and for her "social structure" we need only substitute "institutions."

To Douglas, collective representations are systems of classification which serve institutional purposes only. The real issue is not whether classifications favor punishment or pleasure, but whether they prop up institutional power. Douglas agrees with Foucault that the power of institutions is insidious, forcing its way deep into human consciousness:

Institutions systematically direct individual memory and channel our perceptions into forms compatible with the relations they authorize. They fix processes that are essentially dynamic, they hide their influence, and they rouse our emotions to a standardized pitch on standardized issues. (1986: 92).

It follows that institutional expansion can vitiate conflictive democratic participation. For example, William Graebner claims that institutionalized controls render much American political participation toothless as a force of popular sovereignty. Graebner targets as illustrations of his thesis Boys' Clubs, scouting, Golden Age Clubs, psychotherapy, Spockian childrearing, the YMCA, and corporate programs in industrial relations (1987: chaps. 3–6). To Graebner, all these phenomena constitute "a method of social engineering that operates within 'private,' informal, and voluntary spheres" (1987: 6). This "democratic social engineering" helped control the large number of Americans uprooted by the late nineteenth-century processes of industrialization, urbanization, and immigration. A newly rootless population posed serious dangers to social order. So "democratic social engineering" emerged to reduce the danger (Graebner 1987: chap. 1) and, in the process, destroyed the private well-springs of true democracy.

These several critiques share the premise that all-powerful institutions create legitimizing collective representations, and that collective representations have no other social function. This argument is debatable. For one thing, recent political history in Britain, Canada, and the United States is full of cultural movements which not only originated outside mainstream institutions, but also altered the behavior of such institutions and, in the bargain, redefined collective representations. For example, the American civil rights movement of the 1960s generated novel collective representations of black power. These images eventually penetrated into the evening news, into social studies texts, and even into product advertising. Such representations also paved the way for television sitcoms such as *Julia* and *The Cosby Show*. Thus, extrainstitutional protest created new collective representations within these mainstream institutions.

The same phenomenon occurred in Canada and Britain. The Quiet Revolution was not some media conjurer's ratings gimmick, but a powerful nationalist movement which helped reshape Canadian media imagery, producing, for example, social studies texts which pay Quebecois aspirations close and respectful attention. Similarly, Commonwealth immigration into England was not a British media invention but a real political event which caused a crisis of ethnic assimilation in a class-based, traditionalistic culture. Eventually such television series as *Till Death Us Do Part, The Lenny Henry Show,* and even *Coronation St.* found in these political events the grist of dramatically evocative, change-making collective representations.

Of course, institutions are not the playthings of collective representations and political events. I have no wish to oversimplify the relationship between institutions and collective representations. I assert only that political events and collective representations provide grist for the institutional mill and that, in milling this grist, institutions do not have a free hand to project their own special interests outward.

Moreover, institutional interests are themselves uncertain. Advertising agencies, book publishers, sitcom producers, corporate public relations specialists — all are actually combinations of partially competitive subgroups. Advertising agencies bring together writers, graphic artists, salespeople, pollsters, market researchers, and designers, each of whom sees the institutional world through a particular set of lenses. Similarly, textbooks are the joint products of academics, salespeople, editors, and publishers — and even of state school boards, teachers, administrators, librarians, standardized testing agencies, and admissions officers in universities. No wonder textbook publishers' "interests" and policies shift over time.

Because collective representations often *create* institutional responses, and because institutions are often divided among constituent subgroups, it follows that while "institutions do the classifying" (Douglas 1987: 91), it is the larger culture which often calls the tune. Thus, if IBM and Xerox now disseminate collective representations of affirmative action, it is partially because collective representations of equality actually reshaped the corporations' practices. Similarly, collective representations of Quebecois nationalism helped produce a Canadian public school structure markedly more receptive than its predecessor to the interests of Francophones and "new Canadians."

These culture-driven alterations in dominant institutions are not window dressing; they are substantial. Consider American public schools, which perform very differently depending upon the proportion of minority teachers on the staff. In integrated schools where there are large precentages of minority teachers, black students are not relegated to the lowest educational tracks. But in integrated schools where whites predominate among teachers, proportionately more black students find themselves in academic dead ends (Meier, Stewart, and England 1989). Of course, had not the power and culture of the civil rights movement penetrated schools, there would be no schools of the first kind. Externally generated political struggle, coupled with new collective representations of blacks, has altered culture-creating institutions such as the school. In the process, culture has helped redistribute political power.

Finally, even if dominant institutions could freely construct collective representations, the ultimate test of institutional success would remain public acceptance. Collective representations must reach beyond the institutions of their birth. After all, these images depict few textbook writers, ad men, corporate executives, or sitcom producers. Instead, they depict taxicab drivers, computer programmers, janitors, attorneys, environmental advocates, and the police — in short, the people who make up the audience. Therefore, translating institutional power into dramatically satisfying, legitimizing narratives is not easy. Indeed, insofar as they represent their audience successfully, these representations will recoil upon the institutions of their origin.

Cultural Dynamics and Political Change

Finally, do "partial visons" help to produce political change? In this study, the problem of change stands out in bold relief; after all, the partial visions I have described are only snapshots, restricted as to media and period. Even if the snapshots are accurate, we cannot know whether they capture a static cultural process "frozen" by liberal democracy, or a fluid cultural process in which these particular visions are but phases.

Most observers argue that a cultural approach to politics yields a prognosis of stasis rather than change. As Harry Eckstein has recently stated, "Criticisms of culturalist political theories certainly have emphasized the occurrence of certain changes in political structures, attitudes, and behavior . . . in order to impugn the approach" (1988: 789). A verdict of change often impugns cultural approaches because culture has so often served to support a prognosis of stasis. Therefore, instances of change apparently discredit cultural analysis.

Though Eckstein himself attempts to propose a cultural theory of political change, he too fails. He admits, for example, that, "the postulates of the [cultural] approach all lead to the expectation of political continuity; they make political continuity the 'normal' state" (1988: 790). Eckstein offers two reasons for this view: first, "orientations are not superstructural reflections of objective structures, but themselves invest structures and behavior with cognitive and normative meaning" (1988: 792); second, "orientations are formed through processes of socialization. To the extent that socialization is direct (by precept), generational continuity must occur . . ." (1988: 792).

Given these two assumptions, it is hardly surprising that Eckstein believes cultural change to be infrequent, adaptational, reactive to events, and exogenous. As for revolutionary change in politics, only "despotic or legalistic" measures—not culture—matters (1988: 799). The main conclusion to be drawn from Eckstein's account is that the partial visions of culture are not dynamic and that they offer no real promise for promoting the political change conflictive democratic participation entails.

The argument that cultural explanations in politics must tilt towards political continuity is quite disputable. A number of recent theories of culture and politics propose change as a central feature (e.g., Ingelhart 1990). Such theories assist the present study to envisage three sorts of culturally induced political change: cyclical, configurational, and structural. Moreover, each of these forms of change has implications for conflictive democratic participation.

As to cyclical change, Namenwirth and Weber analyzed 120 years worth of American political party platforms and discovered two distinctive cycles of culturally induced political change. Namenwirth and Weber interpret these cultural cycles from a Parsonian, functionalist perspective (1987). Culture pushes society through these adaptational phases; it does not simply react to dynamic forces generated elsewhere. "Culture . . . is in large part prophetic and therefore critical of the status quo. It is a design of the good society and thus not necessarily of the prevailing one . . . so most cultures exist in opposition to the established social order" (Namenwirth and Weber 1987: 19).

Namenwirth and Weber characterize culturally induced change as cyclical rather than linear because culture never solves all the problems it attacks; old problems recur in new forms, and thus trigger new cycles. Although Namenwirth and Weber's version of American culture differs considerably from "institutionalized individualism," their idea of culturally engendered political cycles can be applied equally, if speculatively, to institutionalized individualism in the United States. We can, in fact, envisage a three-phase cultally engendered cycle of American political change.

First, because the ideas of personal choice, development, and growth are central components of institutionalized individualism, Americans are prone to distinguish sharply between societies where they believe individual choice flourishes and societies where they believe it does not. Indeed, the idea of individual choice helps Americans to distinguish between the United States (the "home" of choice) and other societies. Only a small cognitive displacement is necessary for Americans to perceive multiple and sometimes exaggerated distinctions between themselves and "less free" societies, such as the Soviet Union. Let us call this tendency *cultural displacement.*

But what about group constraint *within* American society? Many Americans do recognize that stubborn economic and social inequalities prevent some of their fellow citizens from exercising meaningful personal choice (Moynihan 1986). However, Americans often explain this culturally dissonant phenomenon by distinguishing between a "real world" of necessary economic inequality that motivates "practical people" to produce efficiently, and an "ideal world" of relaxed equality, in which domestic relations and friendship flower (Lasch 1977). The real thus takes leave of the ideal; Americans become simultaneously the most pragmatic and the most romantic of peoples, a paradox which baffles foreigners only slightly more than it baffles Americans themselves. Let us call this tendency *cultural bifurcation.*

Finally, the strain between the real and the ideal occasionally becomes unbearable, creating reform movements which attempt to extend the range of free choice. But there are limitations upon such efforts, for the movements which undertake reform not only engender opposition, but also must first ensure free choice and the right to dissent in their own ranks. Soon intragroup fragmentation and intergroup conflict develop; as a result, culturally conditioned reform efforts always fall short of their targets. This tendency may be called *incomplete reform* (Huntington 1981).

These three tendencies may combine to form irregular cycles in American history, altering the surface contours of American political culture and motivating major political change. Periods of cultural bifurcation (e.g., the 1870s–80s; the 1920s; the late 1950s; possibly the 1980s) generate moral revulsion and the desire among many to extend the ideal to the real, thus eradicating "unfair" inequalities. This impulse produces periods and movements of incomplete reform (e.g., the Populist-Progressive era of 1890–1910; the New Deal; the Civil Rights Movement of the 1960s). But fragmentation within and opposition without eventually destroy these movements, leaving their adherents bitter and their opponents suspicious. Residual fear and suspicion motivate bursts of cultural displacement, often associated with foreign wars (e.g., World War I and the "crusade for democracy;" antifascist World War II, followed by the Cold War of the late 1940s and early 1950s). The Civil War and Reconstruction may also have constituted a phase of cultural displacement in expunging slavery from the South, following an incomplete reform period of Abolitionist agitation beginning in the 1840s. This phase itself followed a period of cultural bifurcation and economic expansion, which lasted from the late 1830s until the late 1840s. In all these cases, military episodes discharged reform-generated pressures of bitterness and fear, preparing the way for a return to cultural bifurcation and the beginning of a new cycle.

Cyclical changes triggered by a cultural pattern create new and enduring institutions. Movements for reform in the United States have left institutional residues in the form of new civil rights agencies and an expanded court system. Comparable cycles in Canada deposit new institutions designed to implement demands for bi- and multiculturalism in that country. Finally, comparable cycles in Britain might periodically create new class-based institutions. An example is the cooperative movement during the period of Labour party formation; cooperatives attempted to broaden class politics into a total way of life, an institutional development wholly compatible with a society whose cultural visions apparently embody "ways of life" based on class.

A second possible form of culturally induced political change is configurational. The three partial visions this work describes are configurations of several interrelated collective representations. Change in any one component representation might well alter the entire configuration. The idea of configurational cultural change is not outlandish. Consider architecture, for example. Miller observes, "in aesthetics whole styles may alter, as in the transition from Gothic to Classical architecture" (1987: 98). Perhaps the same thing holds for the partial visions of national culture. Take Canada, for example. If Canadian sitcom producers were to incorporate American familial depictions into their own creations, their work would take on a more intense emotional texture. Given the bicultural configuration of Canadian collective representations, this newfound infusion of private emotion might encourage outbursts of group conflict. A result might be that instead of simply sponsoring cultural subidentities, the Canadian state would be forced to take a more activist stance, serving both as policy mediator and symbolic focus. Eventually, a fully *Canadian* identity might appear, driven by culturally induced conflictive democratic participation. Alternatively, of course, a stronger Canadian state might destroy the fragile confederational framework of Canadian unity. In either case, however, substantial political change would be the result.

As this example suggests, configurational change in culture is potentially more consequential than cyclical change. Of still greater potential power, however, is structural change, that is, political change generated by a fundamentally new cultural vision. A shift in the balance of power within a partial vision is not strong enough to create structural change in politics. Instead, destruction and reconstruction of cultural visions must occur. Are there forces currently visible in Britain, Canada, and the United States that might create new visions and major political change?

Several contemporary discussions of culture and politics in the West yield a plausible affirmative response to this question. Relevant theory identifies four agents of major cultural change; change in all four factors together could create major cultural and political effects.

Emmanuel Todd has identified the first two of these change agents: literacy and family structure. Todd argues that increases in rates of literacy both in Europe and the Third World initiated industrialization and demographic change (1987: 1–11). In turn, increases in literacy occurred because women altered their position in families. As Todd puts it, "the cultural level tends to be higher in places where women marry late and are treated neither as children nor as objects. Female age at marriage defines the nature of the relationship between the spouses: it is closely connected with the degree of feminism that is present in any society" (1987: 16). Todd argues that women who married late and enjoyed independent family power secured education for their children. The rate of literacy rose, thus paving the way for major political change, including revolution toward liberal democracy (1987: 135–36).

Today in Britain, Canada, and the United States, literacy is once more undergoing change. In the United States, while unprecedented numbers attend colleges, many people remain "functionally" illiterate. More important, however, is the fact that in all three countries literacy has come to be as much "visual" as "literary." While overwhelming majorities of adults can read, increasing percentages rely for their information not on reading, but on television and other visual devices, such as computerized graphic displays.

Family structure is also in flux. All three countries have recently experienced significant alterations in the status of women; large percentages of women from every social class now enter the workforce, and laws now promote the status of women as fully independent members of society. Finally, "nontraditional" families, running the gamut from single-parent families to homosexual unions, have also proliferated, and even in "traditional" families, spouses now share familial burdens differently.

A third agent of cultural change is industrialization. Just as many nineteenth-century sociologists premised their theories on a transition from preindustrial to industrial society, so in the 1970s many sociologists described a "postindustrial" society, which they characterized as fundamentally dissimilar culturally from industrial society. Kumar describes the postindustrial perspective this way: "A transformation . . . which will eventually produce societies as different from the classically conceived industrial societies as those are from the earlier agrarian societies" (1978: 191).

Although Kumar is critical of postindustrial theory, he does not deny the existence of transitional qualities in the contemporary West. He describes "a disillusion with the fruits of continuous economic growth, with its natural agent, large-scale technology, and . . . with the very mode of cognition of industrial society, science itself. There seems, in other words, to be a reaction against industrialism at its most pervasive and compelling level of operation, that of ideology" (1978: 296).

Ironically, perhaps the most characteristic expression of this reaction *embraces* the products of industrialism. I refer to mass consumption of material goods. According to Daniel Miller, it is the unprecedented level of mass consumption which most distinguishes our time. Miller argues that mass consumption encourages the emergence of new, more flexible forms of culture. Contrary to most readings of Marx, Hegel, and Bourdieu, Miller argues that "consumption is developing as one of the major sites through which the necessary autonomy of the objects of commerce and of the modern states might be made compatible with the specific demands of dynamic social groups. An analysis of consumption may then once more become a critical theory of the status quo . . ." (1987: 216).

Yet how can mass consumption, itself a product of advanced industrialism, become the media for creating a cultural critique of advanced industrialism, much less for creating new cultural visions? Contemporary mass consumption not only alters *material* culture, as Miller discerns; but it may also alter collective representations. Among the flood of consumer goods, there now exist new culture-creating instruments: home video cameras, VCRs, tape recorders, desktop computers, cable television — in short, a media technology that is for the first time available to a mass public.

In a now-classic essay on democratic culture published in mid-century, Karl Mannheim asked, "How does the shape, the physiognomy of a culture change when the stratum actively participating in cultural life, either as creators or as recipients, becomes broader and more inclusive?" (1956: 175) One answer Mannheim proposed was increased intimacy between those who traditionally wielded power and this new stratum (1956: 206ff). Mannheim wisely argued that the closer scrutiny of leaders would not yield greater public satisfaction or trust; instead, he foresaw a "resentment-laden 'unmasking' of the evil practices of power-holders. Such a response is understandable when people see for the first time the profane reality behind the sacred symbols that they had been led to adore from afar" (1956: 216). Mannheim clearly predicted the contemporary "crisis of confidence" in politics.

But beneath the crisis of political confidence, new conditions for cultural restructuring may well be in place. These include alterations in patterns of literacy; new family structures; disillusionment with industrialization; mass consumption of diverse consumer goods; and a technology for creating new cultural visions. True, the democratization of goods is not yet matched by conflictive democratic participation. Our partial visions retain their hold, indispensable, yet incomplete; partly liberating, yet ultimately frustrating. But perhaps there is now a chance for "partial visions" finally to achieve completion in conflictive democratic participation.

Methodological Appendix

The material chosen for the analysis in chapters 3–5 consists of the following.

Television Programs

United States: from 1984 to 1987

1   "Kate and Allie"—five episodes
2   "Murder She Wrote"—three episodes
3   "Dynasty"—four episodes
4   "Growing Pains"—two episodes
5   "Highway to Heaven"—three episodes
6   "The Golden Girls"—six episodes
7   "Family Ties"—five episodes
8   "Who's the Boss"—eight episodes
9   "Cheers"—eleven episodes
10 "The Cosby Show"—eleven episodes
11 "Newhart"—three episodes
12 "Night Court"—three episodes
13 "Dallas"—four episodes
14 "Moonlighting"—three episodes

Total: seventy-one episodes. These programs were chosen on the basis of audience size ratings for each series in the previous television week, as reported in *TV Guide*.

Canada: from 1985 to 1987

1   "Anne of Green Gables"—four episodes
2   "The Beachcombers"—two episodes
3   "Danger Bay"—two episodes
4   "He Shoots, He Scores"—two episodes
5   "De Grassi Junior High"—five episodes

Total: fifteen episodes. These series are among the highest-rated Canadian Broadcasting Corporation series in English, and were kindly made available by Glen Luff, CBC, Toronto.

Great Britain: from 1985 to 1987

1   "Lenny Henry Show"—two episodes
2   "Emmerdale Farm"—five episodes
3   "Eastenders"—four episodes
4   "Only Fools and Horses"—two episodes
5   "Brookside"—two episodes
6   "Coronation Street"—six episodes
7   "Howard's Way"—two episodes
8   "Andy Capp"—one episode
9   "Crossroads"—four episodes

Total: twenty-eight episodes. These programs were chosen on the basis of audience size ratings as reported by television rating services, and were made available through BBC and Independent Television on videotape. I also wish to thank Melanie Grant for additional taping.

Each episode was summarized in terms of plot and action. Each was then analyzed for representation of individual/collectivity, public/private, and group tension by the investigator.

Corporate Publications

United States

Sample house organs, recruitment brochures, and annual reports were examined from Xerox, Exxon, General Electric, Amoco, Dupont, General Motors, IBM, Texaco, and Mobil from 1984 to 1986. These materials were obtained from each company. The companies were chosen from their top corporate values as reported in the *Fortune 500* for those years.

Canada

Sample house organs, recruitment brochures, and annual reports were examined from Stelco, British Columbia Hydro, Canada Packers, Ford of Canada, General Motors of Canada, Canada Life, and Alcan. Efforts to obtain material from other companies were unavailing. Most of these corporations were chosen from their corporate values as reported in *The Fortune International 500*, 19 August 1985: 182–201.

Great Britain

Sample house organs, recruitment brochures, and annual reports from 1984 to 1986 were examined from British Gas, Esso UK, National Coal Board, Marconi, Unilever, Grand Metropolitan, British Petroleum, Dalgety, and General Electric. These companies were chosen from their large corporate values as reported in *The Fortune International 500*, 19 August 1985: 182–201.

Each publication was analyzed by individual article, and coded for major theme, images of public/private, collectivity/individual, and group tensions, as well as other distinguishing characteristics. The investigator coded each article.

Textbooks

United States

1   Daniel Boorstin and Brooks Kelly, *A History of the United States* (Lexington, Mass.: Ginn, 1986).

2   Stephen Jenkins and Susan Spiegel, *Excel in Civics: Lessons in Citizenship* (St. Paul, Minn.: West, 1985).

3   James West Davison and Mark H. Lytle, *The United States: A History of the Republic* (Englewood Cliffs, N.J.: Prentice-Hall, 1986).

4   Winthrop D. Jourdan, *The Americans: The History of a People and a Nation* (Evanston, Ill.: McDougal, Littell, 1985).

5   Carol Berkin and Leonard Wood, *Land of Promise: A History of the United States* (Glenview, Ill.: Scott, Foresman, 1983).

6   Joseph R. Conlin, *Our Land, Our Time: A History of the United States* (San Diego: Coronado, 1985).

7   Lewis Paul Todd and Merle Curti, *Triumph of the American Nation* (New York: Harcourt Brace Jovanovich, 1986).

8   Judith Gillespie and Stuart Lazarus, *American Government: Comparing Political Experiences* (Englewood Cliffs, N.J.: Prentice-Hall, 1979).

9   Allan Kownslar and Terry Smart, *American Government* (New York: McGraw-Hill, 1980).

10 Richard Gross, *American Citizenship: The Way We Govern* (Menlo Park, Calif.: Addison-Wesley, 1979).

11 Steven Jantzen et al., *Scholastic American Citizenship Program* (New York: Scholastic Book Services, 1977).

12 John J. Patrick and Richard Remy, *Civics for Americans* (Glenview, Ill.: Scott, Foresman, 1980).

13 James Clark and Robert Rimini, *We the People: A History of the United States* (Beverly Hills: Glencoe Press, 1975).

14 Armin Rosencranz et al., *American Government* (New York: Holt, Rinehart, and Winson, 1982).

15 *Macgruder's American Government*, revised by Wm. A. McGlenahan (Boston: Allyn and Bacon, 1983).

16 Howard B. Wildes, Robert Ludlum, and Harriett Brown, *This is America's Story* (Boston: Houghton Mifflin, 1983).

These books were chosen from reports of current usage from state education officers in Texas, Illinois, and California, based on their own statistics (supplied to the author). In addition, other books were chosen from private contacts with the Social Studies Consortium, Boulder, Colorado, which suggested additional titles. The Consortium monitors text usage around the country.

Canada

1   Daniel McDevitt et al., *Canada Today* (Scarborough: Prentice-Hall, 1979).

2   Fred McFadden, Don Quinlan, and Rich Life, *Canada: The Twentieth Century* (Toronto: Fitzhenry and Whiteside, 1982).

3   Allan S. Evans and I. L. Martinello, *Canada's Century* (Toronto: McGraw-Hill, Ryerson, 1978).

4   Allen Hux and Fred Jarman, *Canada: A Growing Concern*, rev. ed. (Globe/Modern Canadian: Curriculum Press, 1987).

5   Joseph Lower, *A Nation Developing: A Brief History of Canada* (Toronto: The Ryerson Press, 1970).

6   Ronald C. Kirbyson et al., *Discovering Canada: Shaping an Identity and Developing a Nation* (Scarborough, Ontario: Prentice-Hall, 1983).

7   George K. Grearson and Roy L. King, *Canadian Democracy at Work*, 3d ed. (Toronto: Macmillan, 1971).

8   E. A. Mitchner et al., *Forging a Destiny: Canada Since 1945* (Sage Publishers, 1976).

9   Allan S. Evans and Lawrence Diachun, *Canada: Towards Tomorrow* (Toronto: McGraw-Hill, Ryerson: 1976).

These materials were chosen from those prescribed by the provinces of Alberta, Ontario, Saskatchewan, and British Columbia. Material on usage was provided by prominent educational authorities to the investigator. I am grateful to Fred Headon of the Canadian Association for the Social Studies, who also assisted in identifying these texts.

Great Britain

1   Kathleen Allsop, *Local and Central Government*, 4th ed., revised by Tom Brennan (London: Hutchison, 1984).

2   Philip Gabriel and Andrew Maslen, *British Politics* (Burnt Mill, Harlow: Longman, 1986).

3   Philip Gabriel, *British Government: An Introduction to Politics*, 3d ed., Series One (Burnt Mill, Harlow: Longman, 1986).

4   J. Harvey, *How Britain Is Governed*, 3d ed. (Basingstoke and London: Macmillan, 1985).

5   David Roberts, *Politics: A New Approach* (Ormshirk, Lancashire: Causeway, 1986).

6   D. M. M. Scott and D. L. Kobrin, *O Level British Constitution*, 3d ed. (London: Butterworths, 1979).

7   Lynton Robins, Tom Brennan, and John Sutton, *People and Politics in Britain* (London and Basingstoke: Macmillan, 1985).

8   Peter Lane, *British Social and Economic History from 1760 to the Present Day* (Oxford: Oxford Univ. Press, 1987).

9   Christopher Culpin, *Making Modern Britain* (London: Collins Educational, 1987).

10   R. J. Cootes, *Britain Since 1700*, 2d ed. (Burnt Mill, Harlow, Essex: Longman, 1983).

11   Denis Richards and J. W. Hunt, *An Illustrated History of Modern Britain, 1783–1980* (Burnt Mill, Harlow, Essex: Longman, 1983).

12   John Robottom, *A Social and Economic History of Industrial Britain* (Burnt Mill, Harlow, Essex: Longman, 1987).

No central listing of widely used British secondary school texts is kept by either publishers or educational officers in Great Britain. This sample was compiled by personal contacts with school heads and/or social studies heads at eight comprehensive secondary schools chosen for their geographical and ethnic diversity within England. I am grateful to Finnessa Ferrel-Smith, who gathered this information.

Each text was analyzed using standard coding analysis forms to cover each of the subjects discussed in chapters 3–5. The investigator analyzed each text.

Magazine Ads

United States: magazines from 1986 to 1987

1   *Better Homes and Gardens*—four issues
2   *National Geographic*—four issues
3   *Ms.*—four issues (1986–1987)
4   *Esquire*—three issues
5   *Ladies' Home Journal*—four issues
6   *McCall's*—four issues
7   *Family Circle*—four issues
8   *Reader's Digest*—four issues
9   *Atlantic*—three issues
10   *New Yorker*—four issues
11   *Time*—four issues

Total: forty-two issues. These were chosen on the basis of their circulation figures as supplied in *The World Almanac. Ms., Atlantic, National Geographic,* and the *New Yorker* were chosen for their appeal to elite audiences.

Canada: magazines from 1986 to 1987

1   *Maclean's*—four issues
2   *Canadian Business*—four issues
3   *Canadian Geographic*—four issues
4   *Select Homes*—four issues
5   *Equinox*—four issues
6   *Canadian Living*—four issues
7   *Saturday Night*—four issues
8   *Outdoor Canada*—four issues

Total: thirty-two issues. These were chosen on the basis of national circulation figures, as supplied for the mid-1980s by the *Audit Bureau of Circulation,* Schaumburg, Illinois.

Great Britain: magazines from 1986 to 1987

1   *British Cosmopolitan*—four issues
2   *The Economist*—four issues
3   *Punch*—three issues

4   *Woman*—four issues
5   *Reader's Digest*—four issues
6   *TV Times*—four issues
7   *Living*—four issues

    Total: twenty-seven issues. These were chosen based on circulation figures. *The Economist* and *Punch* were chosen for their appeal to elite audiences. Information supplied by Periodical Publishers Association, London.

    Each advertisement was analyzed with the use of a code sheet that assessed depictions of individuals, particular advertising appeals, and the settings in which the product was placed. The investigator coded each ad.

Bibliography

Abercrombie, Nicholas, Stephen Hill, and Bryan S. Turner. 1980. *The Dominant Ideology Thesis*. London and Boston: Allen and Unwin.

Abramowitz, Alan. 1980. "The United States: Political Culture Under Stress." In Almond and Verba 1980: 177–212.

Abramson, Jeffrey B., F. Christopher Arterton, and Gary R. Orren. 1988. *The Electronic Commonwealth*. New York: Basic Books.

Abramson, Paul. 1983. *Political Attitudes in America*. San Francisco: W. H. Freeman.

Aguirre, B. E. 1984. "The Conventionalization of Collective Behavior in Cuba." *American Journal of Sociology* 90: 541–67.

Alford, Robert. 1963. *Party and Society*. New York: Rand-McNally.

Allsop, Kathleen. 1984. *Local and Central Government*. 4th ed. London: Hutchinson.

Almond, Gabriel, and Sidney Verba, eds. 1980. *The Civic Culture Revisited*. Boston: Little, Brown.

Ang, Ien. 1985. *Watching Dallas: Soap Opera and the Melodramatic Imagination*. Trans. Della Couling. London: Methuen.

Anyon, Jean. 1978. "Elementary Social Studies Textbooks and Legitimating Knowledge." *Theory and Research in Social Education* 6: 40–55.

Anyon, Jean. 1979. "Ideology and United States History Textbooks." *Harvard Educational Review* 49: 361–86.

Anyon, Jean. 1981. "Social Class and School Knowledge." *Curriculum Inquiry* 11: 3–43.

Archer, Margaret. 1988. *Culture and Agency*. Cambridge: Cambridge Univ. Press.

Arnold, Thurman. 1935. *The Symbols of Government*. New Haven: Yale Univ. Press.

Aronowitz, Stanley. 1981. *The Crisis of Historical Materialism*. New York: Praeger.

Asad, T. 1979. "Anthropology and the Analysis of Ideology." *Man* 14: 607–27.

Atwood, Margaret. 1972. *Survival: A Thematic Guide to Canadian Literature*. Toronto: Anansi.

Audley, Paul. 1983. *Canada's Cultural Industries: Broadcasting, Records and Film*. Toronto: Lorimer.

Axelrod, Robert. 1986. "Presidential Election Coalitions in 1984." *American Political Science Review* 80: 281–84.

253

254   Bibliography

Axworthy, Lloyd. 1988. "The Federal System: An Uncertain Path." *Daedalus* 117, no. 4 (Fall): 129–55.

Bailey, F. G., ed. 1971. *Gifts and Poison.* Oxford: Blackwell.

Balkin, J. M. 1987. "Deconstructive Practice and Legal Theory." *The Yale Law Journal* 96: 743–86.

Barber, Benjamin. 1984. *Strong Democracy: Participatory Politics for a New Age.* Berkeley and Los Angeles: Univ. of California Press.

Barnes, Samuel, Max Kaase et al. 1979. *Political Action: Mass Participation in Five Western Democracies.* Beverly Hills: Sage.

Barry, Brian. 1970. *Sociologists, Economists, and Democracy.* London: Collier-Macmillan.

Baudrillard, Jean. 1983. *In the Shadow of the Silent Majorities . . . or The End of the Social.* Trans. Paul Foss, Paul Patton, and John Johnston. New York: Semiotext(e).

BBM (Bureau of Measurement). 1987

Beach, Joseph Warren. 1956. *The Concept of Nature in Nineteenth-Century English Poetry.* New York: Pageant.

Beer, Samuel H. 1969. *British Politics in the Collectivist Age.* New York: Vintage.

Beer, Samuel H. 1982. *Britain against Itself.* New York: Norton.

Bell, Daniel. 1976. *The Cultural Contradictions of Capitalism.* New York: Basic Books.

Bell, David, and Lorne Tepperman. 1979. *The Roots of Disunity: A Look at Canadian Political Culture.* Toronto: McClelland and Stewart.

Bellah, Robert P. 1967. "Civil Religion in America." *Daedalus* 96: 1–21.

Bellah, Robert P., et al. 1985. *Habits of the Heart: Individualism and Commitment in American Life.* Berkeley and Los Angeles: Univ. of California Press.

Bennett, W. Lance, and Martha S. Feldman. 1981. *Reconstructing Reality in the Courtroom.* New Brunswick, N.J.: Rutgers Univ. Press.

Bensman, Joseph. 1967. *Dollars and Sense: Ideology, Ethics, and the Meaning of Work in Profit and Non-Profit Organizations.* New York: Macmillan.

Benson, Lee. 1961. *The Concept of Jacksonian Democracy.* Princeton: Princeton Univ. Press.

Berger, Bennett. 1981. *The Survival of a Counterculture: Ideological Work and Everyday Life Among Rural Communards.* Berkeley and Los Angeles: Univ. of California Press.

Berkin, Carol, and Leonard Wood. 1983. *Land of Promise: A History of the United States.* Glenview, Ill.: Scott, Foresman.

Berry, Jeffrey M. 1989. *The Interest Group Society.* 2d ed. Glenview, Ill.: Scott, Foresman.

Black, Earl, and Merle Black. 1987. *Politics and Society in the South.* Cambridge: Harvard Univ. Press.

Bloom, Allan. 1987. *The Closing of the American Mind.* New York: Simon & Schuster.

Boorstin, Daniel, and Brooks Kelly. 1986. *A History of the United States.* Lexington, Mass.: Ginn.

Bourdieu, Pierre. 1984. *Distinction: A Social Critique of the Judgement of Taste.* London: Routledge and Kegan Paul.

Bourdieu, Pierre, and Jean-Claude Passeron. 1977. *Reproduction in Education, Society and Culture.* Trans. Richard Nice. London and Beverly Hills: Sage.

Bowles, Samuel, and Herbert Gintis. 1986. *Democracy and Capitalism.* New York: Basic Books.

Brennan, Tom. 1981. *Political Education and Democracy.* Cambridge: Cambridge Univ. Press.

British Gas. 1985. "Report to Employees 1984/5."

British Gas Personnel Division. n.d. "British Gas Apprenticeships."

British Petroleum. 1985. *Shield* no. 4.

British Steel Corporation. 1984. "The British Steel Corporation." Mimeo. September.

Brody, Richard. 1980. "The Puzzle of Political Participation in America." In Anthony King, ed., *The New American Political System.* Washington: American Enterprise Institute: 287–325.

Bruce-Gardyne, Jock. 1986. *Ministers and Mandarins: Inside the Whitehall Village.* London: Sidgwick and Jackson.

Buker, Eloise A. 1987. *Politics Through a Looking-Glass: Understanding Political Cultures Through a Structuralist Interpretation of Narratives.* New York: Greenwood Press.

Bullock, Alan. 1960. *The Life and Times of Ernest Bevin.* Vol. 1. London: Heinemann.

Bunce, Richard. 1976. *Television in the Corporate Interest.* New York: Praeger.

Burawoy, Michael. 1979. *Manufacturing Consent.* Chicago: Univ. of Chicago Press.

Burke, Mavis E. 1984. "Educational Implications of Cultural Diversity." In Ronald Samuda, John W. Berry, and Michel Laferriere, eds., *Multiculturalism in Canada: Social and Educational Perspectives.* Toronto: Allyn and Bacon: 3–18.

Burnham, Walter Dean. 1970. *Critical Elections and the Mainsprings of American Politics.* New York: Norton.

Burnham, Walter Dean. 1982. *The Current Crisis in American Politics.* New York and London: Oxford Univ. Press.

Butler, David, and Dennis Kavanaugh. 1988. *The British General Election of 1987.* Houndsmills and London: Macmillan.

Butsch, Richard, and Lynda M. Glennon. 1983. "Social Class: Frequency Trends In Domestic Situation Comedies, 1946–1978." *Journal of Broadcasting* 27, no. 1 (Winter): 77–81.

Campbell, Angus, et al. 1960. *The American Voter.* New York: Wiley.

Canadian Broadcasting Corporation. 1986. *Seeing Things . . . Canadian.* CBC Head Office: August.

Cantor, Muriel, and Suzanne Pingree. 1983. *The Soap Opera.* Beverly Hills: Sage.

Carmines, Edward, and James Stimson. 1982. "Racial Issues and the Structure of Mass Belief Systems." *Journal of Politics* 44: 2–20.

Carmines, Edward, and James Stimson. 1989. *Issue Evolution: Race and the Transformation of American Politics*. Princeton: Princeton Univ. Press.

Carnoy, Martin, and Henry M. Levin. 1985. *Schooling and Work in the Democratic State*. Stanford: Stanford Univ. Press.

Carroll, James, et al. 1987. "We the People: A Review of U.S. Government and Civics Textbooks." Washington: People for the American Way.

Cawelti, John. 1965. *Apostles of the Self-Made Man*. Chicago: Univ. of Chicago Press.

Cawelti, John. 1984. *The Six-Gun Mystique*. 2d ed. Bowling Green: Bowling Green Univ. Press.

Children's World. 1985. "Children's World, A Loving Place to Learn." Evergreen, Colo.: Children's World.

Christensen, Terry. 1987. *Reel Politics: American Political Movies from "Death of a Nation" to "Platoon"*. Oxford: Basil Blackwell.

Christolph, James B. 1984. "Rubbing Up or Running Down? Dilemmas of Civil Service Reform in Britain." In Studlar and Waltman 1984.

Clark, James, and Robert Rimini. 1975. *We the People: A History of the United States*. Beverly Hills: Glencoe Press.

Clarke, Harold D. et al. 1979. *Political Choice in Canada*. Toronto: McGraw-Hill, Ryerson.

Clarke, Peter, ed. 1973. *New Models for Mass Communication Research*. Beverly Hills: Sage.

Clarke, Simon. 1981. *The Foundations of Structuralism*. Brighton, Sussex: The Harvester Press.

Clemens, John. 1983. *Polls, Politics and Populism*. Aldershot, Hans.: Gower.

Cohen, Joshua, and Joel Rogers. 1983. *On Democracy: Toward a Transformation of American Society*. Harmondsworth, Middlesex, England: Penguin.

Commission on Party Structure and Delegate Selection to the Democratic National Committee. 1970. *Mandate for Reform*. Washington: Democratic National Committee.

Conlin, Joseph R. 1985. *Our Land, Our Time: A History of the United States*. San Diego: Coronado.

Connolly, William. 1987. *Politics and Ambiguity*. Madison: Univ. of Wisconsin Press.

Conover, Pamela Johnson, and Virginia Gray. 1983. *Feminism and the New Right: Conflict Over the American Family*. New York: Praeger.

Conway, John. 1988. "An 'Adapted Organic Tradition'." *Daedalus* 117, no. 4 (Fall): 381–96.

Conway, M. Margaret. 1985. *Political Participation in the United States*. Washington: Congressional Quarterly Press.

Cook, Timothy. 1988. "Democracy and Community in American Children's Literature." In Ernest J. Yanarella and Lee Sigelman, eds., *Political Mythology and Popular Fiction*. New York: Greenwood Press: 39–61.

Cooper, Barry, Allan Kornberg, and William Mishler. 1988. "The Resurgence of Conservatism in Britain, Canada, and the United States: An Overview."

In Cooper, Kornberg, and Mishler, eds., *The Resurgence of Conservatism in Anglo-American Democracy.* Durham: Duke Univ. Press: 1–25.

Cootes, R. J. 1982. *Britain Since 1700.* 2d ed. Burnt Mill, Harlow, Essex: Longman.

Coser, Lewis G., et al. 1982. *Books: The Culture and Commerce of Publishing.* New York: Basic Books.

Coughlin, Richard M. 1980. *Ideology, Public Opinion and Welfare Policy: Attitudes toward Taxes and Spending in Industrialized Societies.* Berkeley: Institute of International Studies.

Crewe, Ivor. 1986. "On the Death and Resurrection of Class Voting: Some Reflections on *How Britain Votes.*" *Political Studies* 34: 620–38.

Crewe, Ivor, Tony Fox, and Jim Alt. 1977. "Non-Voting in British General Elections." In Colin Crouch, ed., *Participation in Politics, British Political Sociology Yearbook 3.* London: Croom Held: 38–110.

Crewe, Ivor, and Donald Searing. 1988. "Ideological Change in the British Conservative Party." *American Political Science Review* 82, no. 2 (June): 361–85.

Crotty, William. 1978. *Decision for the Democrats.* Baltimore: Johns Hopkins Univ. Press.

Culpin, Christopher. 1987. *Making Modern Britain.* London: Collins Educational.

Cusick, Philip. 1983. *The Egalitarian Ideal and the American High School.* New York: Longman.

Czitron, Daniel J. 1982. *Media and the American Mind.* Chapel Hill: Univ. of North Carolina Press.

Dahl, Robert A. 1985. *A Preface to Economic Democracy.* Berkeley and Los Angeles: Univ. of California Press.

Dahl, Robert A. 1986. *Democracy, Liberty, and Equality.* Oslo: Norwegian Univ. Press.

Dahl, Robert A., ed. 1966. *Political Oppositions in Western Democracies.* New Haven: Yale Univ. Press.

Dahl, Robert A., and Edward Tufte. 1973. *Size and Democracy.* Stanford: Stanford Univ. Press.

D'Andrade, Roy G. 1984. "Cultural Meaning Systems." In Richard A. Shweder and Robert A. Levine, eds., *Cultural Theory: Essays on Mind, Self, and Emotion.* Cambridge: Cambridge Univ. Press: 88–123.

Davidson, James West, and Mark H. Lytle. 1986. *The United States: A History of the Republic.* Englewood Cliffs, N.J.: Prentice-Hall.

Davis, O. L. Jr., et al. 1986. "Looking at History: A Review of Major U.S. History Textbooks." Washington, D.C.: People for the American Way.

Davison, W. Phillips. 1983. "The Third-Person Effect in Communication." *Public Opinion Quarterly* 47: 1–15.

Deal, Terence, and Allan A. Kennedy. 1982. *Corporate Culture.* Reading, Mass.: Addison-Wesley.

De Brizzi, John A. 1983. *Ideology and the Rise of Labor Theory in America.* Westport, Conn.: Greenwood Press.

Delli Carpini, Michael X. 1986. *Stability and Change in American Politics.* New York and London: New York Univ. Press.

Dennis, Jack. 1986. "Public Support for the Party System: 1964–1984." Paper delivered to the Annual Meeting of the American Political Science Association, Washington, D.C., 28–31 August.

Dick, Ronald S. 1983. "Political Support and the Mass Media: The Publicly Financed Communications Agencies." In Allan Kornberg and Harold D. Clarke, eds., *Political Support in Canada: The Crisis Years.* Durham: Duke Univ. Press: 124–52.

Diggins, John. 1984. *The Lost Soul of American Politics.* New York: Basic Books.

DiMaggio, Paul. 1987. "Classification in Art." *American Sociological Review* 52: 440–55.

Dion, Leon. 1988. "The Mystery of Quebec." *Daedalus* 117, no. 4 (Fall): 282–317.

Dittmer, Lowell. 1976–77. "Political Culture and Political Symbolism: Toward a Theoretical Synthesis." *World Politics* 29: 552–83.

Doise, Willem. 1978. *Groups and Individuals: Explanations in Social Psychology.* Cambridge: Cambridge Univ. Press.

Donovan, Robert J. 1982. *Tumultuous Years: The Presidency of Harry S. Truman.* New York: Norton.

Douglas, Mary. 1966. *Purity and Danger.* London: Routledge and Kegan Paul.

Douglas, Mary. 1970. *Natural Symbols.* Harmondsworth: Penguin.

Douglas, Mary, ed. 1982a. *Essays in the Sociology of Perception.* London: Routledge and Kegan Paul.

Douglas, Mary. 1982b. *In the Active Voice.* London: Routledge and Kegan Paul.

Douglas, Mary, ed. 1984. *Food and Culture.* New York: Russell Sage.

Douglas, Mary. 1986. *How Institutions Think.* Syracuse: Syracuse Univ. Press.

Douglas, Mary, and Baron Isherwood. 1979. *The World of Goods.* New York: Basic Books.

Downs, Anthony. 1957. *An Economic Theory of Democracy.* New York: Harper and Row.

Drabble, Margaret. 1977. *The Ice Age.* London: Weidenfeld and Nicolson.

Dumont, Louis. 1986. *Essays on Individualism.* Chicago: Univ. of Chicago Press.

Duncan, Graeme. 1978. "Comments on Some Radical Critiques of Liberal-Democratic Theory." In Pierre Birnbaum, Jack Lively, and Geraint Parry, eds., *Democracy, Consensus, and Social Contract.* Beverly Hills: Sage.

Dunleavy, Patrick, and Christopher T. Husbands. 1985. *British Democracy at the Crossroads: Voting and Party Competition in the 1980s.* London: George Allen and Unwin.

Dunn, John. 1979. *Western Political Theory in the Face of the Future.* Cambridge: Cambridge Univ. Press.

Durkheim, Emile. 1951. *Suicide: A Study in Sociology.* Trans. George Simpson. Glencoe: The Free Press.

Durkheim, Emile. 1957a. *Professional Ethics and Civic Morals.* Trans. Cornelia Brookfield. London: Routledge and Kegan Paul.

Durkheim, Emile. 1957b. *The Rules of the Sociological Method.* Glencoe: The Free Press.

Durkheim, Emile. 1960. *Montesquieu and Rousseau*. Trans. Ralph Manneheim. Ann Arbor: Univ. of Michigan Press.

Durkheim, Emile. [1912] 1965. *The Elementary Forms of the Religious Life*. New York: The Free Press.

Durkheim, Emile, and Marcel Mauss. 1963. *Primitive Classification*. Ed. Rodney Needham. Chicago: Univ. of Chicago Press.

Eckstein, Harry. 1988. "A Culturalist Theory of Political Change." *American Political Science Review* 82: 789–805.

Edelman, Murray. 1964. *The Symbolic Uses of Politics*. Urbana: Univ. of Illinois Press.

Edelman, Murray. 1984. "The Political Language of the Helping Professions." In Michael Shapiro, ed., *Language and Politics*. New York: New York Univ. Press: 44–61.

Edelman, Murray. 1988. *Constructing the Political Spectacle*. Chicago: Univ. of Chicago Press.

Eliot, T. S. 1949. *Notes Toward the Definition of Culture*. New York: Harcourt, Brace.

Elkins, David J., and Richard E. B. Simeon. 1979. "A Cause in Search of Its Effect, or What Does Political Culture Explain?" *Comparative Politics* 11: 127–46.

Ellington, Lucien. 1986. "Blacks and Hispanics in High School Economics Texts." *Social Education* 50: 64–66.

Elliott, B., and D. McCrone. 1987. "Class, Culture, and Morality: A Sociological Analysis of Neo-Conservatism." *Sociologial Review* 35: 485–515.

Emmerdale Farm: Celebration Edition. n.d. London: London Editions.

Engelman, Frederick C., and Mildred A. Schwartz. 1975. *Canadian Political Parties*. Scarborough, Ont.: Prentice-Hall.

Epstein, Leon. 1986. *Political Parties in the American Mold*. Madison: Univ. of Wisconsin Press.

Esslin, Martin. 1982. *The Age of Television*. San Francisco: W. H. Freeman.

Evans, Allan S., and Lawrence Diachun. 1976. *Canada: Towards Tomorrow*. Toronto: McGraw-Hill, Ryerson.

Evans, Allan S., and I. C. Martinello. 1978. *Canada's Century*. Toronto: McGraw-Hill, Ryerson.

Evans. Robert G. 1988. "'We'll Take Care of It for You': Health Care in the Canadian Community." *Daedalus* 117, no. 4 (Fall): 155–89.

Ewen, Stuart. 1988. *All Consuming Images: The Politics of Style in Contemporary Culture*. New York: Basic Books.

Ewen, Stuart, and Elizabeth Ewen. 1982. *Channels of Desire*. New York: McGraw-Hill.

Exoo, Cavin F., ed. 1987. *Democracy Upside Down: Public Opinion and Cultural Hegemony in the United States*. New York: Praeger.

Fantasia, Rick. 1988. *Cultures of Solidarity*. Berkeley and Los Angeles: Univ. of California Press.

Ferguson, Thomas, and Joel Rogers. 1986. *Right Turn*. New York: Hill and Wang.

Feuer, Jane. 1984. "The MTM Style." In Feuer, Paul Kerr, and Tise Vahimagi, eds., *MTM 'Quality Television'*. London: BFI Books.

Fidler, John. 1984. *The British Business Elite: Its Attitudes to Class, Status, and Power*. London: Routledge and Kegan Paul.

"Finance Graduate Scheme, The Berni and Host Group Ltd." N.d., n.p.

Fiorina, Morris P. 1981. *Retrospective Voting in American National Elections*. New Haven: Yale Univ. Press.

Fiske, John. 1987a. "British Cultural Studies and Television." In Robert C. Allen, ed., *Channels of Discourse: Television and Contemporary Culture*. Chapel Hill: Univ. of North Carolina Press: 254–91.

Fiske, John. 1987b. *Television Culture*. London and New York: Methuen.

Fitzgerald, Frances. 1979. *America Revised*. Boston: Little, Brown.

Flaherty, David H. 1988. "Who Rules Canada?" *Daedalus* 117, no. 4 (Fall): 99–129.

Flanders, Allan. 1970. *Trade Unions*. London: Hutchinson.

Flanigan, William H., and Nancy H. Zingale. 1987. *Political Behavior of the American Electorate*. 6th ed. Boston: Allyn and Bacon.

Forgas, Joseph, et al. 1983. "Lay Explanations of Wealth: Attributions for Economic Success." *Journal of Applied Social Psychology* 13: 381–97.

Foucault, Michel. 1972. *The Archeology of Knowledge*. Trans. A. M. Sheridan Smith. New York: Pantheon.

Foucault, Michel. 1977. *Discipline and Punish: the Birth of the Prison*. Trans. Alan Sheridan. New York: Pantheon.

Fowler, Roger. 1977. *Linguistics and the Novel*. London: Methuen.

Fox, John, and Michael Ornstein. 1986. "The Canadian State and Corporate Elites in the Post-War Period." *Canadian Review of Sociology and Anthropology* 23: 481–506.

Frank, Helmut J., and John J. Schanz, Jr. 1978. *U.S./Canadian Energy Trade*. Boulder: Westview Press.

Franklin, Charles. 1984. "Issue Preferences, Socialization, and the Evolution of Party Identification." *American Journal of Political Science* 28: 459–78.

Franklin, Mark N. 1984. "How the Decline of Class Voting Opened the Way to Radical Change in British Politics." *British Journal of Political Science* 14: 483–508.

Franklin, Mark N. 1985. *The Decline of Class Voting in Britain: Changes in the Basis of Electoral Choice, 1964–1983*. Oxford: Clarendon Press.

Freeden, Michael. 1986. *Liberalism Divided: A Study in British Political Thought, 1914–1939*. Oxford: Clarendon Press.

Fussell, Paul. 1975. *The Great War and Modern Memory*. New York: Oxford Univ. Press.

Gabriel, Philip. 1986. *British Government: An Introduction to Politics*. 3d ed. Series One. Burnt Hill, Harlow, Essex: Longman.

Gabriel, Philip, and Andrew Maslen. 1986. *British Politics*. Burnt Hill, Harlow, Essex: Longman.

Gagnon, Paul. 1988. "Why Study History?" *The Atlantic* (November): 43–74.

Galbraith, John Kenneth. 1964. *The Scotch*. Boston: Houghton Mifflin.

Gans, Herbert. 1974. *Popular Culture and High Culture*. New York: Basic Books.

Gans, Herbert. 1980. *Deciding What's News*. New York: Vintage.

Gardner, Howard. 1985. *The Mind's New Science: A History of the Cognitive Revolution*. New York: Basic Books.

Garfinkel, Andrew. 1983. "A Pragmatic Approach to Truth in Advertising." In Richard Jackson Harris, ed., *Information Processing Research in Advertising*. Hillsdale, N.J.: Lawrence Erlbaum Associates: 175–95.

Gaventa, John. 1980. *Power and Powerlessness*. Champaign: Univ. of Illinois Press.

Geertz, Clifford. 1973. *The Interpretation of Cultures*. New York: Basic.

Geertz, Clifford. 1983. *Local Knowledge*. New York: Basic Books.

General Electric Company. 1986. "A National Asset for a Hundred Years."

Gerbner, George, and Larry Gross. 1981. "The Violent Face of Television and Its Lessons." In Edward L. Palmer and Aimee Dorr, eds., *Children and the Faces of Television*. New York: Academic Press: 149–62.

Gillespie, Judith, and Stuart Lazarus. 1979. *American Government: Comparing Political Experiences*. Englewood Cliffs, N.J.: Prentice-Hall.

Ginsberg, Benjamin. 1986. *The Captive Public*. New York: Basic Books.

Gitlin, Todd. 1980. *The Whole World Is Watching*. Berkeley and Los Angeles: Univ. of California Press.

Gitlin, Todd. 1983. *Inside Prime Time*. New York: Pantheon.

Godelier, Maurice. 1982. "Myths, Infrastructures and History in Lévi-Strauss." In Ino Rossi et al., *The Logic of Culture: Advances in Structural Theory and Methods*. So. Hadley, Mass.: J. F. Bergin: 232–61.

Goffman, Erving. 1979. *Gender Advertisements*. New York: Harper Colophon Books.

Gold, Philip. 1987. *Advertising, Politics and American Culture*. New York: Paragon.

Goldfarb, Jeffrey. 1982. *On Cultural Freedom: An Exploration of Public Life in Poland and the United States*. Chicago: Univ. of Chicago Press.

Golding, Peter, and Sue Middleton. 1983. *Images of Welfare: Press and Public Attitudes to Poverty*. Oxford: Martin Robertson.

Goody, Jack. 1977. *The Domestication of the Savage Mind*. Cambridge: Cambridge Univ. Press.

Graber, Doris. 1984. *Processing the News*. New York: Longman.

Graebner, William. 1987. *The Engineering of Consent: Democracy and Authority in Twentieth Century America*. Madison: Univ. of Wisconsin Press.

Grafstein, Robert. 1982. "Structure and Structuralism." *Social Science Quarterly* 63: 617–33.

Grearson, George K., and Roy C. King. 1971. *Canadian Democracy at Work*. 3d ed. Toronto: Macmillan.

Greenstein, Fred, and Sidney Tarrow. 1970. "Political Orientations of Children: The Use of a Semi-Projective Technique in Three Nations." Beverly Hills: Sage.

Gregory, C. A. 1982. *Gifts and Commodities*. London: Academic Press.

Gross, Richard. 1979. *American Citizenship: The Way We Govern*. Menlo Park, Calif.: Addison-Wesley.

Gutman, Herbert. 1987. *Power and Culture: Essays on the American Working Class*. New York: Pantheon.

Gutmann, Amy. 1987. *Democratic Education*. Princeton: Princeton Univ. Press.

Hairston, Maxine. 1982. *A Contemporary Rhetoric*. 3d ed. Boston: Houghton Mifflin.

Hall, Stuart. 1988. *The Hard Road to Renewal: Thatcherism and the Crisis of the Left*. London: Verso.

Halle, David. 1984. *America's Working Man*. Chicago: Univ. of Chicago Press.

Halsey, A. H., A. F. Heath, and J. M. Ridge. 1980. *Origins and Destinations: Family, Class, and Education in Modern Britain*. Oxford: Clarendon Press.

Hamilton, Charles. 1975. *The Trade Relations between England and India*. Delhi: Idarah-i Adabiyat-i Delhi.

Handler, Richard. 1988. *Nationalism and the Politics of Culture in Quebec*. Madison: Univ. of Wisconsin Press.

Hanson, Russell L. 1985. *The Democratic Imagination in America: Conversations with Our Past*. Princeton: Princeton Univ. Press.

Hare, F. Kenneth. 1988. "Canada: The Land." *Daedalus* (Fall): 31–51.

Harney, Robert F. 1988. "'So Great a Heritage as Ours': Immigration and the Survival of the Canadian Polity." *Daedalus* 117, no. 4 (Fall): 51–99.

Harris, Marvin. 1979. *Cultural Materialism*. New York: Random House.

Hart, Roderick P. 1984. *Verbal Style and the Presidency: A Computer-Based Analysis*. Orlando: Academic Press.

Hart, Roderick P. 1987. *The Sound of Leadership*. Chicago and London: Univ. of Chicago Press.

Hart, Vivien. 1978. *Distrust and Democracy*. Cambridge: Cambridge Univ. Press.

Hartcup, Adeline. 1984. *Love and Marriage in the Great Country Houses*. London: Sidgwich and Jackson.

Hartley, John. "Encouraging Signs." In Rowland and Watkins 1984.

Hartz, Louis. 1955. *The Liberal Tradition in America*. New York: Harvest.

Harvey, J. 1983. *How Britain Is Governed*. 3d ed. London and Basingstoke: Macmillan.

Heath, A. F. et al. 1985. *How Britain Votes*. New York: Pergamon.

Held, David. 1987. *Models of Democracy*. Cambridge: Polity Press.

Hirszowicz, Maria. 1982. *Industrial Sociology: An Introduction*. New York: St. Martin's Press.

Hixon, Sheila, and Ruth Rose, eds. 1972. *The Official Proceedings of the Democratic National Convention 1972*. Washington: Library of Congress: 174–81, 196–210.

Hochschild, Jennifer. 1981. *What's Fair?* Cambridge: Harvard Univ. Press.

Hochschild, Jennifer. 1984. *The New American Dilemma*. New Haven: Yale Univ. Press.

Hockin, Thomas A. 1975. *Government in Canada*. London: Weidenfeld and Nicolson.

Hofstadter, Richard. 1955. *The Age of Reform*. New York: Knopf.

Hofstadter, Richard. 1965. *The Paranoid Style in American Politics*. New York: Knopf.

Hoggart, Richard. 1957. *The Uses of Literacy*. London: Chatto and Windus.

Horowitz, Gad. 1966. "Conservatism, Liberalism, and Socialism in Canada: An Interpretation." *Canadian Journal of Economics and Political Science* 32: 143–71.

Howarth, Christine. 1984. *The Way People Work: Job Satisfaction and the Challenge of Change*. Oxford: Oxford Univ. Press.

Hunt, Geoffrey, and Saundra Satterlee. 1987. "Darts, Drinks, and the Pub: The Culture of Female Drinking." *Sociological Review* 35: 575–602.

Huntington, Samuel. 1981. *American Politics: The Promise of Disharmony*. Cambridge, Mass.: Belknap Press.

Huntington, Samuel, 1968. *Political Order in Changing Societies*. New Haven and London: Yale Univ. Press.

Hutchison, Robert, and Susan Forrester. 1987. *Arts Centres in the United Kingdom*. London: Policy Studies Institute.

Hux, Allan, and Fred Jarman. 1987. *Canada: A Growing Concern*. Rev. ed. Markham: Globe/Modern Canadian Curriculum Press.

Ingelhart, Ronald. 1977. *The Silent Revolution*. Princeton: Princeton Univ. Press.

Ingelhart, Ronald. 1990. *Culture Shift in Advanced Industrial Society*. Princeton: Princeton Univ. Press.

Inglis, Fred. 1988. *Popular Culture and Political Power*. New York: St. Martin's Press.

Innis, Hugh R., ed. [1969] 1973. *Bilingualism and Biculturalism: An Abridged Version of the Royal Commission Report*. Toronto: McClelland and Stewart.

Iyengar, Shanto, and Donald R. Kinder. 1987. *News that Matters: Television and American Opinion*. Chicago: Univ. of Chicago Press.

Jackman, Mary, and Michael Muha. 1984. "Separate, Therefore Unequal." *American Sociological Review* 49: 751–70.

Jackman, Robert. 1987. "Political Institutions and Voter Turnout in the Industrial Democracies." *American Political Science Review* 81, no. 2 (June): 405–24.

Jackman, Robert, and Mary Jackman. 1983. *Class Awareness in the United States*. Berkeley and Los Angeles: Univ. of California Press.

Jaenen, Cornelius J. 1977. "Multiculturalism and Public Education." In Hugh A. Stevenson and J. Donald Wilson, eds., *Precepts, Policy and Process: Perspectives on Contemporary Canadian Education*. London, Ontario: Alexander, Blake: 77–97.

Jahoda, Gustav. 1982. *Psychology and Anthropology*. London: Academic Press.

Janowitz, Morris. 1983. *The Reconstruction of Patriotism*. Chicago: Univ. of Chicago Press.

Jantzen, Steven et al. 1977. *Scholastic American Citizenship*. New York: Scholastic Book Services.

Jenkins, Alan. 1979. *The Social Theory of Claude Lévi-Strauss*. London: Academic Press.

Jenkins, Stephen, and Susan Spiegel. 1985. *Excel in Civics: Lessons in Citizenship*. St. Paul, Minn.: West.

Johnson, William, and Michael Ornstein. 1985. "Social Class and Political Ideology in Canada." *Canadian Review of Sociology and Anthropology* (August): 369–94.

Jones, Nicholas. 1986. *Strikes and the Media*. Oxford: Basil Blackwell.

Jordan, Mary. 1975. *Survival: Labour's Trials and Tribulations in Canada*. Toronto: McDonald House.

Jordan, Winthrop D. 1985. *The Americans: The History of a People and a Nation*. Evanston, Ill.: McDougal, Littell.

Kaminsky, Stuart N., and Jeffrey H. Mahan. 1985. *American Television Genres*. Chicago: Nelson Hall.

Kelley, Robert. 1977. "Ideology and Political Culture from Jefferson to Nixon." *American Historical Review* 82: 531–62.

Kelley, Robert. 1979. *The Cultural Pattern in American Politics: The First Century*. New York: Knopf.

Kelso, William. 1978. *American Democratic Theory*. Westport, Conn.: Greenwood Press.

Kermode, Frank. 1979. *The Genesis of Secrecy*. Cambridge: Harvard Univ. Press.

Kertzer, David L. 1988. *Ritual, Politics, and Power*. New Haven and London: Yale Univ. Press.

Key, V. O., Jr. 1956. *American State Politics: An Introduction*. New York: Knopf.

Kielty, Frank, Clara Hatton, and Peter Munsche. [1980] n.d. *Canadians Speak Out: The Canadian Gallup Polls, 1980 Edition*. Toronto: McNamara.

Kinder, Donald. 1986. "The Continuing American Dilemma: White Resistance to Racial Change 40 Years After Myrdal." *Journal of Social Issues* 42, no. 2: 151–71.

Kinzer, Bruce. 1982. *The Ballot Question in Nineteenth-Century English Politics*. New York and London: Garland.

Kirbyson, Ronald *et al.* 1983. *Discovering Canada: Shaping an Identity*. Scarborough, Ontario: Prentice-Hall.

Kishima, Takako. 1987. "Political Life Reconsidered: A Post-Structuralist View of the World of Man in Japan." Unpublished Ph.D. Diss., Univ. of Wisconsin–Madison.

Kornberg, Alan, and Marianne C. Stewart. 1983. "National Identification and Political Support." In Allan Kornberg and Harold D. Clarke, eds., *Political Support in Canada: The Crisis Years*. Durham, N.C.: Duke Univ. Press: 73–103.

Kownslar, Allan, and Terry Smart. 1980. *American Government*. New York: McGraw-Hill.

Kracauer, Sigfried. 1947. *From Caligari to Hitler*. Princeton: Princeton Univ. Press.

Krieger, Joel. 1986. *Reagan, Thatcher, and the Politics of Decline*. Cambridge: Polity Press.

Kumar, Krishan. 1978. *Prophecy and Progress: The Sociology of Industrial and Post-Industrial Society.* London: Allen Lane.

Labour Party. 1982. *Report of the Annual Conference, 1980.*

Laitin, David. 1986. *Hegemony and Culture.* Chicago: Univ. of Chicago Press.

Laitin, David. 1988. "Political Culture and Political Preferences." *American Political Science Review* 82: 589–96.

Landes, Ronald. 1977. "Political Socialization among Youth: A Comparative Study of English-Canadian and American School Children." *International Journal of Comparative Sociology* 18: 63–80.

Lane, Christel. 1981. *The Rites of Rulers.* Cambridge: Cambridge Univ. Press.

Lane, Peter. 1987. *British Social and Economic History from 1760 to the Present Day.* Oxford: Oxford Univ. Press.

Lane, Robert E. 1983. "Political Observers and Market Participants: The Effects on Cognition." *Political Psychology* 4: 445–82.

Lanzetta, John T., and Scott Orr. 1986. "Excitatory Strength and Expressive Fear: Effects of Happy and Fear Expressions and Context on the Extinction of a Conditional Fear Response." *Journal of Personality and Social Psychology* 50 (January): 190–94.

Laponce, Jean. 1981. *Left & Right: The Topography of Political Perceptions.* Toronto: Univ. of Toronto Press.

Lasch, Christopher. 1977. *Haven in a Heartless World: The Family Besieged.* New York: Basic Books.

Lasch, Christopher. 1984. *The Minimal Self: Psychic Survival in Troubled Times.* New York: Norton.

Leach, Edmund. 1973. "Structuralism in Social Anthropology." In David Robey, ed., *Structuralism: An Introduction.* Oxford: Clarendon Press: 37–57.

Leach, Edmund. 1976. *Culture and Communication: The Logic by Which Symbols Are Connected.* Cambridge: Cambridge Univ. Press.

Leach, Edmund, and D. Alan Aycock, eds. 1983. *Structuralist Interpretations of Biblical Myth.* Cambridge: Cambridge Univ. Press.

Leahy, Robert. 1983. "Development of the Conception of Economic Inequality: II. Explanations, Justifications, and Concepts of Social Mobility and Change." *Developmental Psychology* 19: 111–25.

Leavis, F. R. 1948. *The Great Tradition.* London: Chatto and Windus.

Leavis, F. R., and Denys Thompson. 1937. *Culture and Environment: The Training of Critical Awareness.* London: Chatto and Windus.

Le Duc, L. 1985. "Partisan Change and Dealignment in Canada, Great Britain, and the United States." *Comparative Politics* 17: 379–98.

Leitch, Vincent B. 1983. *Deconstructive Criticism: An Advanced Introduction.* New York: Columbia Univ. Press.

Leming, James S. 1985. "Research on Social Studies Curriculum and Instruction: Interventions and Outcomes in the Socio-Moral Domain." In William B. Stanley et al., *Review of Research in Social Studies Education, 1976–1983.* Washington, D.C.: National Council for the Social Studies: 123–215.

Levin, Murray B. 1987. *Talk Radio and the American Dream.* Lexington, Mass.: D. C. Heath.

Lévi-Strauss, Claude. 1963. *Structural Anthropology.* Trans. Claire Jacobson and Brooke Grundfelt Schoerf. New York: Basic Books.

Lévi-Strauss, Claude. 1973a. *From Honey to Ashes.* Trans. John and Doreen Weightman. New York: Harper and Row.

Lévi-Strauss, Claude. 1973b. *Tristes Tropiques.* Trans. John and Doreen Weightman. London: Cape.

Leymore, V. Langhorne. 1975. *Hidden Myth.* London: Heinemann.

Leymore, V. Langhorne. 1982. "The Structural Factor in Systems of Communication." *British Journal of Sociology* 33, no. 3 (September): 421–34.

Leys, Colin. 1983. *Politics in Britain.* Toronto and Buffalo: Univ. of Toronto Press.

Lidz, Charles W. 1982. "Toward a Deep Structural Analysis of Moral Action." In Ino Rossi, ed., *Structural Sociology.* New York: Columbia Univ. Press: 229–56.

Lipset, Seymour Martin. 1950. *Agrarian Socialism.* Berkeley and Los Angeles: Univ. of California Press.

Lipset, Seymour Martin. 1963. *The First New Nation.* New York: Basic Books.

Lipset, Seymour Martin. 1989. *Continental Divide: The Values and Institutions of the United States and Canada.* Toronto, Ontario: C. D. Howe Institute.

Lipset, Seymour Martin, and William Schneider. 1987. *The Confidence Gap.* Rev. ed. Baltimore: Johns Hopkins Univ. Press.

Lipsky, Michael, and David J. Olson. 1977. *Commission Politics: The Processing of Racial Crisis in America.* New Brunswick, N.J.: Transaction Books.

Lister, Ian. 1988. "Civic Education for Positive Pluralism." Paper Presented to the Conference on Education for Citizenship in Multiethnic Societies. Rutgers Univ., New Brunswick, N.J. (September).

Lock, Andrew. 1981. "Universals in Human Conception." In Paul Heelas and Andrew Lock, eds., *Indigenous Psychologies: The Anthropology of the Self.* London: Academic Press. 19–39.

Lodge, Paul, and Tessa Blackstone. 1982. *Educational Policy and Educational Inequality.* Oxford: Martin Robertson.

Lower, Arthur R. M. 1958. *Canadians in the Making.* Toronto: Longmans, Green.

Lower, Joseph. 1970. *A Nation Developing: A Brief History of Canada.* Toronto: Ryerson.

Lowi, Theodore. 1969. *The End of Liberalism.* New York: Norton.

Lucaites, John Louis, and Celeste Michelle Condit. 1985. "Re-constructing Narrative Theory: A Functional Perspective." *Journal of Communication* 35: 90–109.

Lukes, Stephen. 1973. *Individualism.* Oxford: Basil Blackwell.

Lunch, William M. 1987. *The Nationalization of American Politics.* Berkeley and Los Angeles: Univ. of California Press.

McAllister, Ian, and Anthony Mughan. 1987. "Class, Attitudes, and Electoral Politics in Britain, 1974–1983." *Comparative Political Studies* 20: 47–71.

McCloskey, Donald N. 1985. *The Rhetoric of Economics*. Madison: Univ. of Wisconsin Press.

McClosky, Herbert, and Alida Brill. 1983. *Dimensions of Tolerance*. New York: Russell Sage.

McClosky, Herbert, and John Zaller. 1984. *The American Ethos: Public Attitudes Toward Capitalism and Democracy*. Cambridge: Harvard Univ. Press.

McDevitt, Daniel et al. 1979. *Canada Today*. Scarborough: Prentice-Hall.

McFadden, Fred, Don Quinlan, and Rich Life. 1982. *Canada: The Twentieth Century*. Toronto: Fitzhenry and Whiteside.

McGlenehan, William A. 1983. *Macgruder's American Government*. Rev. ed. Boston: Allyn and Bacon.

McGregor, Gaile. 1986. "A View from the Fort: Erving Goffman as Canadian." *Canadian Review of Sociology and Anthropology* 23: 531–43.

Mack, Joanna, and Stewart Lansley. 1985. *Poor Britain*. London: George Allen and Unwin.

McKenzie, Robert. 1982. "Power in the Labour Party: The Issue of 'Intra-Party Democracy.'" In Dennis Kavanaugh, ed., *The Politics of the Labour Party*. London: George Allen and Unwin: 191–202.

McLean, Ian. 1982. *Dealing in Votes*. New York: St. Martin's Press.

McNeil, Linda M. 1986. *Contradictions of Control: School Structure and School Knowledge*. New York and London: Routledge and Kegan Paul.

MacPherson, C. B. 1973. *Democratic Theory: Essays in Retrieval*. Oxford: Clarendon Press.

McRae, Kenneth D. 1964. "The Structure of Canadian History." In Louis Hartz, ed., *The Founding of New Societies*. New York: Harcourt, Brace and World: 219–75.

Malcolm, Andrew H. 1985. *The Canadians*. Toronto: Bantam.

Mander, Mary S. 1983. "Dallas: The Mythology of Crime and the Moral Occult." *Journal of Popular Culture* 17: 44–51.

Mann, Michael. 1970. "The Social Cohesion of Liberal Democracy." *American Sociological Review* 35: 422–39.

Mannheim, Karl. 1956. "The Democratization of Culture." In *Essays on the Sociology of Culture*. London: Routledge and Kegan Paul: 171–247.

Mansbridge, Jane. 1980. *Beyond Adversary Democracy*. New York: Basic Books.

Marchand, Roland. 1985. *Advertising the American Dream: Making Way for Modernity, 1920–1940*. Berkeley and Los Angeles: Univ. of California Press.

Marcus, George E. and Michael M. J. Fischer. 1986. *Anthropology as Cultural Critique: An Experimental Moment in the Human Sciences*. Chicago: Univ. of Chicago Press.

Marsh, Alan. 1977. *Protest and Political Consciousness*. Beverly Hills: Sage.

Marsh, Catherine. 1982. *The Survey Method*. London: Allen and Unwin.

Marwell, Gerald, and Ruth E. Ames. 1979. "Experiments on the Provision of

Public Goods. I. Resources, Interest, Group Size and the Free-Rider Problem." *American Journal of Sociology* 85: 1335–60.

Marwell, Gerald, and Ruth E. Ames. 1980. "Experiments on the Provision of Public Goods. II. Provision Points, Stakes, Experience, and the Free-Rider Problem." *American Journal of Sociology* 86: 926–37.

Marwick, Arthur. 1980. *Class.* New York: Oxford Univ. Press.

Marx, Leo. 1964. *The Machine in the Garden.* London: Oxford Univ. Press.

Matheson, W. A. 1976. *The Prime Minister and the Cabinet.* Toronto: Methuen.

Maxwell, Grant. 1976. "Attitudes at the Canadian Grassroots." Ottawa: Canadian Catholic Conference.

Mead, Lawrence. 1986. *Beyond Entitlement: The Social Obligations of Citizenship.* New York: Free Press.

Meier, Kenneth J., Joseph Stewart, Jr., and Robert England. 1989. *Race, Class, and Education: The Politics of Second-Generation Discrimination.* Madison: Univ. of Wisconsin Press.

Meisel, John. 1975. *Working Papers on Canadian Politics.* 2d. ed. Montreal and London: McGill-Queen's Univ. Press.

Menzies, Heather. 1978. *The Railroad's Not Enough: Canada Now.* Toronto/Vancouver: Clarke, Irwin.

Merelman, Richard M. 1984. *Making Something of Ourselves: On Culture and Politics in the United States.* Berkeley and Los Angeles: Univ. of California Press.

Merelman, Richard M. 1988. "Cultural Displays: An Illustration from American Immigration." *Qualitative Sociology* (Winter): 335–55.

Merquior, J. G. 1979. *The Veil and the Mask: Essays on Culture and Ideology.* London: Routledge and Kegan Paul.

Miller, Arthur, et al. 1981. "Group Consciousness and Political Participation." *American Journal of Political Science* 25: 203–13.

Miller, Daniel. 1987. *Material Culture and Mass Consumption.* Oxford: Basil Blackwell.

Miller, Mark Crispin. 1988. *Boxed In: The Culture of TV.* Evanston: Northwestern Univ. Press.

Mishler, William, Marilyn Hoskin, and Roy E. Fitzgerald. 1988. "Hunting the Snark: On Searching for Evidence of that Widely Touted but Highly Elusive Resurgence of Public Support for Conservative Parties in Britain, Canada, and the United States." In Cooper, Kornberg, and Mishler 1988: 54–96.

Mitchner, E. A., et al. 1976. *Forging a Destiny: Canada Since 1945.* Gage.

Moore, Stanley W., James Lare, and Kenneth Wagner. 1985. *The Child's Political World.* New York: Praeger.

Morris, Milton D. 1985. *Immigration: The Beleaguered Bureaucracy.* Washington, D.C.: Brookings Institution.

Morris, Raymond N. 1984. "Canada as a Family: Ontario Reposonses to the Quebec Independence Movement." *Canadian Review of Sociology and Anthropology* 24: 181–201.

Moynihan, Daniel. 1986. *Family and Nation.* New York: Harcourt Brace Jovanovich.

Mughan, Anthony. 1986. *Party and Participation in British Elections*. New York: St. Martin's Press.

Mutz, Diana C. 1989. "The Influence of Perceptions of Media Influence: Third Person Effects and the Public Expression of Opinions." *International Journal of Public Opinion Research* 1, no. 1: 3–23.

Nagel, Jack H. 1987. *Participation*. Englewood Cliffs, N.J.: Prentice-Hall.

Nagel, Jack H. 1988. "The Marriage of Normative Values and Empirical Concepts: Mutual Integrity or Reciprocal Distortion?" In Ian Shapiro and Grant Reeher, eds., *Power, Inequality, and Democratic Politics: Essays in Honor of Robert A. Dahl*. Boulder and London: Westview Press: 73–80.

Namenwirth, J. Zvi, and Robert Philip Weber. 1987. *Dynamics of Culture*. Boston: George Allen and Unwin.

Natchez, Peter B. 1985. *Images of Voting/Visions of Democracy*. New York: Basic Books.

National Coal Board. 1985. "Your Project Is Coal." Eagle House Press.

Nichols, Theo, and Huw Beynon. 1977. *Living With Capitalism: Class Relations and the Modern Factory*. London: Routledge and Kegan Paul.

Nimmo, Dan, and James E. Combs. 1985. *Nightly Horrors: Crisis Coverage by Television Network News*. Knoxville: Univ. of Tennessee Press.

Noelle-Neumann, Elisabeth. 1981. *The Spiral of Silence*. Chicago: Univ. of Chicago Press.

Norton, Anne. 1986. *Alternative Americas*. Chicago: Univ. of Chicago Press.

Nown, Graham, ed. 1985. *Coronation Street, 1960–1985*. London: Ward Lock.

Nye, David. 1985. *Image Worlds: Corporate Identities at General Electric, 1890–1930*. Cambridge: The MIT Press.

Oestereicher, Emil. 1982. "Form and Praxis: A Contribution to the Theory of Cultural Forces." *Social Research* 668–89.

Okun, Arthur. 1975. *Equality and Efficiency: The Big Trade-Off*. Washington, D.C.: Brookings Institution.

Olsen, Marvin. 1982. *Participatory Pluralism*. Chicago: Nelson-Hall.

Olson, Mancur. Jr. 1965. *The Logic of Collective Action*. Cambridge: Harvard Univ. Press.

Ornstein, Michael. 1986. "The Political Ideology of the Canadian Capitalist Class." *Canadian Review of Sociology and Anthropology* 26: 182–209

Page, Benjamin. 1979. *Choices and Echoes in Presidential Elections*. Chicago: Univ. of Chicago Press.

Page, Benjamin. 1983. *Who Gets What from Government?* Berkeley and Los Angeles: Univ. of California Press.

Paletz, David, and Robert Entman. 1981. *Media, Power, Politics*. New York: The Free Press.

Parenti, Michael. 1986. *Inventing Reality: The Politics of the Mass Media*. New York: St. Martins Press.

Parkin, Frank. 1971. *Class Inequality and Political Order*. New York: Praeger.

Patrick, John J., and Sharrl Davis Hawke. 1982. "Curriculum Materials." In

Irving Morrisett, ed., *Social Studies in the 1980s*. Alexandria, Va.: Association for Supervision and Curriculum Development: 39–51.

Patrick, John J., and Richard Remy. 1980. *Civics for Americans*. Glenview, Ill.: Scott, Foresman.

Pelletier, Gerard. 1988. "Quebec: Different, But in Step with North America." *Daedalus* 117, no. 4 (Fall) 265–83.

Pennock, J. Roland. 1979. *Democratic Political Theory*. Princeton: Princeton Univ. Press.

Pennock, J. Roland, and John W. Chapman, eds. 1975. *Participation in Politics*. New York: Atherton.

Perin, Constance. 1988. *Belonging in America*. Madison: Univ. of Wisconsin Press.

Peter, Karl. 1981. "The Myth of Multiculturalism and Other Political Fables." In Jorgen Dahlie and Tissa Fernando, eds. *Ethnicity, Power, and Politics in Canada*. Toronto: Methuen: 56–68.

Piaget, Jean. 1971. *Structuralism*. Trans. Chaninch Maschler. London: Routledge and Kegan Paul.

Pitkin, Hanna. 1972. *Wittgenstein and Justice*. Berkeley: Univ. of California Press.

Pollard, Michael. 1984. *The Hardest Work under Heaven: The Life and Death of the British Coal Miners*. London: Hutchinson.

Polsby, Nelson, and Aaron Wildavsky. 1988. *Presidential Elections*. 7th ed. New York: The Free Press.

Pope, Daniel. 1983. *The Making of Modern Advertising*. New York: Basic Books.

Popkin, Samuel. 1979. *The Rational Peasant*. Berkeley and Los Angeles: Univ. of California Press.

Powell, G. Bingham. 1982. *Contemporary Democracies: Participation, Stability, and Violence*. Cambridge: Harvard Univ. Press.

Powell, G. Bingham. 1986. "American Voter Turnout in Comparative Perspective." *American Political Science Review* 80: 17–43.

Prentice, Alison. 1975. "Education and the Metaphor of the Family: The Upper Canadian Example." In Michael B. Katz and Paul Mattingly, eds., *Education and Social Change: Themes from Ontario's Past*. New York: New York Univ. Press: 110–33.

Presthus, Robert. 1973. *Elite Accommodation in Canadian Politics*. Cambridge: Cambridge Univ. Press.

Rabinowitz, Peter J. 1987. *Before Reading: Narrative Conventions and the Politics of Interpretation*. Ithaca, N.Y.: Cornell Univ. Press.

Ranney, Austin. 1975. *Curing the Mischiefs of Faction: Party Reform in America*. Berkeley and Los Angeles: Univ. of California Press.

Redfield, Robert. 1955. *The Little Community*. Chicago: Univ. of Chicago Press.

Reinarman, Craig, 1987. *American States of Mind: Political Beliefs and Behavior Among Private and Public Workers*. New Haven & London: Yale Univ. Press.

Richards, David, and J. S. Hunt. 1983. *An Illustrated History of Modern Britain, 1783–1980*. 3d ed. Burnt Mill, Harlow, Essex: Longman.

Riley, Patricia. 1983. "A Structurationist Account of Political Culture." *Administrative Science Quarterly* 28: 414–37.

Roberts, David. 1986. *Politics: A New Approach.* Ormskirk, Lancashire: Causeway.

Robertson, David. 1984. *Class and the British Electorate.* Oxford: Basil Blackwell.

Robins, Lynton, Tom Brennan, and John Sutton. 1985. *People and Politics in Britain.* London and Basingstoke: Macmillan.

Robottom, John. 1987. *A Social and Economic History of Industrial Britain.* Burnt Mill, Harlow, Essex: Longman.

Rogin, Michael. 1987. *Ronald Reagan, The Movie.* Berkeley and Los Angeles: Univ. of California Press.

Rosaldo, Michelle Z. 1984. "Toward an Anthropology of Self and Feeling." In Richard A. Shweder and Robert A. Levine, eds., *Culture Theory: Essays on Mind, Self, and Emotion.* Cambridge: Cambridge Univ. Press: 137–58.

Rose, Richard. 1985. *Politics in England: Persistence and Change.* London: Faber and Faber.

Rosencranz, Armin, and James B. Chapin. 1982. *American Government.* New York: Holt, Rinehart, and Winston.

Rowland, Willard D., Jr., and Bruce Watkins, eds. 1984. *Interpreting Television.* Beverly Hills: Sage.

Runciman, W. G. 1966. *Relative Deprivation and Social Justice.* Berkeley and Los Angeles: Univ. of California Press.

Ruthrof, Horst. 1981. *The Reader's Construction of Narrative.* London: Routledge and Kegan Paul.

Sahlins, Marshall. 1976. *Culture and Practical Reason.* Chicago: Univ. of Chicago Press.

Sahlins, Marshall. 1981. *Historical Metaphors and Mythical Realities: Structure in the Early History of the Sandwich Islands Kingdom.* Ann Arbor: Univ. of Michigan Press.

Sandel, Michael, ed. 1984. *Liberalism and Its Critics.* New York: New York Univ. Press.

Sarlvik, Bo, and Ivor Crewe. 1983. *Decade of Dealignment.* Cambridge: Cambridge Univ. Press.

Sartori, Giovanni. 1987. *The Theory of Democracy Revisited.* Chatham, N.J.: Chatham House.

Sass, Louis A. 1986. "Anthropology's Native Problems." *Harper's* May: 49–58.

Saussure, Ferdinand de. 1966. *Course in General Linguistics.* New York: McGraw-Hill.

Schattschneider, E. E. 1960. *The Semi-Sovereign People.* New York: Holt, Rinehart, and Winston.

Schlozman, Kay Lehman. 1984. "What Accent the Heavenly Chorus? Political Equality and the American Pressure System." *Journal of Politics* 46: 1006–32.

Scholes, Robert. 1985. *Textual Power: Literary Theory and the Teaching of English.* New Haven and London: Yale Univ. Press.

Schudson, Michael. 1984. *Advertising: The Uneasy Persuasion: Its Dubious Impact on American Society*. New York: Basic Books.

Schumann, Howard, Charlotte Steeh, and Lawrence Bobo. 1985. *Racial Attitudes in America: Trends and Interpretations*. Cambridge: Harvard Univ. Press.

Schutz, Alfred. 1944. "The Stranger." *American Journal of Sociology* 50: 499–508.

Schwartz, Barry. 1981. *Vertical Classification: A Study in Structuralism and the Sociology of Knowledge*. Chicago: Univ. of Chicago Press.

Schwartz, Mildred. 1967. *Public Opinion and Canadian Identity*. Berkeley and Los Angeles: Univ. of California Press.

Schwarz, John. 1983. *America's Hidden Success: A Reassessment of Twenty Years of Public Policy*. New York: Norton.

Scitovsky, Tibor. 1976. *The Joyless Economy*. New York: Oxford Univ. Press.

Scott, D. M. M., and D. L. Kobrin. [1979] 1983. *O-Level British Constitution*. 4th ed. London: Butterworths.

Scott, James C. 1985. *Weapons of the Weak*. New Haven: Yale Univ. Press.

Sears, David O., Carl Hensler, and L. K. Speer. 1979. "Whites' Opposition to Busing: Self-Interest or Symbolic Politics?" *American Political Science Review* 73: 369–84.

Sennett, Richard. 1970. *Families against the City*. Cambridge: Harvard Univ. Press.

Sennett, Richard. 1976. *The Fall of Public Man*. New York: Knopf.

Shafer, Byron E. 1983. *Quiet Revolution: The Struggle for the Democratic Party and the Shaping of Post-Reform Politics*. New York: Russell Sage.

Shafer, Byron E. 1984. "The New Cultural Politics." *PS* 18 no. 2: 221–31.

Shaw, Eric. 1988. *Discipline and Discord in the Labour Party: The Politics of Managerial Control in the Labour Party, 1951–87*. Manchester: Manchester Univ. Press.

Shienbaum, Kim Ezra. 1984. *Beyond the Electoral Connection*. Philadelphia: Univ. of Pennsylvania Press.

Shils, Edward. 1975. *Centre and Periphery*. Chicago: Univ. of Chicago Press.

Shils, Edward, and Michael Young. 1953. "The Meaning of the Coronation." *Sociological Review* 1–2: 63–81.

Smiley, Donald V. 1967. *The Canadian Political Nationality*. Toronto and London: Methuen.

Smith, Anthony, ed. 1974. *British Broadcasting*. Newton Abbot: David and Charles.

Smith, Henry Nash. 1950. *Virgin Land: The American West as Symbol and Myth*. New York: Vintage.

Sniderman, Paul, and Philip Tetlock. 1986a. "Interrelationship of Political Ideology and Public Opinion." In Margaret G. Hermann, ed., *Political Psychology*. San Francisco: Jossey-Bass: 62–97.

Sniderman, Paul, and Philip Tetlock. 1986b. "Symbolic Racism: Problems of Motive Attribution in Political Analysis." *Journal of Social Issues* 42: 129–50.

Sofer, Cyril. 1970. *Men in Mid-Career*. Cambridge: Cambridge Univ. Press.

Soucie, Rolande. 1987. "Official Bilingualism in Canada: The Second Decade." Current Issue Review, 86-11E, Research Branch, Library of Parliament.

Sperber, Dan. 1982. "Is Symbolic Thought Prerational?" In Michael Izard and Pierre Smith, eds., *Between Belief and Transgression: Structuralist Essays in Religion, History, and Myth.* Chicago: Univ. of Chicago Press: 245–65.

Stein, Colman Brez, Jr. 1986. *Sink or Swim: The Politics of Bilingual Education.* New York: Praeger.

The Story of Emmerdale Farm, 15th Anniversary Special. N.d. Granada Television.

Studlar, Donley, and Jerold L. Waltman, eds. 1984. *Dilemmas of Change in British Politics.* Jackson: Univ. Press of Mississippi.

Sullivan, John. et al. 1978. "Ideological Constraint in the Mass Public: A Methodological Critique and Some New Findings." *American Journal of Political Science* May: 233–49.

Sullivan, John, et al. 1982. *Political Tolerance and American Democracy.* Chicago: Univ. of Chicago Press.

Susman, Warren I. 1984. *Culture as History: The Transformation of American Society in the Twentieth Century.* New York: Pantheon.

Sutton, Francis, et al. 1956. *The American Business Creed.* Cambridge: Harvard Univ. Press.

Swann, Lord. 1985. *Education for All.* London: Her Majesty's Stationary Office.

Szalay, Loran B., Rita M. Kelly, and Won T. Moon. 1972. "Ideology: Its Meaning and Measurement." *Comparative Political Studies* July: 151–74.

Tajfel, Henri, ed. 1978. *Differentiation between Social Groups.* London: Academic Press.

Tajfel, Henri, ed. 1982. *Social Identity and Intergroup Relations.* Cambridge: Cambridge Univ. Press.

Tapper, Ted. and Brian Salter. 1978. *Education and the Political Order.* London: Macmillan.

Taylor-Gooby, Peter. 1985. *Public Opinion, Ideology, and State Welfare.* London: Routledge and Kegan Paul.

"Testing Time for the NDP." *Maclean's,* 15 August 1988: 12.

Thompson, E. P. 1964. *The Making of the English Working Class.* New York: Pantheon.

Tinker, Jack. 1985. *Coronation St.* London: Octopus Books.

Todd, Emmanuel. 1987. *The Causes of Progress: Culture, Authority and Change.* Trans. Richard Boulind. Oxford: Basil Blackwell.

Todd, Lewis Paul, and Merle Curti. 1986. *Triumph of the American Nation.* New York: Harcourt Brace Jovanovich.

Tocqueville, Alexis de. 1969. *Democracy in America.* Ed. Phillips Bradley. New York: Vintage.

Trudel, Marcel, and Genevieve Jain. 1970. *Canadian History Textbooks: A Comparative Study.* Studies of the Royal Commission on Bilingualism and Biculturalism, 5. Ottawa: Queen's Printer for Canada.

274   Bibliography

Tunstall, Jeremy, and David Walker. 1981. *Media Made in California*. New York: Oxford Univ. Press.
Turner, Victor. 1967. *The Forest of Symbols*. Ithaca, N.Y.: Cornell Univ. Press.
Turner, Victor. 1969. *The Ritual Process: Structure and Anti-Structure*. Chicago: Aldine.
Turner, Victor, and Edith Turner. 1978. *Image and Pilgrimage in Christian Culture*. New York: Columbia Univ. Press.
United States Commission on Civil Rights. 1975. *A Better Chance to Learn: Bilingual-Bicultural Education*. Publication 51. Washington: United States Commission on Civil Rights.
Ursell, Gill. 1983. "The Views of British Managers and Shop Stewards on Industrial Democracy." In C. Crouch and F. Heller, eds., *Organizational Democracy and Political Processes*. London: Wiley: 327–53.
Vanneman, Reeve, and Lynn Cannon. 1987. *The American Perception of Class*. Philadephia: Temple Univ. Press.
Varenne, Herve. 1977. *Americans Together: Structural Diversity in a Midwestern Town*. New York: Teachers College Press.
Verba, Sidney, Norman Nie, and Jae-on Kim. 1978. *Participation and Political Equality*. Cambridge: Cambridge Univ. Press.
Verba, Sidney, and Gary Orren. 1985. *Equality in America: The View from the Top*. Cambridge: Harvard Univ. Press.
Verba, Sidney, Norman Nie, and John Petrocik. 1980. *The New American Electorate*. Cambridge: Cambridge Univ. Press.
Verney, Douglas V. 1986. *Three Civilizations, Two Cultures, One State: Canada's Political Traditions*. Durham: Duke Univ. Press.
Vestergaard, Torben, and Kim Schroder. 1985. *The Language of Advertising*. Oxford, Basil Blackwell.
Vincent, Andrew, and Raymond Plant. 1984. *Philosophy, Politics and Citizenship: The Life and Thought of the British Idealists*. Oxford: Basil Blackwell.
Vitz, Paul C. 1986. "Religion and Traditional Values in Public School Textbooks." *The Public Interest* Summer: 79–90.
Vogel, David. 1986. *National Styles of Regulation: Environmental Policy in Great Britain and the United States*. Ithaca: Cornell Univ. Press.
Wagner-Pacifici, Robin Erica. 1986. *The Moro Morality Play*. Chicago: Univ. of Chicago Press.
Walzer, Michael. 1980. *Radical Principles*. New York: Basic Books.
Warner, William Lloyd. 1959. *The Living and the Dead*. New Haven: Yale Univ. Press.
Wattenburg, Martin. 1984. *The Decline of American Political Parties, 1952–1980*. Cambridge: Harvard Univ. Press.
Weber, Max. 1958. *The Protestant Ethic and the Spirit of Capitalism*. Trans. Talcott Parsons. New York: Scribner.
Weber, Max. 1963. *The Sociology of Religion*. Trans. Ephraim Fischoff. Boston: Beacon.

Weiler, Peter. 1982. *The New Liberalism: Liberal Social Theory in Great Britain, 1889–1914.* New York and London: Garland.

White, James Boyd. 1985. *Heracles' Bow: Essays on the Rhetoric and Poetics of the Law.* Madison: Univ. of Wisconsin Press.

Wildavsky, Aaron. 1987. "Choosing Preferences by Constructing Institutions: A Cultural Theory of Preference Formation." *American Political Science Review* 81, no. 1 (March): 3–21.

Wildes, Howard B., Robert P. Ludlum, and Harriett Brown. 1983. *This is America's Story.* Boston: Houghton Mifflin.

Wilkinson, Rupert. 1969. *Governing Elites: Studies in Training and Selection.* New York: Oxford Univ. Press.

Wilkinson, Rupert. 1984. *American Tough: The Tough-Guy Tradition and American Character.* Westport, Conn.: Greenwood Press.

Williams, Juan. 1987. *Eyes on the Prize: America's Civil Rights Years, 1954–1965.* New York: Viking.

Williams, Raymond. 1960. *Culture and Society, 1780–1950.* Garden City, N.Y.: Anchor.

Williams, Raymond. 1961. *The Long Revolution.* Westport, Conn.: Greenwood Press.

Williams, Raymond. 1974. *Television: Technology and Cultural Form.* London: Fontana.

Williams, Raymond. 1981. *The Sociology of Culture.* New York: Schocken Books.

Williamson, Judith. 1986. *Consuming Passions: The Dynamics of Popular Culture.* London: Marion Boyars.

Wilmott, Peter, and Michael Young. 1960. *Family and Class in a London Suburb.* London: Routledge and Kegan Paul.

Wilson, Graham K. 1985. *Business and Politics: A Comparative Introduction.* Chatham, N.J.: Chatham House.

Wilson, William H. 1978. *The Declining Significance of Race.* Chicago: Univ. of Chicago Press.

Wolfe, Morris. 1985. *Jolts: The TV Wasteland and the Canadian Oasis.* Toronto: James Lorimer.

Wolfinger, Raymond, and Stephen Rosenstone. 1980. *Who Votes?* New Haven: Yale Univ. Press.

Wright, James D. 1976. *The Dissent of the Governed.* New York: Academic Press.

Wuthnow, Robert et al. 1984. *Cultural Analysis.* London: Routledge and Kegan Paul.

Yankelovich, Daniel. 1974. *The New Morality.* New York: McGraw-Hill.

Young, Michael, and Peter Willmott. 1957. *Family and Kinship in East London.* Baltimore: Penguin.

Index